Criminal Appeals Handbook

Criminal Appeals Handbook

Daniel Jones
Barrister, Dyers Chambers

Gregory Stewart
Solicitor and Higher Courts Advocate,
GT Stewart Solicitors & Advocates

Joel Bennathan QC
Barrister, Doughty Street Chambers

with (on chapter 5)
Emily Bolton and Sophie Walker
Solicitors, Centre for Criminal Appeals

and (on chapter 9)
Rebecca Penfold
Barrister, Dyers Chambers

Bloomsbury Professional

**Bloomsbury Professional Limited, Maxwelton House,
41–43 Boltro Road, Haywards Heath, West Sussex, RH16 1BJ**

© Bloomsbury Professional Ltd 2015

A CIP Catalogue record for this book is available from the British Library.

ISBN 978 1 78043 463 6

Typeset by Phoenix Photosetting, Chatham, Kent
Printed and bound in Great Britain by CPI Group (UK) Ltd, Croydon, CR0 4YY

Foreword

Apart from a few specialists, advocates practising in crime spend the vast majority of their time dealing with criminal cases in the Magistrates' and Crown Courts. Forays to the Court of Appeal Criminal Division can be few and far between and I suspect these infrequent appearances often engender feelings of uncertainty and apprehension. I vividly recall the challenge that is presented when all three members of the court are seemingly unimpressed by an argument, and proceed to fire difficult questions in rapid succession. The advocate can feel very lonely and ill equipped. Furthermore, appellate proceedings are in many ways a wholly different exercise to conducting first instance cases, and the procedure, the conventions and the jurisprudence are voluminous and can feel positively byzantine, especially to the uninitiated.

In order for the Court of Appeal Criminal Division to function efficiently and effectively, it is crucial that the advocates understand and apply the rules, and that the procedures of these courts are loyally followed. A relatively small number of judges deal with a high volume of work, and this is only possible if the applicants/appellants and the respondents prepare and present these cases in accordance with the established modus operandi. There are many elephant traps lying in wait for those who have not done their homework in advance. For the judiciary, it is a joy when cases are properly prepared, presented and economically argued and there is a risk that good points may be obscured if the court is forced to wrestle with a chaotically prepared case or when unfocussed submissions fail to distinguish between good and bad points.

This book is a wholly welcome addition to the relatively few guides that are available for advocates in this field. One of its great strengths is that it has been presented in a rigorously practical and intelligent way, and as a consequence it provides an impressive mix of purely practical assistance on basic procedure, along with detailed insight into some of the more legally challenging issues. The layout of the book means that it will be easy to use – the different stages are clearly delineated and it provides 'cradle to grave' assistance. It offers a clear route through the labyrinth and it is packed with excellent legal analysis. In the result, I suspect that many members of the judiciary will have it close at hand as a critical point of reference.

The Rt. Hon. Lord Justice Fulford
Deputy Senior Presiding Judge

Preface

Appealing against a conviction or a sentence that was imposed in the Crown Court can be a daunting business. There is a striking contrast to be found between the ease with which an appeal can be brought against a decision of the Magistrates' Court and the difficulties and uncertainties involved in appealing from the Crown Court.

A defendant who wishes to appeal against a conviction or a sentence that was imposed in the Magistrates' Court simply has to lodge a notice of appeal. He is then entitled to a complete re-hearing in the Crown Court. In contrast, appealing a conviction or sentence that was imposed in the Crown Court, which is always to the Court of Appeal, requires an application to be made for leave to the Court of Appeal. If leave is allowed, what is being granted is the right to a hearing at which the appellant has the opportunity to persuade the Court to allow the appeal. That opportunity is a narrow one. It often consists of a short hearing before a Court that has read the papers and may already have formed a clear preliminary view of the merits of the case.

This is a process that poses particular challenges for defendants and their lawyers. Defendants who have acclimatised themselves to the pace and formality of the Crown Court find themselves having to adjust to new and very different proceedings; there is a new set of legal terms to grapple with, further delays, a process from which they seem to be excluded, and that may culminate in a hearing at which trials that may have lasted for weeks are considered in minutes, and matters that seemed so crucial at trial are barely mentioned.

Their lawyers must seek to persuade a Court in which the swift, sometimes brutal dispatch of business and a ruthless focus on essentials replaces the comparatively relaxed pace of life in the Crown Court. It requires a different approach and even a different set of skills in order to achieve the best result for their clients.

The aim of this book is to assist those who seek to challenge a conviction or sentence, including a confiscation order, which was imposed in the Crown Court. It is intended for defence lawyers but also for defendants and their families who want a better understanding of the appeal process. For those who choose to represent themselves we hope to provide assistance. But it is not our intention to encourage anyone to do so. The need for effective legal representation is never more important than at the appeal stage. That effectiveness can only be increased when clients understand what they should expect of their lawyers and both lawyers and clients appreciate and can focus on the questions that will be of importance to the Court.

Because convictions and sentences that have been imposed on the Crown Court can only be appealed to the Court of Appeal, the focus of this book is largely on appealing to that Court. Chapter 1 provides a brief introduction to the Court, its judges, constitution, rules and administration. Chapter 2 considers the sources of law that it applies. Chapters 3 and 4 consider the tests for appeal, potential grounds and the powers of the Court in relation to conviction and sentence (including confiscation), respectively.

Chapters 5 to 8 then address the practicalities of appealing. Chapter 5 considers the important but often overlooked question of defence investigations, often the source of new material that provides the basis for an appeal. Chapter 6 deals with the practicalities of preparing the case; applying for leave, renewal of such applications and extensions of time, whilst Chapter 7 considers preparation for hearings. Chapter 8 deals with applying for legal aid to cover legal advice or representation whilst touching on the other ways of obtaining legal assistance, through private instruction, innocence projects and charities.

One of the most important features of the appeals process is the Criminal Cases Review Commission, which has the power to refer cases back to the Court of Appeal that have previously been considered and refused. Chapter 9 focuses on applying to the Commission whilst Chapter 10 sets out the procedure for appealing from the Court of Appeal to the Supreme Court.

Although a decision of the Court of Appeal or, very occasionally, the Supreme Court, will conclude the domestic appeal process, it need not always exhaust the search for justice. If a defendant's rights have been violated, he may apply for the case to be heard by the European Court of Human Rights. Chapter 11 addresses when and how such an application can be made and what can be achieved by doing so.

We have concluded with three chapters on subjects with which the defence practitioner will occasionally have to grapple. Chapter 12 deals with interlocutory appeals. Chapter 13 addresses the issue of responding to prosecution appeals against sentence (or 'Attorney General's references') and against acquittal. Chapter 14 deals with appeals against certain findings and orders made in the Crown Court against defendants who are found to be suffering from serious mental disorders.

In retaining the focus on appeals in relation to serious criminal offences we have deliberately omitted two topics. First, appeals from the Magistrates' Court. As already indicated, the process of appealing from the Magistrates' Court to the Crown is straightforward. Lawyers will find what they need to know in the general criminal practitioner's textbooks. Self-representing should also be able to comply with the procedural requirements for an appeal, perhaps with some assistance from the local Crown Court in relation to the completion of the relevant forms and time limits for doing so.

The second topic is that of judicial review of the decisions of the Magistrates' Court and judicial review of certain decisions of the Crown Court.[1] It is a topic of considerable scope and complexity. The law is covered briefly in the established practitioner's textbooks but more extensively in judicial review textbooks and now in a textbook devoted to judicial review in criminal proceedings.[2] We could not hope, in the limited space that might have been devoted to the topic in this book, to match the guidance that is to be found in such publications.

It should by now also be obvious that this book is not intended to be a comprehensive guide to the Court of Appeal and its wide array of powers. It is intended for those who act for those who have suffered a miscarriage of justice in the Crown Court and who seek redress. It was Parliament's purpose in creating the Court of Appeal to ensure that when such injustices occurred in the Crown Court there should be a remedy. We seek to assist defendants and their representatives to make best use of the rights of appeal that Parliament has provided.

Any practitioner in the criminal courts will have had the experience of getting a bad result, either the loss of a trial that should have been won or a sentence far harsher than predicted. Very soon, someone will ask, 'What next?' By combining our experience, knowledge and ideas in this book, we hope to assist in arriving at the right answer.

Joel Bennathan QC
Gregory Stewart
Daniel Jones
February 2015

---

1   Decisions in relation to trial on indictment may only be appealed to the Court of Appeal by virtue of the Senior Courts Act 1981, s. 29(3). However, decisions in relation to bail at an early stage in criminal proceedings (*R (M) v Isleworth Crown Court* [2005] EWHC 363 (Admin)), custody time limits, production orders and decisions in relation to appeals from the Magistrates' Court fall outside the scope of that section and may be challenged by way of judicial review.

2   Von Berg, P. (ed.) (2014) *Criminal Judicial Review*, Oxford: Hart Publishing.

Acknowledgements

We would like to thank Sally Berlins and Justin Hawkins of the CCRC for their helpful comments on the draft Chapter 9. We are equally grateful to Kiran Goss, Hannah Johnson and Rebecca Cupit from Bloomsbury for patiently guiding us from initial proposal to publication. Finally, we would like to thank our families for their support during the writing of this book.

Contents

Contents

Contents

Table of Statutes

All references are to paragraph numbers

Table of Statutes

Table of Statutory Instruments

All references are to paragraph numbers

Table of Cases

All references are to paragraph numbers

A

Part 1
The Law

Chapter 1

Introduction to the Court of Appeal

INTRODUCTION

1.1   The Court of Appeal (Criminal Division) ('the Court') sits in the gothic setting of the Royal Courts of Justice, London, in courtrooms of dark and intimidating antiquity. This should not mislead us into thinking that the Court is itself one of our ancient institutions. It was created in the 20th century, following years of campaigning by legal reformers and fierce opposition from successive governments and members of the judiciary.[1] Its core function then, as now, is to hear appeals from the Crown Court against conviction and sentence (including appeals against confiscation orders). However, Parliament has since loaded the Court with powers to hear appeals from a variety of other decisions of the Crown Court and Courts Martial. Although the focus of this book is on appeals against conviction and sentence, the additional powers that are most significant for general criminal litigation are also considered.[2]

THE DEVELOPMENT OF THE COURT OF APPEAL

1.2   The roots of the jury trial can be traced back to the middle ages. But if the jury system was one of the historic strengths of the English system of justice, the absence of a system of appeal against decisions of the jury was one of its great weaknesses. Before 1907 those who wished to challenge a conviction or a sentence imposed in the Assize and Sessions Courts (the predecessors of today's Crown Court) had two potential avenues of redress,

---

1   See Cornish, W. and Clarke, G. (1989) *Law and Society in England 1750–1950*, London: Sweet & Maxwell, pp. 619–623.
2   The prosecution's own rights of appeal, which are considered in Chapter 13; appeals against interlocutory rulings, which are considered in Chapter 12; appeals against restraint, receivership and foreign confiscation requests, which are considered in Chapter 4.

neither of them satisfactory.[3] The principle argument against the creation of a criminal court of appeal that was made in the 19th century (in which some 50 bills for the creation of a Court of Appeal were introduced to Parliament but failed to become law[4]) was that the role of the jury would be undermined if judges could, on appeal, overturn, the jury's decisions.[5] However, opposition was also driven by the perceived need for finality in criminal litigation[6] and a refusal, among some, to accept that the existing system was the cause of significant injustices.[7]

1.3   When Parliament finally bowed to public pressure and passed the Criminal Appeal Act 1907, these concerns found expression in the requirements for leave (or 'permission' as it is referred to in civil cases) to appeal in certain cases and also in the limited grounds upon which the Court could quash a conviction. Although the 1907 Act was repealed, it set the mould in which subsequent legislation was cast.

1.4   The 1907 Act created the 'Criminal Court of Appeal', which had the power to determine appeals against conviction and sentence from cases that had been heard on indictment in the Assize and Sessions Courts. An appeal against conviction could be brought without the need for leave of the Court when it was based upon a question of law. However, the leave of the Court or the certificate of the trial judge was required when an appeal was brought on a question of fact alone.

1.5   The Court had the power to set aside a conviction if it was:

(a)   unreasonable;

(b)   did not accord with the evidence;

(c)   was wrong in law.

---

3   From 1848 onwards a convicted person could ask the trial judge to refer the case to the Court for Crown Cases Reserved, which was established by the Crown Cases Reserved Act 1848, but only if the correctness of the conviction rested on a point of law. If the trial judge declined to refer the case, the only alternative was to fall back on the ancient practice of petitioning the government to grant a royal pardon. In contrast all but one US state had a criminal appeals court by 1840 (Grossberg, M. and Tomlins, C. (eds) (2008) *The Cambridge History of Law in America*, Vol. 2, New York: Cambridge University Press).

4   Radzinowicz, L. and Hood, R. (1986) *A History of English Law and it Administration from 1750*, Vol. V, London: Stevens & Sons, p. 758.

5   Cornish and Clarke (1989), pp. 619–623.

6   As R. Spencer noted in Delmas-Marty, M. and Spencer, J. R. (eds) (2002) *European Criminal Procedures*, Cambridge: Cambridge University Press, at p. 28: 'In England the Jury was introduced as a substitute for the Judgment of God pronounced through the ordeal, and like the Judgment of God it was not open to challenge on the ground that it has given an answer that was wrong'.

7   Radzinowicz and Hood (1986), p. 763.

1.6   Even if the Court found that any of these criteria were satisfied, it did not have to set aside the conviction if 'no substantial miscarriage of justice had occurred'.[8]

1.7   A number of reforms were introduced by the Criminal Appeal Acts 1964, 1966 and 1967. Most notably, the 1966 Act re-constituted the Court as a branch of the existing civil Court of Appeal, enabling all High Court judges and Lord Justices of Appeal to sit in both Courts. Thereafter the Court was known as the Court of Appeal (Criminal Division).

1.8   These changes were consolidated by the Criminal Appeal Act 1968 ('CAA 1968') which (much amended by later legislation) contains the powers of today's Court of Appeal in relation to appeals against conviction and sentence.

1.9   The Senior Courts Act 1981 contains the overarching framework that now governs the Court of Appeal (Criminal Division) in all its activities. The need for such a framework is a testament to the many other appeals from the decisions of the Crown Court with which, since 1968, Parliament has empowered the Court to determine.

1.10   The last major reforms of the Court's powers are contained in the Criminal Appeal Act 1995, which made a number of amendments to the 1968 Act, the most important of which were:

(a)   The introduction of a new test for appeal against conviction. Whilst the original criteria from section 4(1) of the 1907 Act (see **1.5**, above) had been preserved in section 2(1) of the Criminal Appeal Act 1968, the Criminal Appeal Act 1995 amended section 2(1) by replacing that criteria with a single test: the Court has to ask whether the conviction is 'safe'.

(b)   The removal of the automatic right of appeal against conviction in those cases where appeal is based on a point of law. Thereafter, either leave to appeal from the Court of Appeal or a certification from the trial judge would be required for all criminal appeals.

(c)   The creation of the Criminal Cases Review Commission ('the Commission') (the role of which is considered in Chapter 9).

---

8   Criminal Appeals Act 1907, s. 4(1).

Appeals from cases which pre-date the coming into force of CAA 1995

1.11   The test of unsafety applies to appeals against all convictions, whether they took place before or after the commencement of CAA 1995.[9] However, the pre-1995 rules in relation to leave remain in force in respect of appeals against convictions that took place before 1 January 1996. If one appeals against such a historic conviction there will be no requirement for leave where the appeal involves a question of law only.[10]

THE CURRENT STATUTORY REGIME

1.12   The jurisdiction of the Court is set out in section 53(2) of the Senior Courts Act 1981. It provides that the Criminal Division of the Court of Appeal shall exercise:

(a)   all jurisdiction of the Court of Appeal under Parts I and II of the Criminal Appeal Act 1968;

(b)   the jurisdiction of the Court of Appeal under section 13 of the Administration of Justice Act 1960 (appeals in cases of contempt of court) in relation to appeals from orders and decisions of the Crown Court;

(c)   all other jurisdiction expressly conferred on that division by this or any other Act; and

(d)   the jurisdiction to order the issue of writs of *venire de novo* (a rarely used remedy that can be used to remit a case to the Crown Court where the Court is satisfied that the proceedings were so irregular that they did not constitute a proper trial).

1.13   Part 1 sets out the Court's powers when determining appeals against conviction or sentence from the Crown Court. Part II sets out its powers when determining applications for leave to appeal from that Court to the Supreme Court.

PROCEDURAL RULES AND GUIDANCE

1.14   Although the Court is a creature of statute and its powers are limited to those which Parliament has provided it, it does have the power to regulate its own procedures. Therefore, the statutory provisions relating to the conduct

---

9   By virtue of the Criminal Appeal Act 1995 (Commencement No. 1 and Transitional Provisions) Order 1995 (SI 1995/3061).

10   See *DPP v Majewski* [1975] 3 All ER 296 for the meaning of 'a question of law'.

of appeals are supplemented by detailed procedural rules and guidelines from the following sources:

(a) The Criminal Procedure Rules ('CPR')[11] – Part 1 contains the rules that apply to all criminal proceedings. Parts 65 to 72 contain the rules which apply to appeals to the Court of Appeal. Part 68 contains those rules which specifically apply to appeals against conviction and sentence in the Court of Appeal.

(b) The Criminal Practice Direction ('the Practice Direction')[12] – Part 68 of the Practice Direction is specifically concerned with Appeals to the Court of Appeal Against Conviction and Sentence. The Practice Direction is updated periodically.

(c) The 'Guide to Commencing Proceedings in the Court of Appeal (Criminal Division)' ('the Guide') was published in October 2008. It was prepared by Court of Appeal lawyers under the direction of the then Registrar. Guidance notes are produced by the Court for appellants, lawyers and others with an interest in the appeal process.[13]

(d) The case law of the Court – The Lord Chief Justice or Vice President of the Criminal Division occasionally use particular cases to provide guidance on what the Court expects from the parties. These individual decisions are often incorporated into the Practice Direction when it is updated.

THE JUDGES OF THE COURT OF APPEAL

1.15   The Court of Appeal is presided over by the Lord Chief Justice who is appointed by the Lord Chancellor. He may in turn appoint another judge as Vice President of the Criminal Division to assist him.[14]

1.16   The other permanent judges of the Court are a small number of holders or former holders of certain high judicial offices, and a larger number of 'ordinary' judges who on appointment to the Court of Appeal are known as Lord or Lady Justices of Appeal.[15] In addition, the Lord Chief Justice may ask

---

11 The Criminal Procedure Rules are set out in statutory instruments that are promulgated under the Courts Act 2003, s. 69. The Criminal Procedure Rules Committee, which is chaired by the Lord Chief Justice, is responsible for drawing them up. Unless otherwise stated, references to 'CPR' are to the 2014 Rules.

12 The Lord Chief Justice has the power, under the Courts Act 2003, s. 74 and the Constitutional Reform Act 2005, Sch. 2, Pt 1 to make directions as to the practice and procedure of the criminal courts.

13 They can be found at: www.justice.gov.uk/courts/rcj-rolls-building/court-of-appeal/criminal-division.

14 Senior Courts Act 1981, s. 3.

15 Senior Courts Act 1981, s. 2.

High Court judges (referred to in the legislation as 'puisne judges') or judges who sit in the Crown Court ('circuit judges') to sit in the Court of Appeal.[16]

1.17 When a judge is sitting in the Court of Appeal, he or she should be addressed as my Lord or My Lady.

The composition of the Court

1.18 The Court is constituted, for the purposes of exercising any of its powers, when it sits as an uneven number of judges, not less than three.[17] In practice it usually sits as a Court of three judges, presided over by a Lord or Lady Justice of Appeal. A court of five judges will occasionally sit on important cases when the Lord Chief Justice deems it appropriate. There may never be more than one circuit judge sitting in any one court.

1.19 A Court of two judges may be constituted by two High Court judges or a High Court judge and a Circuit judge.[18] It may only hear the following appeals:

(a)   an appeal against sentence;

(b)   a renewed application for leave to appeal against conviction or sentence where the single judge has already refused leave.

The 'single judge'

1.20 An application for leave to appeal against conviction or sentence is generally considered by a single judge, in practice this will be a High Court judge. The single judge may determine other applications (for example, an application for bail) that are made along with or following the application for leave. Alternatively, he may refer applications on to the full Court for its determination. Although his decisions are usually made on paper he may choose to hold oral hearings.

THE REGISTRAR OF CRIMINAL APPEALS AND THE CRIMINAL APPEALS OFFICE

1.21 The role of the Registrar of Criminal Appeals ('the Registrar') is to assist the Court in the effective management of cases. It is an administrative but also a judicial role in that he (as the current occupier of the office is) has a

---

16   Senior Courts Act 1981, s. 9.
17   Senior Courts Act 1981, s. 55(2).
18   Senior Courts Act 1981, s. 55(6).

number of case management powers, some of which are considered in Chapters 6 and 7 of this book.

1.22   The Registrar himself is assisted by the lawyers and administrative staff at the 'Criminal Appeals Office'. Cases will be assigned to a lawyer and caseworker who will then take responsibility for preparing the case and communicating with the parties.

1.23   Their work is undertaken in the name of 'the Registrar', and it is the 'the Registrar' to whom correspondence with the Court should generally be addressed. However, it should be assumed that routine casework is undertaken without the Registrar's personal involvement.[19]

WHERE AND WHEN THE COURT SITS

1.24   The Court may sit anywhere in England and Wales but it is based in the Royal Courts of Justice in the Strand (sitting usually in Courts 4 to 9) along with the Registrar and the Criminal Appeals Office.

1.25   It sits at the following times of year:[20]

(a)   the Michaelmas sittings, which begin on 1 October and end on 21 December;

(b)   the Hilary sittings, which begin on 11 January and end on the Wednesday before Easter Sunday;

(c)   the Easter sittings, which begin on the second Tuesday after Easter Sunday and end on the Friday before the spring holiday; and

(d)   the Trinity sittings, which begin on the second Tuesday after the spring holiday and end on 31 July.

COMMUNICATING WITH THE COURT

1.26   Correspondence to the Court should be addressed to:

The Registrar of Criminal Appeals
The Royal Courts of Justice
Strand
London
WC2A 2LL
DX 44451 Strand

---

19   Senior Courts Act 1981, s. 31A(2)(b).
20   Civil Practice Direction 39B.

1.27   All correspondence to the Court should contain the case reference number which is to be found on all correspondence from the Court.

1.28   In practice, most correspondence will be considered and replied to by the lawyer or the caseworker who has been assigned to the case. The lawyer may pass on correspondence to the Registrar himself if the nature of the issues requires his consideration. If the case is being prepared for hearing and a presiding judge has already been assigned, the lawyer may pass correspondence on to the judge's clerk.

SUMMARY OF KEY POINTS

- The Court of Appeal (Criminal Division) hears all appeals against conviction and sentence from the Crown Court. It also has power to hear a number of other appeals from decisions of the Crown Court and the Courts Martial.

- The Court was created by statute. Its powers and jurisdiction are therefore defined by statute. Its overarching framework is contained in the Senior Courts Act 1981.

- Its powers in relation to appeals against conviction or sentence are to be found in the Criminal Appeals Act 1968 as amended by subsequent legislation, most notably the Criminal Appeals Act 1995. However, appeals against decisions that were made before 1 January 1995 take place under the provisions that were then in force.

- It has the power to regulate its own procedures. The legislation is supplemented by a number of procedural rules and guidelines that are to be found in the relevant Criminal Procedural Rules, the relevant parts of the Criminal Practice Direction, decisions of the Court itself and the Court's written guidance for advocates.

- It is based in the Royal Courts of Justice (sitting usually in Courts 4 to 9) where the Registrar of Criminal Appeals and the Criminal Appeals Office are also based.

- Communication with the Court should be through written correspondence addressed to the Registrar and should contain the Court's own case reference number.

Chapter 2

Applying the law: recent developments

INTRODUCTION

2.1   The Court interprets and applies law from the following sources:

(a)   Acts of Parliament;

(b)   Statutory Instruments;

(c)   decisions of the Superior Courts;

(d)   the European Convention on Human Rights and decisions of the European Court of Human Rights;

(e)   European Union law and international law.

2.2   The overriding requirement to apply statutes remains a constant feature of our criminal law. However, in the last 20 years a once crystal clear hierarchy of norms has become clouded as the Human Rights Act and the growing impact of European Union law and international law has added complexity to the business of interpreting the domestic criminal law. It has also been a period in which the Court of Appeal has returned on several occasions to the question of when it is entitled to depart from its own previous decisions. The focus of this chapter is upon these developments.

STARE DECISIS[1] AND THE COURT OF APPEAL

2.3   The Court of Appeal must follow the decisions of the Supreme Court and those of its predecessor, the Judicial Committee of the House of Lords.[2] The judges who sit in the Supreme Court also sit in the Judicial Committee of the Privy Council which hears appeals from a number of Commonwealth countries. Its decisions are not strictly binding on the Court of Appeal but will carry great weight and are likely to be followed unless there is very good reason to depart from them.

---

1   The doctrine of *stare decisis* means that a court is bound to follow the decisions of a higher court and other courts of equal standing.

2   The Supreme Court was created by the Constitutional Reform Act 2005. It came into existence on 1 October 2009.

2.4 *Applying the law: recent developments*

2.4 As a general rule the Court of Appeal is bound to follow its own decisions. However, there are exceptions to that rule. It is the scope of those exceptions that needs to be considered.

2.5 In *Young v Bristol Airplane Co Ltd*[3] the Court of Appeal (Civil Division) held that the Court of Appeal was bound to follow a previous decision of the Court unless one of the following exceptions applied:

(a) There is a conflict between two Court of Appeal authorities and the Court must decide which to follow.

(b) The decision of the Court of Appeal cannot stand with a decision of the Supreme Court.

(c) The decision was *per incuriam* (taken without consideration of relevant statutory provision or binding case law (*Morelle Ltd v Wakeling*[4])).

2.6 It has since been established that the Criminal Division of the Court of Appeal also has a residual discretion to decline to follow a previous decision for reasons that lie outside those categories. The scope of that discretion has been considered in three cases in which the Court was presided over by successive Lord Chief Justices (*R v Simpson*,[5] *R v Rowe*[6] and *R v Magro*[7]). These cases indicate differing approaches to the scope of the discretion. However, the following principles emerge:

(a) It is only in very rare cases that the Court will decline to follow a previous decision of the Court of Appeal.

(b) If it is considering doing so it will usually sit as a Court of five judges rather than the usual two or three. Such a Court will usually be presided over by the Lord Chief Justice.

(c) If the effect of refusing to follow a previous decision would be to render the appellant guilty of a crime of which he would not otherwise be guilty, the Court will be bound to follow the decision in question.

(d) If failing to follow the previous decision has the effect of exposing the appellant to some lesser disadvantage, that may be a powerful factor against departing from the decision.

(e) If the previous decision can be said to be *per incuriam*, very broadly understood (for example, if the matter in issue was not properly argued or if all the relevant authorities were not drawn to the Court's attention), the Court may in those circumstances decide not to follow that decision.

---

3   [1944] KB 718.
4   [1955] 2 QB 379.
5   [2003] EWCA Crim 1499.
6   [2007] EWCA Crim 635.
7   [2010] EWCA Crim 1575.

(f)   However, if the previous decision was reached following full argument on the point and careful consideration of all the relevant authorities and statutory provisions, the Court may regard itself as being bound to follow that decision.

JUDGMENTS OF THE EUROPEAN COURT OF HUMAN RIGHTS

2.7   The European Convention on Human Rights ('the Convention') is a Convention between European states which was incorporated by the Human Rights Act 1998 ('HRA 1998') into domestic law. The effect of HRA 1998 is to require the Courts to:

(a)   Interpret legislation in so far as possible to give effect to the Convention. However, Parliament remains the ultimate source of law. Therefore if the Court is unable to interpret a statute so as to render it compatible with the Convention, it must make a declaration of incompatibility that will require Parliament to consider amending the legislation.

(b)   Interpret statutory instruments in accordance with the requirements of the Convention or refuse to apply them if they cannot be interpreted in a way that is compatible with the Convention.

(c)   Develop the common law so as to give effect to the Convention.

2.8   The European Court of Human Rights ('ECtHR') determines cases brought against a state that is a signatory to the Convention. HRA 1998 requires that in determining the scope of Convention rights the domestic courts must 'take account' of any relevant judgment of the ECtHR.[8]

2.9   This requirement is interpreted by the domestic courts as meaning that they should give great weight to the judgments of the ECtHR and strive to follow them. However, they do not regard themselves as bound to follow the ECtHR. If, after careful consideration, the domestic courts reach a different conclusion as to what the Convention requires, the courts should not follow the jurisprudence of the ECtHR.[9]

2.10   The case law[10] suggests that when the Court of Appeal is contemplating disagreeing with the ECtHR it will sit as a Court of five judges presided over by the Lord Chief Justice or the Vice President. Faced with a conflict of approach between the Supreme Court and the ECtHR the Court of Appeal is bound by the doctrine of precedent to follow the Supreme Court.

---

8   Human Rights Act 1998, s. 2(1)(a).
9   *R v Horncastle* [2009] UKSC 14.
10   *R v Horncastle* [2009] EWCA Crim 964; *R v McLoughlin* [2014] EWCA Crim 188.

2.11   Whether the ECtHR provides a useful avenue of redress, when an appeal against conviction or sentence is refused is considered in Chapter 11, below.

EUROPEAN UNION LAW AND INTERNATIONAL LAW

2.12   The European Union now has explicit but limited powers to legislate in matters of substantive criminal law[11] and criminal procedure.[12] It may only do so through directives. They must usually be incorporated into domestic law by legislation in order to have effect. Clearly, EU law will be an important aid to the interpretation of legislation that seeks to bring it into domestic effect. However, EU law may also shape our domestic criminal law even in the absence of such domestic legislation, if and when it confers rights on individuals that may be relied on in court.[13]

2.13   International law consists of customary international law (general international practice which is accepted as law) and international treaties. Like European Union law, it too may shape the common law even when it has not been incorporated into domestic law, when the effect of a rule or principle of international law is to create individual rights.

2.14   An important example of the role that both EU and international law can play in the criminal law lies in the protection of victims of human trafficking. International conventions[14] and an EU Directive on human trafficking[15] require the UK to take steps to ensure that victims of trafficking who have been compelled to commit an offence as a direct consequence of having been trafficked are not prosecuted for those offences. In *R v L, HVN, THN & T*[16] the Court found that, in order to comply with its international and EU obligations, the domestic courts should stay, as an abuse of process, the prosecution of a victim of trafficking whose offending was carried out as a direct result of having been trafficked.

2.15   Although international and EU law may be sources of rights, it is a well-recognised principle that criminal offences may now only be created by Parliament. Whilst there are several old common law offences which the

---

11   Treaty of the European Union, Art. 83.
12   Treaty of the European Union, Art. 82(2).
13   *Van Duyn v Home Office* (Case C-226/07) [1974] ECR 1337.
14   Council of Europe Convention on Action against Trafficking in Human Beings 2005 (CETS No. 197) and the Protocol to Prevent, Suppress and Punish Trafficking in Persons, especially Women and Children ('the Palermo Protocol'), supplementing the United Nations Convention against Transnational Organised Crime 2000.
15   EU Directive 2011/36/EU on Preventing and Combating Trafficking in Human Beings and Protecting its Victims.
16   [2013] EWCA Crim 991.

courts still recognise, the courts will not recognise new offences unless they are created by domestic legislation. Therefore, neither EU law (absent a major EU Treaty change) nor international law can be used to establish or extend the bounds of criminal liability without being incorporated into domestic law by Parliament.

SUMMARY OF KEY POINTS

- The Court of Appeal (Criminal Division) is bound to follow the decisions of the Supreme Court and its predecessor, the Judicial Committee of the House of Lords.

- It is generally bound to follow previous decisions of the Court of Appeal. However, there are certain exceptions that would allow it to depart from such a decision.

- The Court is bound to interpret the law in accordance with the requirements of the European Convention on Human Rights. If it cannot interpret a statute in accordance with the requirements of the Convention it must make a declaration of incompatibility.

- In interpreting the requirements of the Convention, it must have regard to the decisions of the European Court of Human Rights. However, it is not bound by them.

- The Court may take into account important principles of EU and international law when interpreting the requirements of our criminal law, even when it has not been incorporated into domestic law by statute.

- However, although there are several old common law offences that are recognised by the courts, statute is now the only source of new criminal liability.

Chapter 3

Appeals against conviction

INTRODUCTION

3.1   The application form for a reference from the Criminal Cases Review Commission asks applicants to describe 'what went wrong and what is new?' This question captures the many potentially overlapping grounds of appeal against conviction that are advanced before the Court of Appeal. The Court expects an applicant to clearly identify either some irregularity in the trial process or some new development such as fresh evidence or (more rarely) some change in the law. But, whilst the identification of grounds may be necessary, it is never sufficient. The grounds must meet a single test: whether the conviction is unsafe.

THE MEANING OF 'UNSAFE'

3.2   Section 2(1) of CAA 1968, as amended by CAA 1995, provides that:

'Subject to the provisions of this Act, the Court of Appeal –

(a)   shall allow an appeal against conviction if they think that the conviction is unsafe; and

(b)   shall dismiss such an appeal in any other case.'

3.3   The meaning of the term 'unsafe' was considered by Lord Bingham CJ, as he then was, in the judgment of the Court in *R v Criminal Cases Review Commission, ex p. Pearson*[1] at para 10:

'The expression "unsafe" in section 2(1)(a) of the 1968 Act does not lend itself to precise definition. In some cases unsafety will be obvious, as (for example) where it appears that someone other than the appellant committed the crime and the appellant did not, or where the appellant has been convicted of an act that was not in law a crime, or where a conviction is shown to be vitiated by serious unfairness in the conduct of the trial

---

1   [2000] 1 Cr App R 141.

or significant legal misdirection, or where the jury verdict, in the context of other verdicts, defies any rational explanation. Cases however arise in which unsafety is much less obvious: cases in which the court, although by no means persuaded of an appellant's innocence, is subject to some lurking doubt or uneasiness whether an injustice has been done (*R v Cooper [1969] 1 QB 267 at 271*). If, on consideration of all the facts and circumstances of the case before it, the court entertains real doubts whether the appellant was guilty of the offence of which he has been convicted, the court will consider the conviction unsafe. In these less obvious cases the ultimate decision of the Court of Appeal will very much depend on its assessment of all the facts and circumstances.'

3.4   An unsafe conviction, then, can be considered a wrongful conviction. Although Lord Bingham was careful not to seek to provide a comprehensive definition of the factors that might lead the Court to regard a conviction as unsafe, the passage outlines some of the key features of the test.

Error or new evidence giving rise to doubt as to guilt

3.5   Is a conviction unsafe only when there are grounds to doubt the guilt of the convicted person or does it involve wider questions of fairness and procedural regularity in the trial process? As Lord Bingham's speech from *Pearson* indicates, the Courts have come to embrace the broad understanding of the test; a conviction may be unsafe even where there is no doubt as to guilt, where the conviction has been obtained following a trial that was unfair.

3.6   However, it is only in rare cases that the Court will be prepared to find a conviction unsafe in the absence of any real doubt as to guilt. In most appeals, the Court's approach is to consider whether, had the error or irregularity not occurred, 'the only proper and reasonable verdict be one of guilty.' (*R v Davis, Rowe and Johnson*[2]). If the Court concludes that the verdict would still have been one of guilty, it is likely to find that the conviction is safe.

3.7   This approach involves the Court placing itself in the position of the jury and asking how the matter that is the subject of the appeal may have led to its returning a different verdict.

3.8   In relation to grounds of appeal concerning a failure of disclosure, the Court should ask whether 'there was a real possibility of a different outcome – if the jury might reasonably have come to a different view on the issue to

---

2   [2001] 1 Cr App R 8 at 132.

which it directed its verdict if the withheld material had been disclosed to the defence.'[3]

The jury impact test

3.9   The correctness of this 'jury impact' approach was considered in appeals that turned on the admission of fresh evidence. In *Stafford v DPP*,[4] the House of Lords held that when fresh evidence was received by the Court, the Court itself had to assess the impact of that evidence on the safety of the conviction and not what effect it might have had upon the jury.

3.10   In *R v Pendleton*,[5] the majority of the House of Lords found that whilst the fundamental question of whether the conviction was safe was for the Court itself, the Court might be at a disadvantage in relating that evidence to the evidence that the jury had heard. Therefore, in all but the clearest cases, it would be wise for the Court to consider whether the evidence might reasonably have affected the verdict of the jury.

3.11   In the subsequent case law differently constituted Courts emphasised either the potential jury impact of fresh evidence or the Court's own task of assessing for itself the potential impact of the evidence (see *R v Noye*[6]).

3.12   Although the two approaches will generally produce the same result there may be some benefit to the defence to frame arguments in terms of the potential jury impact of the error or new evidence that is the subject of the grounds of appeal. It may be cited so long as it is couched in the terms that were recognised as correct in *Pendleton* and the latter case law.

'Unsafe' and 'unfair'

3.13   Article 6(1) of the European Convention of Human Rights, provides the right to a fair trial, with Article 6(3) providing a number of specific fair trial guarantees. After the Human Rights Act bought the Convention into domestic force, an unfair trial was an unlawful trial and a conviction following such a trial is unsafe. This logic was not immediately recognised by the Court of Appeal in *R v Davis, Rowe and Johnson*[7] which, at para 135 stressed that an unfair trial and an unsafe conviction were two distinct concepts. However,

---

3   Lord Kerr, speaking in an extra judicial capacity, at the Justice Scotland International Human Rights Day Lecture 2013, Miscarriage of Justice – When Should an Appellate Court Quash Conviction? 10 December 2013.

4   [1974] AC 878.

5   [2001] UKHL 66.

6   [2011] EWCA Crim 650.

7   See fn 2, above

without eliding the two tests, the Court has since made it clear that a trial that is unfair will almost certainly also be unsafe.

3.14 In *R v Togher*,[8] Lord Woolf CJ said: 'we consider that if a defendant has been denied a fair trial it will almost be inevitable that the conviction will be regarded as unsafe.'

3.15 This principle was confirmed in subsequent cases such as *R v Forbes*[9] and the Privy Council case of *R v Randall*,[10] in which Lord Bingham made clear that in the absence of a fair trial a conviction was likely to be unsafe even in the face of strong evidence of guilt:

> 'There will come a point where the departure from good practice is so gross, or persistent, or prejudicial, or irremediable that an appellate Court will have no choice but to condemn the trial as unfair and quash the conviction as unsafe, however strong the grounds for believing the defendant to be guilty.'

3.16 This jurisprudence is consistent with the law in relation to abuse of process, which recognises that a prosecution may give rise to abuse of process if either a fair trial was not possible or it would not be fair to try the defendant (*R v Horseferry Road Magistrates' Court, ex p. Bennett*[11]). The refusal of the trial judge to stay a case as an abuse of process may itself be the subject of appeal.

3.17 However, it is not every breach of the right to a fair trial that will render a conviction unsafe. It will only be if the trial itself could be said to be unfair that the conviction would be considered unsafe *(R v Togher*[12]*)*.

3.18 This is not to say that individual breaches of Article 6, particularly Article 6(3), could not form the basis of successful grounds as long as the appellant was able to show that had these breaches not taken place there was a real chance that he would not have been convicted.

Procedural irregularity

3.19 When the Court can be satisfied that a procedural irregularity in the trial process materially disadvantaged a defendant such that in the absence of the defect the jury may have had a doubt as to his guilt, then the usual approach of considering whether there are real grounds to doubt the appellant's

---

8   [2001] 1 Cr App R 33, para 30.
9   [2001] 1 Cr App R 31.
10   [2002] UKPC 19.
11   [1993] 3 All ER 138 (HL).
12   See fn 8, above.

guilt can be applied without difficulty. An example of this approach in action can be found in relation to the judge's decision to allow an amendment to the indictment in *R v O'Connor*,[13] where the applicant would be expected to explain how the amendment was unfair and how it disadvantaged him in the conduct of his case.

3.20   In such cases, it will be important to be able to explain whether the procedural flaw was raised at trial and if so, why not. The Court will wish to know that the defence did not make a deliberate tactical decision not to raise the point, in the belief that this would give the defendant some advantage at trial, only to switch tactics on appeal.

3.21   If the defendant has suffered no clear disadvantage, will procedural irregularity lead to the conviction being quashed? The approach of the Courts is to ask whether it was the intention of Parliament that the failure to follow the procedure in question should render the proceedings a nullity. If so, then it is likely that the conviction will be unsafe. An example of this principle at work can be found in *R v Clarke and McDaid*[14] in which the House of Lords held that the failure to sign an indictment rendered the trial process a nullity because Parliament had provided in sections 1 and 2 of the Administration of Justice (Miscellaneous Provisions) Act 1993 that an indictment must be signed to be valid and a trial could only take place on the basis of a valid indictment.[15]

3.22   A further example is to be found in relation to misjoinder. When charges wrongly joined are therefore in breach of rule 9 of the Indictment Rules (*R v Smith (Brian Peter)*[16]), the misjoined charge will be quashed. However, this misjoinder will not render the proceedings a nullity and the remaining charges will be unaffected, unless prejudice is caused to the defence.

'Lurking doubt'

3.23   Despite all that has been said above about the need to advance particular grounds, the Court may in rare circumstances be prepared to conclude that a conviction is unsafe, in the absence of either irregularity at trial or new evidence, if it nonetheless has some doubt or uneasiness about the verdict which makes the Court wonder if an injustice had been done.

3.24   This was recognised as a proper basis to quash a conviction in *R v Cooper*.[17] That this ground has survived the introduction of the new test of

---

13   [1997] Crim LR 516 (CA).
14   [2008] UKHL 8.
15   However, following the Coroners and Justice Act 2009, s.116, it is no longer the case that an indictment must be signed in order for it to be valid.
16   [1997] 1 Cr App R 390 (CA).
17   [1969] 1 QB 267 (CA) at 271.

unsafety was indicated by Lord Bingham in *Pearson* although in *R v Pope*[18] the Court indicated that it would only be in the most exceptional circumstances that a conviction would be found to be unsafe on this ground alone.

Conclusion: 'unsafe' as a flexible test

3.25   The above comments are illustrations of how the Court has approached the question of unsafety in particular circumstances. They should not be regarded as immutable doctrines. The Court has repeatedly emphasised that there is a single statutory test of unsafety and has shown considerable flexibility in its application.

3.26   The Court does not always elaborate on the basis upon which it has concluded that the conviction is unsafe. This is often so when the Court finds that the conviction is unsafe because of the cumulative effect of a number of errors that are detailed in a number of distinct grounds.

3.27   When the Court's basis for finding a conviction to be unsafe is set out, the Court may approach the issue of fairness and jury impact in a number of different ways. For example, the closer that the error complained of goes to a core feature of a fair trial, the more likely it is that the Court will be prepared to find that the conviction was unsafe without extensive enquiry as to what the verdict might have been if the error had not been made. So, when the judge fails to direct the jury on the balance and burden of proof, it has been held only when the case was overwhelming that the conviction would be regarded as safe (*Davis, Rowe and Johnson*[19])

3.28   This does not make it easy for lawyers who are asked to advise on appeal against conviction. Given that an unsafe conviction is a wrongful conviction, it may be helpful to consider, in each case, why is it that the conviction must be regarded as wrongful. This is likely to provide the best guide to the way in which the Court will approach the case.

THE COURT'S APPROACH TO COMMON ISSUES

Appeal following a guilty plea

3.29   The fact that a defendant has pleaded guilty does not act as a bar to any appeal against conviction. However, the guilty plea is likely to be regarded by the Courts as a very significant factor in favour of the safety of the conviction.

---

18   [2013] EWCA Crim 2241.
19   See fn 2, above.

The Court has been prepared to allow appeals against conviction following a guilty plea, in the following circumstances:

(a)   Guilty pleas will be treated as a nullity and quashed where they were equivocal. However, in those circumstances an application should first have been made to the Crown Court to re-open. Any appeal must be against the judge's ruling.

(b)   Guilty plea following flawed legal advice: the advice must go to the heart of the guilty plea. The elements of the offence may do so, advice on the likely length of sentence will not (*R v Saik*[20]).

(c)   Guilty plea following erroneous ruling by the judge may be regarded as giving rise to an unsafe conviction but only where the ruling has the effect of depriving the defendant of a real choice as to whether to plead guilty (*R v Chalkley and Jeffries*[21]).

(d)   In *R v Togher*,[22] other defendants had secured a stay as a result of non-disclosure. At the time when he pleaded guilty, the appellant was not aware of the material upon which the abuse of process application was based. The Court found that it would be iniquitous for the conviction to stand.

(e)   Lack of jurisdiction or procedural irregularity that rendered the proceedings a nullity (*R v Davies*[23]).

Trial rulings

3.30   There is a high threshold to cross when challenging the decision of a judge in relation to a ruling made at trial. How high is less clear. It is not sufficient that the Court may not have reached the same decision. What is less certain is whether the ruling must be so manifestly wrong as to be regarded as *Wednesbury* unreasonable or whether it was sufficient for the Court to form its own view that the decision was wrong. The better view seems to be that when the Court reaches the view that it is 'clearly wrong' it should go on to consider the safety of the conviction. This was the approach adopted in *R vMcCann*[24] in which it was said that:

'To reverse the judge's ruling it is not enough that the members of this Court would have exercised their discretion differently. We must be clearly satisfied that the judge was wrong; but our powers to review the exercise of his discretion is not limited to cases in which he has erred in principle or

---

20   [2004] EWCA Crim 2936.
21   [1998] 2 Cr App R 79.
22   See fn 8, above.
23   [1983] 76 Cr App R 120.
24   (1991) 92 Cr App R 239.

there is shown to have been no material on which he could properly have arrived at his decision. The Court must, if necessary, examine anew the relevant facts and circumstances to exercise a discretion by way of review if it thinks that the judge's ruling may have resulted in injustice to the appellants. See *Evans v. Bartlam [1937] AC 473.'*

3.31   In the subsequent case of *R v Quinn*,[25] it was held that the Court of Appeal would not interfere with a ruling of the trial judge unless and until the judge failed to take into account relevant factors or took account of irrelevant factors. However, in *R v Hanson*[26] in relation to rulings on bad character, the Court held:

'If a judge has directed himself or herself correctly, this Court will be very slow to interfere with a ruling either as to admissibility or as to the consequences of noncompliance with the regulations for the giving of notice of intention to rely on bad character evidence. It will not interfere unless the judge's judgment as to the capacity of prior events to establish propensity is plainly wrong, or discretion has been exercised unreasonably in the *Wednesbury* sense.'

Defective summing up

Judge commenting on the evidence

3.32   The judge is entitled to comment on the facts. It is the role of the judge to provide guidance on factual as well as legal issues. However, these comments should not jeopardise the jury's own consideration of the evidence by being clearly partisan. The judge should direct the members of the jury that they were the judges of fact and should only take into account views expressed by the judge to the extent that it agreed with their own. If this direction is provided, it will be regarded by the Court as an important factor in considering whether any comments made by the judge might have improperly influenced the jury. However, in a case in which the judge's comments were particularly extreme or damaging, the conviction will not be made safe by the parrot-like recitation that 'it is matter for you, the jury'; see Lord Bingham in *R v Bentley*,[27] citing with approval the judgment of Lloyd LJ in *Gilbey.*[28]

3.33   As always, the key test is whether the judge's conduct is such as to render the conviction unsafe. Appeals may succeed if the judge has made clear

---

25   [1996] Crim LR 516.
26   [2005] EWCA Crim 824, para 15.
27   [2001] 1 Cr App R 21.
28   (unreported) 26 January 1990.

his preference for the prosecution case (see *R v Bryant*[29]), has undermined the advocate in the eyes of the jury, or has interrupted so much as to prevent the defence from being able to properly advance its case (see *R v Lashley*,[30] another successful appeal from the same trial judge as in *Bryant)*.

Summing up on a different basis to that advanced at trial

3.34   There is no bar to the judge summing up the prosecution case on a different basis to that which it was put by the prosecution at trial. However, the judge must proceed with caution. There is an obvious danger that the fairness of the trial will be prejudiced where the judge introduces lines of argument to which the defence have had no opportunity to respond to (*R v Falconer-Atlee*[31]).

Leaving alternative verdicts to the jury

3.35   Whether to leave alternative, lesser counts to the jury is a matter that the judge should raise with counsel but is ultimately a matter for the judge himself. It should generally be done where it obviously arises on the evidence. A failure to do so is highly likely to lead to a verdict being quashed (*R v Coutts*[32] and *R v Foster*[33]).

Getting the law wrong

3.36   As discussed above at **3.27**, a failure to properly direct the jury on the balance and burden of proof will be regarded as highly likely to render a conviction unsafe. Other failures in directing the jury on the law, such as to correctly identify the elements of the offence or the defence relied upon may provide powerful grounds of appeal. However, it should never be assumed that such errors will automatically lead the Court to conclude that the conviction is unsafe. If the judge has not provided the correct wording in a particular passage, the Court will look to the summing up as a whole to see whether it provided the jury with the appropriate guidance. Even in those cases where it failed to do so, the Court is likely to consider whether, in the circumstances of the case, there is a real risk that it leads the jury to adopt the wrong approach.

---

29   [2005] EWCA Crim 2079.
30   [2005] EWCA Crim 2016.
31   (1974) 58 Cr App R 348.
32   [2006] UKHL 39.
33   [2007] EWCA Crim 2869.

The significance of 'specimen directions'

3.37   The Court of Appeal has made it clear that the specimen directions are not blueprints that must be slavishly followed (*R v Millard*[34]). In the forward to the *Judicial Studies Board Crown Court Bench Book* (2010), the Lord Chief Justice placed increased emphasis on the importance of the judge crafting his own directions:

> 'We are all familiar with the so-called "specimen directions" for juries. We read of them in the news. We hear much about them in the Court of Appeal. And, of course, we use them in the Crown Court. But the great value of the specimen direction has also the potential to be a weakness. What was intended to provide guidance and assistance to judges has, on many occasions, to all intents and purposes, operated as if judges were bound by them when they were preparing their summing up and sometimes the specimen directions have been incanted mechanistically and without any sufficient link with the case being tried.
>
> In this Benchbook, the objective has been to move away from the perceived rigidity of specimen directions towards a fresh emphasis on the responsibility of the individual judge, in an individual case, to craft directions appropriate to that case.'

3.38   It is clear from this that a failure to follow the specimen directions that are contained in the Bench Book will not itself render a direction defective. A direction will be defective only to the extent that it fails to clearly and accurately set out the relevant law as the jury should apply it (*R v Keene*[35]).

Grounds in relation to the jury

Jury selection

3.39   Irregularities in the selection of the jury may give rise to an appeal. In certain circumstances the failure to follow the correct procedure for jury selection may render the trial a nullity, leading to the issue of the writ of *venire de novo* (*R v Tarrant*[36]). See **3.81–3.82** below, on retrials and *venire de novo*.

Allegations of jury misconduct

3.40   It has been known for a convicted person, his family or his lawyers to be contacted by former jurors who express disquiet at what took place in

---

34   [2003] EWCA Crim 3629.
35   [2010] EWCA Crim 2514, para 20.
36   [1998] Crim LR 342.

the jury room. If this occurs, those taking a statement from the former juror are in danger of committing an offence if they pose questions whose answers would breach section 8 of the Contempt of Court Act 1981, which prohibits the disclosure of a jury's deliberations. The Courts are not subject to that section and can authorise enquiries; see *R v Thompson*.[37] However, evidence in relation to jury deliberations is inadmissible unless the juror's approach involves a complete repudiation of his oath to try the case on the evidence or involves extraneous material being introduced into jury deliberations. It is therefore only in one of these two circumstances that jury deliberations can form a ground of appeal.

3.41   The sensible course for any lawyer coming into possession of complaints about the jury's deliberations from former jurors is to swiftly contact the Registrar to seek guidance and to draft grounds of appeal in reliance on what they have already, then allow the Court to control any further investigations.

3.42   If grounds are drafted based on a former juror's account, the Court may ask the Criminal Cases Review Commission to undertake enquires by tracing the whole jury and taking statements from them. It should not be assumed that these enquiries will be made as a matter of course; in *R v Baybasin*[38] the Lord Chief Justice stated that where a complaint is first raised after verdict, the Court will assume that any genuine problem would have been raised before, and will therefore not order enquiries to be made in the absence of any other 'strong and compelling evidence'.

3.43   Even after an investigation, the Court may be wary of relying on the allegations made by former jurors when those matters were not raised at trial. Usually, the Court will proceed on the basis that a complaint made by a juror after a trial is simply a protest against a verdict with which he disagreed (see *R v Lewis*[39]). All this said, the reservations expressed by the Court are never in absolute terms. If a former juror is able to produce a powerful account such as casts doubt on the safety of the verdict, and if he has a credible explanation for not raising the matter during the trial, such later complaints can be the foundation for an appeal.

Possible jury bias

3.44   Allegations of jury bias will often not require investigation into what occurred in the jury room. That is because the Court's starting point is to consider the appearance of potential bias.

---

37   [2010] EWCA Crim 1623.
38   [2013] EWCA Crim 2357.
39   [2013] EWCA Crim 776.

3.45   The Court will consider whether 'the fair minded and informed observer having considered the facts would conclude that there was a real possibility that the jury were biased' (*Porter v Magill; Weeks v Magill*[40]).

Adverse publicity

3.46   The Court takes the view that jurors know their duty and will be robust in disregarding what they have read or viewed in the media; see the trial direction of Hughes J, as he then was, later cited with approval by the Court in *R v Abu Hamza*.[41] The cases where appeals founded on adverse publicity have met with any success have almost all been where the publicity was during the trial and was focused on the facts of the case itself or had a direct and obvious link, such as *R v McCann*[42] and *R v Taylor*.[43]

Fresh evidence

3.47   The Court has the power to receive fresh evidence after a conviction where it is in the interests of justice to do so. The considerations that the Court must have regard to are set out in section 23(2)(a)–(d) of CAA 1968 and are:

(a)   whether the evidence is capable of belief;

(b)   whether the evidence may afford any ground for allowing the appeal;

(c)   whether the evidence would have been admissible at trial; and

(d)   whether there is a reasonable explanation for the failure to adduce that evidence at trial.

3.48   The Court has emphasised that the application of these considerations is highly fact sensitive but that all four need to be addressed in any application (see *R v Erskine*[44]). In the same case, Lord Judge CJ said at para 39: 'the considerations … are neither exhaustive nor conclusive'.

3.49   The most usual occasions in which one might seek to adduce fresh evidence that does not meet all the section 23 criteria, however, is where there is no sound reason why the evidence was not called at trial (usually an application to adduce such evidence will also be accompanied by criticism of trial lawyers for failing to adduce, see below). This is not to say that the Court encourages such applications, but the comment by Lord Judge in *Erskine* confirms that the

---

40   [2001] UKHL 67.
41   [2006] EWCA Crim 2918.
42   (1991) 92 Cr App R 239.
43   (1994) 98 Cr App R 361.
44   [2009] EWCA Crim 1425.

considerations are not prerequisites and so fresh evidence can be received if it is in the interests of justice to do so even where they are not met.

3.50 The Court has also made clear that it will normally not allow an appellant to run a different case on appeal from the one advanced at trial. For example in *R v H*,[45] Lord Justice Judge, as he then was, said at para 82: 'It follows that this court will only permit an appellant to present a factual case inconsistent with his instructions and sworn testimony at the trial at which he was convicted in the most exceptional circumstances'.

3.51 It is obvious from all the above that the Court is eager not to encourage convicted defendants from trying to appeal by acquiring and deploying further evidence. All that said, when a convicted person or his legal advisors have compelling evidence that suggests he may be innocent of the offence, this type of application for leave to appeal should be pursued. The test that the Court has to apply in determining whether a conviction is unsafe in the light of fresh evidence is considered above at **3.9–3.12**. The procedures for doing so are considered in at **6.31**.

Errors of defence lawyers

3.52 Allegations that the defendant's trial lawyers committed serious errors in the conduct of the defence case can provide a perfectly sound basis for an appeal, but there are three important things to bear in mind. First, the trial lawyers have to be given the chance to explain how they conducted the case. Secondly, the Court will require clear evidence of fault before this ground succeeds, and thirdly (as always), the Court must determine whether the errors make the conviction unsafe.

3.53 There is no one method for seeking the views of trial lawyers, as long as it is done fully and fairly. The applicant will have to waive privilege and the trial lawyers need to be given a clear indication of what questions are being asked of them and what criticisms are being made. The practicalities of obtaining a waiver and communicating with previous representatives are considered at **6.13– 6.14**.

3.54 If the reply by the trial team conflicts with the applicant's account of what took place, the Court is likely to prefer the lawyers' recollections unless there are contemporaneous records that contradict them. So obtaining as many of the trial notes and papers as possible is always a good idea.

3.55 Historically, the Court made clear that the decisions of trial lawyers made in good faith after proper consideration of the competing arguments and,

---

45 [2002] EWCA Crim 730.

where appropriate, after consultation with the defendant, would not make a verdict unsafe even though the Court disagreed with that decision. On the other hand, if a decision was taken in defiance of, or without, proper instruction, or when 'all promptings of reason and common sense pointed the other way', that may render a conviction unsafe (see *R v Clinton*[46]).

3.56   In more recent cases based on the failings of trial lawyers, the Court has moved away from any test of incompetence and instead focused on the single statutory test of safety (see *R v Day*[47]).

3.57   However, *Day* has not altered the Court's traditionally cautious approach to criticism of former representatives. It tends to be robust in finding that trial lawyers who take decisions in the heat of a trial are not to be criticised unless those decisions were very clearly flawed. It is wary of applying the benefit of hindsight to difficult forensic decisions.

3.58   The final requirement is that the failings of the trial lawyers have the effect of making the conviction unsafe. These would have to be major and significant events in the case, for example not calling powerful alibi evidence or not advising the defendant properly about the advantages of giving evidence. Without such a connection, there can be very serious problems with the trial lawyers but no successful appeal will result. In a spectacular example of this principle in action, the Court found that two murder convictions were safe even though trial counsel was under investigation for serious sexual offences and the supply of class A drugs, and was also made bankrupt whilst simultaneously conducting two trials in different parts of the country. In rejecting the appeal, the Court reviewed not only the manner in which the advocate conducted the trials but also the strength of the evidence (which in the case of both appellants was overwhelming) (*R v Bolivar; R v Lee*[48]).

Changes in the law

3.59   Changes in the law since conviction may provide grounds of appeal but only if this change has given rise to substantial injustice (*R v R (Amer)*[49]).

THE COURT'S POWERS

3.60   The Court may either allow or dismiss an appeal. If it allows the appeal it must quash the conviction. Unless it orders a re-trial the effect of the

---

46   (1993) 97 Cr App R 320.
47   [2003] EWCA Crim 1060.
48   [2003] EWCA Crim 1167.
49   [2006] EWCA Crim 1974.

conviction being quashed is to require the Crown Court to record a judgment and verdict of acquittal.

3.61   If the Court quashes a conviction it is not required to make any further order. However, it may:

(a)   substitute the conviction with a conviction for an alternative offence upon which he could have been convicted in the Crown Court;

(b)   order that a re-trial take place; or

(c)   re-sentence the appellant in respect of related convictions for which the sentence was not quashed.

3.62   Although CAA 1968 does not expressly frame these as alternatives, it would be difficult to see how they could be fairly combined.

Substituting a conviction

3.63   Where a defendant was convicted of a particular count but might, on the same evidence, have been convicted on an alternative count, the Court of Appeal has the power to substitute the conviction of one offence for a conviction for another.[50]

3.64   In *R v Graham*[51] the Court held that the power could only be exercised when the following criteria were met:

(a)   The jury could, on the indictment, have found the appellant guilty of some other offence, because the allegation in the count of which the appellant was convicted expressly or impliedly included this other count.

(b)   By their verdict of guilty on the count that is subject to appeal, the jury must also have been satisfied of the facts that rendered the appellant guilty of this other offence.

3.65   The Court must impose a sentence for the new count but that sentence cannot be so long as to increase the overall length of sentence above that which was imposed in the Crown Court.

---

50   CAA 1968, s. 3 in respect of offences for which he was convicted by a jury, s. 3A in respect of offences to which the appellant had originally pleaded guilty.

51   (1997) 1 Cr App R 302.

Re-trials

The circumstances in which a re-trial can be ordered

3.66   The test for whether to order a re-trial is whether it is in the interests of justice to do so.[52] This may involve consideration of a number of factors. The following are commonly considered by the Court:

(a)   how much of the original sentence the appellant has already served;

(b)   the seriousness of the offence;

(c)   the time that elapsed since the commission of the offence and any particular difficulties that the passage of time may cause the parties in now conducting the case;

(d)   whether the appeal was allowed as a result of errors in the original trial which can be easily remedied at a re-trial (for example, errors in the legal directions that were provided to the jury) or whether difficulties in the original trial are likely to be present in any future trial (for example, abuse of process caused by delay, inherent weakness in the prosecution's case); and

(e)   personal circumstances of the appellant (for example, age or poor health).

3.67   The type of convictions that may be subject to a retrial are set out in s 7(2):

'(2)   A person shall not under this section be ordered to be retried for any offence other than –

(a)   the offence of which he was convicted at the original trial and in respect of which his appeal is allowed as mentioned in subsection (1) above;

(b)   an offence of which he could have been convicted at the original trial on an indictment for the first-mentioned offence; or

(c)   an offence charged in an alternative count of the indictment in respect of which the jury were discharged from giving a verdict in consequence of convicting him of the first-mentioned offence.'

The procedure for making an order for re-trial

3.68   Whether to order a re-trial is a matter for the Court. There is no statutory requirement for an application for a re-trial to have been made before the Court

---

52   CAA 1968, s. 7(1).

makes an order. However, it will usually only make it upon application of the prosecution. Therefore, the Court will expect the advocate who is appearing on behalf of the prosecution to have been provided instructions on this point prior to the appeal hearing. The defence advocate should be prepared to make submissions on the matter at the conclusion of the hearing.

3.69 If prosecuting counsel does not have instructions, the Court may put the matter back in order for him to do so. If it puts the case back to a future date for a final hearing to formally pronounce judgment and determine whether to allow a re-trial, it may consider whether to grant bail in the interim.

3.70 Once the decision of the Court to quash the conviction is formally recorded in the Crown Court as an acquittal, the Court of Appeal has no power to order a re-trial. Even if the application for a re-trial is made before this takes place, if by the time that the Court comes to consider the application the verdict of acquittal has been entered, the Court has no power to grant the application prosecution (*R v Blackwood*[53]).

The procedure once an order for re-trial is made

3.71 Once a re-trial is ordered the defendant must be arraigned on a new indictment that has been preferred by direction of the Court of Appeal, in the Crown Court. Arraignment must take place within two months of the order having been made.[54]

3.72 If it is does not take place within two months, it may only take place if the prosecution applies to the Court of Appeal for leave for arrangement to take place and the Court is satisfied both that:

(a) 'The prosecution has acted with all due expedition'; and

(b) 'That there is good and sufficient cause for a retrial' in spite of the lapse of time since the order for a retrial was made.[55]

3.73 The Court may list the matter for legal argument. If it is not satisfied that both conditions are made out, the Court will direct that an order for acquittal be recorded by the Crown Court.

3.74 When it makes an order for a re-trial, the Court has power to grant bail or order that the defendant be remanded in custody.[56] Once an indictment is preferred in the Crown Court, any applications in relation to bail must be

---

53   [2012] EWCA Crim 390.
54   CAA 1968, s. 8(2).
55   CAA 1968, s. 8(1B)(b).
56   Section 8(2).

made to the Crown Court itself. The position during the period between an order being made and an indictment being preferred is unclear. However, there is dicta in *R v X*[57] to suggest that the Crown Court does have the power to deal with bail after an order for re-trial was made.

3.75 Once the Crown Court is seized of the matter it has the power to amend the indictment. However, when considering the fairness of any application to amend, the Crown Court must take into account that the purpose of the order made by the Court of Appeal is to allow the defendant to be retried for the offences that he originally faced, not tried for new matters (*R v Booker*[58]).

3.76 The key limitation upon the power of the Crown Court is that a sentence that is passed in respect of a conviction that was secured following a re-trial may not be more severe than the sentence that was originally imposed by the Crown Court.[59] There is dicta to suggest that when a defendant originally pleaded guilty, successfully appealed his conviction, but then was convicted by a jury, a sentence that was longer than that which was originally imposed (to take account of the fact a discount was originally made to reflect the guilty plea) may not necessarily be regarded as 'more severe' (*R v Skanes*[60]).

3.77 A sentence of imprisonment that is imposed following a re-trial takes effect as if it was imposed on the date of the original sentence. However, time spent on bail following an order for re-trial and time in custody before trial that would not have been counted towards the original sentence is to be deducted from this period.[61]

3.78 Legal aid to cover the re-trial is not granted by the Court of Appeal. Instead, an application must be made to the Legal Aid Authority.

Re-sentencing

3.79 If the appellant was convicted of two or more offences on an indictment, the Court may re-sentence him in respect of those remaining sentences.[62] The power is often exercised to reduce the remaining sentences to take account in the reduction in the total level of criminality following the quashing of a conviction. But the Court may impose harsher sentences for the remaining offences than were originally imposed, including for an offence for which no separate penalty was originally imposed *(R v Dolan*[63]).

---

57 [2010] EWCA Crim 2367.
58 [2011] EWCA Crim 7.
59 By virtue of CAA 1968, Sch. 2, para. 2(1).
60 [2006] EWCA Crim 2309.
61 CAA 1968, Sch. 2, para. 2(3).
62 CAA 1968, s. 4.
63 (1976) 62 Cr App R 36.

3.80   However, the Court may not impose a sentence that would have the effect of rendering the overall length of sentence longer than the overall length of sentence which was originally imposed in the Crown Court.[64]

Retrial and venire de novo

3.81   In a case in which the Court finds that there was never a valid conviction, because the proceedings were so irregular so as not to constitute a proper trial, it may make an order for *venire do novo*. The effect of this is to require proceedings to start again in the Crown Court, with the original 'conviction' set aside. If the Court makes such a finding, any re-trial is free of the procedural constraints in respect of re-trials under section 7 of CAA 1968.

3.82   A writ of *venire* may be issued where the proceedings were not properly commenced or the verdict was not returned by a properly constituted jury. It may also be available in respect of other fundamental procedural errors that render the trial a nullity.

SUMMARY OF KEY POINTS

- In determining appeals against conviction the Court applies the single statutory test of whether the conviction is 'unsafe'.

- A conviction that was obtained following a trial that was fundamentally unfair will usually be considered unsafe regardless of the strength of the evidence. However, not every unfairness that occurs during trial will render a conviction unsafe. In most instances the Court will consider the impact that the error or other unfairness may have had on the verdict of the jury.

- In relation to appeals that turn on fresh evidence the Court has emphasised that the jury impact test may assist the Court but it was ultimately for the Court itself to assess the potential impact of the evidence in question.

- The Court may be prepared to allow an appeal on the basis of its 'lurking doubt', in the absence of other grounds, in the most exceptional of circumstances.

- There are a limited number of circumstances in which a conviction may be appealed following a guilty plea. They include when the plea was entered following incorrect legal advice that went to the heart of the decision to plead guilty.

---

64   CAA 1968, s. 4(3).

- A procedural error may form the basis for grounds of appeal. However, unless the error was of such a serious nature that it rendered the proceedings a nullity, it will usually be necessary to show that it caused serious prejudice to the defence in the conduct of the trial.

- A wrongful trial ruling may provide grounds of appeal. However, the ruling must have been clearly wrong or unreasonable, not merely a ruling that the Court would not itself have made.

- The failure of the defence representative may give rise to grounds of appeal. But they must be given the opportunity to answer any criticism and the Court will distinguish between genuine error and criticism of tactical decisions made with the benefit of hindsight. Any proven or admitted failure must have had the effect of rendering the conviction unsafe.

- If fresh evidence is relied on, the requirements of section 23 of CAA 1968 must be met.

- If the Court allows the appeal and quashes the conviction it may, in certain circumstances, substitute a conviction for another offence or re-sentence the defendant for any offences that remain on the indictment or order a re-trial.

- If a re-trial is ordered, arraignment must take place within two months. Any application to extend this time must be made to the Court of Appeal.

- If the defendant is convicted following a re-trial, any sentence imposed may not be more severe than the sentence that was originally imposed.

Chapter 4

Appeals against sentence

INTRODUCTION

4.1   Under section 9 of the Criminal Appeal Act 1968, a defendant may appeal to the Court of Appeal against any sentence that was imposed by the Crown Court on indictment and, in certain circumstances, against sentences imposed by the Crown Court, following a conviction in the Magistrates' Court (CAA 1968, ss. 9 and 10).

4.2   A 'sentence' is defined as 'an order made on an offender following conviction' (CAA 1968, s. 50). It therefore captures the very wide range of orders that the Crown Court is now empowered to make against those who have been convicted of an offence. The powers of the Court of Appeal when determining appeals against sentence are also broad:

'(3) On an appeal against sentence the Court of Appeal, if they consider that the appellant should be sentenced differently for an offence for which he was dealt with by the court below may –

(a)   quash any sentence or order which is the subject of the appeal; and

(b)   in place of it pass such sentence or make such order as they think appropriate for the case and as the court below had power to pass or make when dealing with him for the offence;

but the Court shall so exercise their powers under this subsection that, taking the case as a whole, the appellant is not more severely dealt with on appeal than he was dealt with by the court below.'

4.3   In order to understand how the Court employs these powers it is necessary to turn from the statute to the body of principles that it has developed. The grounds upon which the Court may be prepared to allow an appeal against sentence overlap and the terms are not always used consistently. The precise classification of grounds is less important than ensuring that the grounds clearly and succinctly identify why the sentence is wrong, by applying the underlying principles to the facts of the case.

4.4   This chapter therefore considers the types of orders that can be appealed as sentences and then sets out the principles to be applied to such appeals. There are distinct principles and powers in relation to appeals against confiscation orders. Therefore, confiscation orders are considered separately in the latter part of the chapter. However, because of the wide range of orders which may be appealed as appeals against sentence, the principles that the Court has developed in relation to appeals against confiscation orders may well also be applicable to other sentence appeals.

APPEAL AGAINST SENTENCE ON INDICTMENT AND FOR CASES SENT FROM THE MAGISTRATES' COURT

4.5   The Court may hear appeals against sentences imposed in the Crown Court following a conviction on indictment. It may also hear appeals against sentence for summary offences that had been sent to the Crown Court under section 41 of the Criminal Justice Act 1988 (power of Crown Court to deal with summary offence where person committed for either way offence) or under paragraph 6 of Schedule 3 to the Crime and Disorder Act 1998 (power of Crown Court to deal with summary offence where person sent for trial for indictable-only offence).[1]

4.6   In addition, the Court may also hear appeals against sentence for other offences sent from the Magistrates' Court in the terms set out in section 10 of CAA 1968:

'(2) The proceedings from which an appeal against sentence lies under this section are those where an offender convicted of an offence by a magistrates' court –

(a)   is committed by the court to be dealt with for his offence before the Crown Court; or

(b)   having been made the subject of an order for conditional discharge or a community order within the meaning of the Powers of Criminal Courts (Sentencing) Act 2000 or given a suspended sentence, appears or is brought before the Crown Court to be further dealt with for his offence; or

(c)   having been released under Part II of the Criminal Justice Act 1991 after serving part of a sentence of imprisonment or detention imposed for the offence, is ordered by the Crown Court to be returned to prison or detention.

(3) An offender dealt with for an offence before the Crown Court in a

---

1   CAA 1968, s. 9(b).

proceeding to which subsection (2) of this section applies may appeal to the Court of Appeal against sentence in any of the following cases:

(a) where either for that offence alone or for that offence and other offences for which sentence is passed in the same proceeding, he is sentenced to imprisonment or to youth custody under section 6 of the Criminal Justice Act 1982 for a term of six months or more; or

(b) where the sentence is one which the court convicting him had not power to pass; or

(c) where the court in dealing with him for the offence makes in respect of him –

   (i)   a recommendation for deportation; or

   (ii) an order disqualifying him for holding or obtaining a licence to drive a motor vehicle under Part II of the Road Traffic Act 1960; or

   (iii) an order under section 119 of the Powers of Criminal Courts (Sentencing) Act 2000 (orders as to existing suspended sentence when person subject to the sentence is again convicted).

   (iv) a banning order under section 14A of the Football Spectators Act 1989; or

   (v)   a declaration of relevance under the Football Spectators Act 1989; or

(cc) where the court makes such an order with regard to him as is mentioned in section 116(2) or (4) of the Powers of Criminal Courts (Sentencing) Act 2000 of the Criminal Justice Act 1991.'

What counts as a sentence?

4.7   Section 50 of CAA 1968 provides:

'(1) In this Act "sentence", in relation to an offence, includes any order made by a court when dealing with an offender including, in particular –

(a) a hospital order under Part III of the Mental Health Act 1983, with or without a restriction order;

(b) an interim hospital order under that Part;

(bb) a hospital direction and a limitation direction under that Part;

(c) a recommendation for deportation;

(d) a confiscation order under the Drug Trafficking Act 1994 other than one made by the High Court;

(e)   a confiscation order under Part VI of the Criminal Justice Act 1988;

(f)   an order varying a confiscation order of a kind which is included by virtue of paragraph (d) or (e) above;

(g)   an order made by the Crown Court varying a confiscation order which was made by the High Court by virtue of section 19 of the Act of 1994; and

(h)   a declaration of relevance under section 31 of the Public Order Act 1986 or under the Football Spectators Act 1989.

(1A) Section 14 of the Powers of Criminal Courts (Sentencing) Act 2000 (under which a conviction of an offence for which an order for a conditional or absolute discharge is made is deemed not to be a conviction except for certain purposes) shall not prevent an appeal under this Act, whether against conviction or otherwise.'

4.8   Since the list at section 50 is not exhaustive, the Court has had to consider whether a number of other orders are sentences.

Costs

4.9   Section 50(3) specifically provides that an order for recovery of defence costs under section 17 of the Access to Justice Act 1999 is not a sentence within the meaning of section 9. However, an order that the defendant pay towards the costs of the prosecution is a sentence within the meaning of the section and may therefore be appealed (*R v Hayden*[2]).

Anti-social behaviour orders

4.10   The making of an anti-social behaviour order following conviction is a sentence within the meaning of section 50 as is a subsequent decision of the Crown Court to vary or refuse an application to vary the order (*R v Preston Crown Court, ex p. Langley*[3])

Making and varying of sexual offences prevention orders

4.11   The making of a sexual offences prevention order and also a subsequent decision of the Crown Court in relation to varying such an order

---

2   (1974) 60 Cr App R 304.
3   [2008] EWHC 2623 (Admin).

is a sentence within the meaning of section 50 (*R v Hoath; R v Standage,*[4] approved in *R v Aldridge; R v Eaton*[5]).

Restraining orders

4.12   A restraining order that is made following conviction is clearly within the scope of section 50. However, by virtue of section 5A(5) of the Protection from Harassment Act 1997, so too is a restraining order that is made following an acquittal.

Financial reporting orders

4.13   Financial reporting orders are sentences for the purposes of section 50 (*R v Adams*[6]).

Appeals in relation to sentences fixed by law

4.14   A defendant who is the subject of a mandatory life sentence may appeal against the minimum term that he must serve.

Appeals by parents and guardians

4.15   Parents and guardians may appeal against:

(a)   an order that they pay a fine, costs or compensation that has been imposed on a child or young person (Powers of Criminal Courts (Sentencing) Act 2000, s. 137 (1));

(b)   an order, under section 150 of the Powers of Criminal Courts (Sentencing) Act 2000 that they enter into a recognisance to take proper care of a child or to pay a fine in lieu;

(c)   a parenting order made pursuant to section 8 of the Crime and Disorder Act 1889 (s. 10(4)).

A single right of appeal – more than one sentence

4.16   There is a single right of appeal against sentence (*R v Pinfold*[7]). A defendant cannot appeal against a particular aspect of his sentence and then

---

4   [2011] EWCA Crim 274.
5   [2012] EWCA Crim 1456.
6   [2008] EWCA Crim 914.
7   (1988) 87 Cr App R 15.

separately appeal against another, unless the case is referred back to the Court by the Criminal Cases Review Commission.

4.17   The significant exception to this relates to orders that are made on different dates as separate sentencing exercises. This occurs mainly in relation to confiscation orders, which may be made weeks or months after the original sentence was imposed. It will also apply to appeals against refusals to vary orders that were made on an earlier occasion. The 28-day time limit will run from the date when the order that is subject to appeal is made.

THE PRINCIPLES: GENERAL

What are the grounds of appeal?

4.18   The grounds upon which the Court has been prepared to allow appeals against sentence are numerous and overlapping. The terminology with which the Court describes sentencing grounds is not always consistently used. The most well-known terms are 'manifestly excessive or wrong in principle'. Although it may be said that the two terms themselves overlap (see *R v Ball*[8]), their meaning is sufficiently clear and broad to capture the variety of grounds that may be advanced. The Court will regard a sentence as manifestly excessive if it is improperly severe as a result, for example, of the judge having failed to apply the relevant guidelines, given too much weight to an aggravating feature or too little weight to a guilty plea or some piece of mitigation. A sentence may be wrong in principle if it was wrong for some other reason: if, for example, it was unlawful, or passed following a procedural failure, breach of legitimate expectation or some other important sentencing principle.

4.19   It may be helpful, therefore, for the grounds of appeal to state whether the sentence is challenged on the basis that it is manifestly excessive or wrong in principle. However, it is far more important that the grounds should go on to state clearly and succinctly exactly why it is said that the sentence is wrong. An appeal against sentence will not fail because the grounds have been misclassified. However, leave to appeal is often refused because the nature of the challenge is simply unclear.

Manifestly excessive

4.20   The term 'manifestly excessive' tends to induce a high degree of caution in the minds of many advocates. If this caution is based on a correct understanding of the term then it is justified. It is intended to exclude those sentences in which different judges might disagree. The Court often states that

---

8   (1951) 35 Cr App R 164.

the test is not whether they would have passed the same sentence but whether it is outside the range that could properly be imposed for the offence.

4.21 However, it is sometimes understood that the term 'manifestly excessive' means very or significantly excessive. It does not. If a sentence can be shown to be clearly outside that range, whether by a substantial or limited period, it is manifestly excessive.

4.22 It is right that the Court does not 'tinker' with sentences, but if a custodial sentence is manifestly excessive by months or even, in the case of shorter sentences, by weeks, then a reduction in sentence by months or weeks will hardly be considered 'tinkering' by the person who has to serve it or by a fair-minded tribunal.

4.23 Whether a sentence is manifestly excessive will depend on the facts of each case. However, the following general principles apply:

The Court will consider whether the total sentence is wrong

4.24 When a defendant is sentenced for a number of offences, the Court of Appeal is generally concerned with the correctness of the overarching sentence (the total length of the sentences imposed in a single sentencing exercise) that was imposed (*R v Razaq*[9]). So, if it can be shown that an individual sentence was excessive but the overarching sentence was correct, an application for leave is likely to be refused.

Failure to follow the guidelines

4.25 When it passes sentence for an offence that was committed before 6 April 2010, the Crown Court must have regard to any sentencing guideline that was promulgated by the Sentencing Guidelines Council.[10]

4.26 However, when the offence in question was committed after that date, the Court is bound by the stronger injunction of section 125(1) of the Coroners and Justice Act 2009 which provides:

'Every court –

(a) must, in sentencing an offender, follow any sentencing guidelines which are relevant to the offender's case, and

---

9 [2011] EWCA Crim 1518.
10 CJA 2003, s. 172, as preserved by the Coroners and Justice Act 2009 (Commencement No. 4, Transitional and Saving Provisions) Order 2010 (SI 2010/816).

(b)   must, in exercising any other function relating to the sentencing of offenders, follow any sentencing guidelines which are relevant to the function,

unless the court is satisfied that it would be contrary to the interests of justice to do so.'

4.27   In addition, section 174(2) of CJA 2003, as amended by paragraph 84 of Schedule 21 to the 2009 Act, makes clear that when sentencing for offences committed after 6 April 2010, the court must:

'(a)   identify any definitive sentencing guidelines relevant to the offender's case and explain how the court discharged any duty imposed on it by section 125 of the Coroners and Justice Act 2009,

(aa)   where the court did not follow any such guidelines because it was of the opinion that it would be contrary to the interests of justice to do so, state why it was of that opinion'[11]

4.28   The effect of this is that if the Crown Court fails to follow the applicable guideline without giving good reason for doing so or if it applies them incorrectly, this may provide a ground for appeal (*R v Mahendran*[12]). However, the sentencing judge is free to apply the guidelines in a flexible manner in order to achieve a just result:

'we have lost count of the number of times when this court has emphasised that these provisions are not intended to be applied inflexibly. Indeed, in our judgment, an inflexible approach would be inconsistent with the terms of the statutory framework ... even when the approach to the sentencing decision is laid down in an apparently detailed and on the face of it intentionally comprehensive scheme, the sentencing judge must achieve a just result.' (*R v Height and Anderson*[13])

4.29   The existence of a specific guideline will supersede previous Court of Appeal case law. However, section 125 has not diminished the weight to be attached to decisions of the Court of Appeal. Therefore the sentencing Court should take into account any significant sentencing guidance that is contained in authorities of the Court of Appeal that post-date the relevant guideline.

---

11   The same provision amends section 174 to cover guidelines issued by the Sentencing Council for England and Wales under section 120 of the 2009 Act. The guidelines which fall within the ambit of section 120 include guidelines issued by the Sentencing Guidelines Council under the 2003 Act which were in effect immediately before section 125 of the 2009 Act came into force, as well as guidelines included in any judgment of the Court given before 27 February 2004 which have not been superseded by new sentencing guidelines (see paragraph 7(1) and (5) of the Coroners and Justice Act 2009 (Commencement No 4, Transitional and Saving Provisions) Order 2010.)

12   [2011] EWCA Crim 608.

13   [2008] EWCA Crim 2500 at para 29.

'The "interests of justice" consideration which now, and we assume always has and always will underpin the work of the Sentencing Guidelines Council (now the Sentencing Council), undoubtedly involves consideration of the subsequent thinking of this court and of the legislature on sentencing issues which may impact on every original definitive guidance. Just as the guidelines are not tramlines – an observation made time and time again – nor are they ring-fenced.' (*R v Thornley*[14])

4.30 A distinction should be drawn between authorities that have an impact upon the guidelines and those cases which merely apply the guidelines to the facts of the case. Advocates should recall the injunction of the Court in *Erskine*[15] about the citation of cases which are merely fact specific. (See **6.24–6.27.**)

Procedural unfairness

4.31 A failure to follow the proper procedures may provide grounds of appeal. However, the general approach of the Court is to decline to interfere with a sentence where, had the correct procedures been followed, the sentence that would have been imposed would have been essentially the same.

Post-sentence developments

4.32 The Court is not confined to considering only the material to which the sentencing judge had access. It may, in its discretion, consider material that was not before the Court or events that have occurred since the sentence took place. The appellant's conduct following sentence will often play an important part in the sentencing process. If leave is granted, the Court may ask for a report from the prison on the appellant's progress on his sentence. The Court can order its own probation report in cases where it is of the view that it may be assisted by one, even if there was no probation report in the lower court.

4.33 When considering new material in an appeal against sentence, the Court generally does not regard itself as bound by the rules in relation to fresh evidence (*R v Roberts*[16]). However, it will usually require good explanation for any failure to place material that is relied upon on appeal before the Crown Court. See **4.50** and **4.51** below for consideration of changes in the law following sentence in relation to confiscation, all of which is likely to be equally applicable to changes in the law in relation to other sentencing cases.

---

14 [2011] EWCA Crim 153.
15 [2010] EWCA Crim 1425.
16 [2006] EWCA Crim 2915.

Disparity in sentence

4.34   An unjustified disparity in sentence between co-defendants may give rise to grounds of appeal but only if 'right thinking members of the public with knowledge of the relevant facts and circumstances, learning of this sentence would consider that something had gone wrong with the administration of justice' (*R v Fawcett*[17]).

Unlawful sentences and the slip rule

4.35   When the Crown Court passes a sentence that is unlawful, in the sense that the Court does not have the power to impose it, the sentence may be appealed. However, consideration should first be given to returning to the Crown Court under the slip rule and asking the sentencing judge to correct the error. Section 155 of the Powers of the Criminal Courts (Sentencing) Act 2000 provides that a sentence that was imposed by the Crown Court can be 'varied or rescinded' up to 56 days from the date when the sentence was passed.

4.36   It is only if the judge refuses, wrongly, to correct the error or the matter is not listed within the time limit for correction that an appeal to the Court of Appeal should be lodged.

4.37   In a case where there are other grounds of appeal, it may be tempting to bypass the Crown Court entirely and have all matters dealt with on appeal. However, the time limit for appeal runs from the date of any variation[18] so nothing is lost by resolving such matters that can be resolved in the Crown Court.

Failure to credit time spent on a qualifying curfew

4.38   Although the sentencing judge is no longer required to specify the number of days spent on remand that should count towards sentence, he must still state the amount of time spent on a qualifying curfew.[19] If the judge fails, without good reason, to state the period on curfew that should be counted to towards the sentence or if the period was miscalculated, the approach outlined by the Court in *R v Gordon*[20] should be followed.

---

17   (1983) 5 Cr App R (S) 158.
18   Powers of the Criminal Courts (Sentencing) Act 2000, s 155(6).
19   Criminal Justice Act 2003, s 240A.
20   [2007] EWCA Crim 165.

POWERS OF THE COURT: GENERAL

4.39   Section 11(3) of CAA 1968 provides:

'On an appeal against sentence the Court of Appeal, if they consider that the appellant should be sentenced differently for an offence for which he was dealt with by the court below may –

(a)   quash any sentence or order which is the subject of the appeal; and

(b)   in place of it pass such sentence or make such order as they think appropriate for the case and as the court below had power to pass or make when dealing with him for the offence;

but the Court shall so exercise their powers under this subsection that, taking the case as a whole, the appellant is not more severely dealt with on appeal than he was dealt with by the Court below.'

4.40   The injunction upon the Court not to impose a more severe sentence than that which was originally imposed is clear and unequivocal. The Court cannot even impose a sentence that would be mandatory for a sentencing Court to impose (*R v Reynolds*[21]). However, whether a sentence is 'more severe' than the sentence that was the subject of appeal is not always clear. A life sentence cannot be imposed in place of a determinate sentence (*R v Whittaker*[22]). However, in *R v Bennett*,[23] the Court held that a hospital order with a restriction with an indefinite period in place of a determinate sentence, was not more severe than a determinate sentence.

RIGHTS OF APPEAL: CONFISCATION ORDERS AND OTHER ORDERS UNDER THE ASSET RECOVERY LEGISLATION

4.41   Section 50 of CAA 1968 provides that an appeal against a confiscation order, whether under the Proceeds of Crime Act 2002 ('POCA 2002') or the Drug Trafficking Act 1994 (except when the order has been made by a High Court judge) or the Criminal Justice Act 1988 is an appeal against sentence. However, there are a number of other orders that a Crown Court can make under this legislation, only some of which attract a right of appeal against sentence.

4.42   A refusal to vary a confiscation order under section 23 of POCA 2002 is not a sentence and there is no appeal to the Court of Appeal. Therefore,

---

21   [2007] EWCA Crim 538.
22   [1967] Crim LR 431.
23   (1968) 52 Cr App R 514.

the only way such an order can be challenged is by way of judicial review. However, as section 50 provides, decisions in relation to a reconsideration of benefit and available amount (POCA 2002, ss. 21 and 22) and variations of orders made whilst the defendant was considered an absconder (s. 29) under POCA 2002 are considered sentences.

4.43   In contrast, any variation or refusal to vary a confiscation order under the Drug Trafficking Act 1994 (except when the confiscation order has been made by a High Court judge) or the Criminal Justice Act 1988 is a sentence within the meaning of section 50.

4.44   Appeals against restraint or receivership orders under POCA are not appeals against sentence. However, they attract their own rights of appeal.[24]

PRINCIPLES: CONFISCATION

Grounds of appeal

4.45   There are no prescribed grounds of appeal against confiscation orders. Common grounds of appeal are that the judge erred in fact or law. The Court is often cautious about interfering with errors of fact, unless they are clear and significant. It normally accords considerable respect to factual findings of the Crown Court judge who heard the case, particularly if his judgment depends to a significant extent on assessment of live evidence that the judge heard in either the course of the confiscation hearing or the preceding trial.

The slip rule

4.46   Section 155 of the Powers of Criminal Courts (Sentencing) Act 2000 (see **4.35–4.37**, above) applies to confiscations orders (*R v Bukhari*[25]).

Fresh evidence

4.47   The statutory rules in relation to fresh evidence apply to confiscation proceedings (*R v Stroud*[26]). A party seeking to adduce fresh evidence must

---

24   Appeals against making or refusing to make a confiscation order may be made either by the person making the application or by a person affected by the order under POCA 2002, s. 43. Parts 71 and 73 of the CPR apply. The rights of Appeal in relation to receivership orders are to be found at POCA 2002, s. 65. Appeals against the registration and subsequent proceedings in relation to an external confiscation order are contained in the Proceeds of Crime Act 2002 (External Requests and Orders) Order (SI 2005/3181).

25   [2008] EWCA Crim 2915.

26   [2004] EWCA Crim 1048.

therefore meet the requirements of section 23 of CAA 1968. Much of the case law on fresh evidence in appeals against conviction is applicable to appeals against confiscation order. (See **3.47–3.51** and **6.31**.)

Appeals against confiscation orders made by consent

4.48   In *R v Mackle*,[27] the Supreme Court held that a confiscation order that had been made with the consent of the defendant but following clearly erroneous legal advice may be appealed. This overturned the decision of the Court of Appeal in *R v Hirani*[28] in which the Court found that in the absence of exceptional circumstances a defendant was bound by an order to which he consented, even if that consent was based on an entirely incorrect understanding of what he was consenting to, following bad legal advice.

4.49   *Mackle* did not provide any guidance as to how the Court of Appeal should now approach appeals based upon allegations of consent being given as a result of flawed legal advice. However, it is likely that the Court will approach in a similar manner to appeals against conviction in which it is argued that a guilty plea was tendered following bad legal advice.

Extension of time to appeal against a confiscation order following a change in the law

4.50   Following the judgment of the Supreme Court in *R v Waya*,[29] in which the Court held that the First Protocol of the Convention required the Crown Court to ensure that any confiscation order represents a proportionate interference with the defendant's property, a number of applications for extension of time within which to appeal against sentence were made by applicants whose confiscation order had been made some time ago and had not appealed because the law, prior to *Waya*, provided no grounds upon which to do so.

4.51   In *Bestel v R*,[30] the Court held that the principle of finality that decisions made under the law as it was then understood should not be disturbed unless this would cause substantial injustice, should be followed in confiscation cases.

POWERS OF THE COURT: CONFISCATION

4.52   The Court has the power under section 11(3) to impose an alternative sentence to that which was subject to appeal (see **4.39**, above). However, it also

---

27   [2014] UKSC 5.
28   [2008] EWCA Crim 1463.
29   [2012] UKSC 51.
30   [2013] EWCA Crim 1305.

has the power, under section 11(3A) to quash a confiscation order and then to remit the case to the Crown Court with a direction that a new confiscation hearing take place. When it does so, the Court of Appeal must give directions to the Crown Court as to the conduct of the new hearing. The Crown Court must not impose a confiscation order that is more severe than that which was subject to appeal.

PROSECUTION RIGHTS OF APPEAL IN CONFISCATION CASES

4.53 The prosecution enjoy rights of appeal against the terms of a confiscation order or the refusal to make a confiscation order under POCA 2002 only. Section 31 of POCA 2002 provides:

'(1) If the Crown Court makes a confiscation order the prosecutor or the Director may appeal to the Court of Appeal in respect of the order.

(2) If the Crown Court decides not to make a confiscation order the prosecutor or the Director may appeal to the Court of Appeal against the decision.

(3) Subsections (1) and (2) do not apply to an order or decision made by virtue of section 19, 20, 27 or 28.'

4.54 The 'Director' referred to is the Director of the Assets Recovery Agency. As subsection (3) provides, the prosecution enjoy none of the rights of appeal against variations of a confiscation order that are enjoyed by the defence.

4.55 The procedure in relation to these appeals is governed by Parts 71 and 72 of the CPR. The usual time limits and requirements for leave apply. The Court's powers when hearing an appeal under section 31(1) are to confirm, quash or vary the order. Its powers under section 31(2) are to make a confiscation order or to remit the case to the Crown Court for a fresh hearing.

SUMMARY OF KEY POINTS

- For the purpose of appeal against sentence, a 'sentence' is widely defined to include 'any order made by a court when dealing with an offender.' Such an order includes a confiscation order.

- The only statutory test is 'that the appellant should be sentenced differently for an offence'.

- The Court had recognised a number of grounds of appeal against sentence, the most well-established of which are that a sentence is 'manifestly excessive' or 'wrong in principle'. Between them these terms cover most of the types of arguments that can be advanced. However, for the applicant, the classification of grounds is less important than ensuring that the grounds clearly identify the way in which it is said that the sentence in question is flawed.

- In determining whether a sentence is manifestly excessive, the Court will consider whether the sentence as a whole is excessive.

- The Court may be prepared to find that a failure to follow the sentencing guidelines renders a sentence manifestly excessive. However, it has reiterated that guidelines are not a straightjacket and may in any event be interpreted in a flexible manner.

- The unjustified disparity in sentence between co-defendants may give rise to grounds of appeal but only if 'right thinking members of the public with knowledge of the relevant facts and circumstances, learning of this sentence would consider that something had gone wrong with the administration of justice'.

- A failure to follow the proper procedures may provide grounds of appeal. However, the general approach of the Court is to decline to interfere with a sentence where, had the correct procedures been followed the sentence that would have been imposed would have been essentially the same.

- An unlawful sentence may be corrected on appeal. However, consideration should first be given to whether the unlawful element of the sentence can be corrected by returning to the Crown Court under the slip rule.

- The Court may consider developments that have occurred since the sentence was passed. Although the strict requirements for adducing fresh evidence do not generally apply to material that is adduced in relation to appeals against sentence, the Court would generally require good explanation for any failure to place before the Crown Court material that is relied upon on appeal.

- If the Court allows an appeal it may quash the sentence and replace it with any sentence that the Crown Court had the power to impose. However, this new sentence must not be more severe than the sentence that was appealed.

- Confiscation orders may be appealed as decisions in relation to the variations of confiscation orders but not variations under section 23 of POCA 2002.

- There are no prescribed grounds of appeal against sentence conviction. However, when appeal is based on alleged errors of fact, the Court may be reluctant to interfere with the findings of the Crown Court judge save in the clearest circumstances.

4.55   *Appeals against sentence*

- Strict rules in relation to fresh evidence do apply to appeals against confiscation orders.

- A confiscation order that has been made with the consent of the defendant may be appealed if it can be shown that, as a result of bad legal advice or some other reason, the defendant did not understand the order he was agreeing to.

- If the Court allows an appeal against a order it may simply quash the order, impose a new order or remit the case to the Crown Court for a new confiscation hearing to take place.

- The prosecution may also appeal against a confiscation order or a refusal to make a confiscation order but only when proceedings are under POCA 2002.

Part 2
The Appeal Process

Chapter 5

Defence investigations

INTRODUCTION

5.1   Defence investigations can play a vital role in correcting miscarriages of justice. However, they are often undervalued or regarded with suspicion by the prosecution, the courts and even some defence lawyers.

5.2   When investigating a crime the police have a duty to pursue all reasonable lines of enquiry and to obtain evidence which points away from as well as towards the suspect.[1] However, by the time a defendant is charged the police will be firmly committed to a particular view of the case. It is inevitable that resources will be focussed on obtaining evidence that will help secure a conviction.

5.3   The defence can pursue other avenues and obtain information from those who may be reluctant to speak to police officers. This is important before trial but becomes indispensable after conviction because at that point most prosecution investigations will cease entirely. It will only be those who act on behalf of the defendant who have an interest in continuing to work on the case. Such investigations may uncover evidence upon which an appeal can be based. Alternatively, they may reveal material that triggers further prosecution disclosure or persuades the Criminal Cases Review Commission to commence its own investigation.

WHAT ARE DEFENCE INVESTIGATIONS? WHO MAY CARRY THEM OUT?

5.4   Defence investigations are simply attempts to obtain material that may be admissible as fresh evidence in such a way as to create the best chance of it being admitted.

---

1   Attorney General's Guidelines on Disclosure, para. 17.

5.5 Although the term 'defence investigations' conjures up complex enquiries in relation to convictions for grave crimes, there are few appeal cases which cannot benefit from new material. For example, in the most straightforward appeal against sentence it may be possible to obtain medical evidence that was never before the Crown Court or a compelling character witness who was never asked to give a statement. Whether the Court will be prepared to allow the admission of this material as fresh evidence is a different matter (see Chapter 3).

5.6 As to who may carry out the investigation, the short answer is 'anyone'. The longer answer is that investigations should be carried out under the direction of the defence lawyers. If investigations can be carried out by a solicitor then so much the better. (They are officers of the Court and subject to the discipline of their professional body so the Court may be more likely to attach weight to the material that they uncover.) However, there is no reason why evidence obtained by non-lawyers should not be admitted as long as it was obtained in a proper manner.

THE ETHICS OF DEFENCE INVESTIGATION

5.7 Obtaining evidence in a manner that protects its integrity maximises the chance of it being admitted by the Court of Appeal. Being aware of potential ethical pitfalls is particularly important in appeal cases. Interviewing witnesses who gave evidence for the Crown at trial is a matter that often gives rise to particular concern. An unwillingness to speak to them often stems from a fear that the defence team could be accused of influencing the witness to change his evidence, particularly if the witness previously gave statements that are inconsistent with what he is now saying.[2]

5.8 These and other concerns can be assuaged by following best practices and the relevant ethical rules that can be found in the solicitor's Code of Conduct. In particular, the investigator should:

(a)   create a careful file note of the meeting or significant conversation with a witness that lays out exactly what was said by all parties;

(b)   never misrepresent who he is, who he works for and why he is asking questions;[3]

---

2   Hannibal, M. and Mountford, L. (2013) *Criminal Litigation Handbook 2013/14*, Oxford: OUP, para. 1.11.6.
3   The people you are interviewing or asking for records from may ask you questions in return about what you are up to. This is part of the natural give and take of conversation and does not mean they are unwilling to talk to you. This does not mean you have to explain things that are confidential to the defendant or things that, strategically, you would rather not have in the public realm. You can simply explain that you are investigating for an appeal on behalf of a defendant, and that you want to hear everyone's side of the story.

(c)   take care not to intimidate a witness in any way and remember that it is the witness's prerogative to refuse to be interviewed;[4]

(d)   never take advantage of an unrepresented third party;[5]

(e)   never interview a represented person without the consent of his legal representative; and

(f)   never give legal advice where there is a conflict of interest.[6]

5.9   The defendant himself should not be involved in questioning potential witnesses nor should any other potential defence witnesses.

THE TECHNIQUES OF INVESTIGATION

Funding for an investigation

5.10   Where leave has not been applied for and the purpose of the investigation is to put the defence in a position to make an application for leave, funding can be requested from the Legal Aid Authority under the Advice and Assistance scheme. (See Chapter 8 for consideration of funding applications under the scheme.) If leave is granted the Court may grant a representation order to allow the appellant's solicitors to undertake particular tasks. (See **6.43** and **8.35–8.37**.)

Conducting the investigation strategically

5.11   Planning an investigation involves:

(a)   knowing what evidence was before the jury and what evidence was available to both the prosecution and the defence at trial;

(b)   prioritising the leads to follow first (given the limited resources available);

---

4   This includes thinking carefully about who is the best person to do the interview, with reference to matters such as age, gender, race, etc. The suspicion that a witness's feeling of being intimidated stems from prejudice does not obviate the fact that he felt intimidated.

5   A lawyer has a duty to represent his client to the best of his ability, but he also has a duty not to take advantage of those who do not have legal representation in order to do so (Solicitors Regulation Authority Code of Conduct, Chapter 11, Outcome 11.1). One way of dealing with this situation may be to ensure that the potential witness has independent legal assistance before formalising what he has to say in a s. 9 witness statement.

6   See the Solicitors Regulatory Authority Code of Conduct, Chapter 3, Outcome 3.5. If someone else wants to confess to the crime, or confess to previous perjury in the case, the defendant's lawyer cannot advise him of the legal implications of doing this. It is necessary to get the information from him about what he would tell the Court (because that is your duty to your client), but the defendant's lawyer can't advise him of the risks he faces. He should obtain independent legal representative before he makes any formal statement.

(c)   working from the outside of the circle to the centre when approaching a sensitive issue or witness, so that as much information as possible is obtained before any evidence is removed from reach (such as a witness refusing to talk or a document being destroyed, etc.).

What you already know

5.12   It is always helpful to start by establishing what material is already in the hands of the defence. This will involve speaking to the defendant, his family and certainly his previous lawyers.[7] It is also important to gather as complete a case file as possible.

5.13   The following material should normally be sought:

(a)   records of arrest and pre-trial custody;

(b)   the defendant's statements;

(c)   the duty solicitor's notes;

(d)   police reports, plus material the police relied on in writing their reports (such as contemporaneous notes);

(e)   witness statements taken by the police;

(f)   forensics reports;

(g)   news media reports;

(h)   recordings of transcribed statements;

(i)   recorded evidence such as CCTV, copies of computer hard drives and the 999 call;

(j)   expert reports plus material experts relied on in reaching their conclusions;

(k)   unused material provided to the trial team by the CPS;

(l)   trial solicitors' working file including notes, correspondence and billing (the latter is useful for working out when/whether material was actually read);

(m)   trial exhibits/material that went before the jury;

(n)   trial transcript (access limited – see below);

(o)   counsel's notebooks;

---

7   The Court of Appeal recently held that speaking with previous legal representatives 'will henceforth be necessary … to ensure that facts are correct, unless there are in exceptional circumstances good and compelling reasons not to do so.' *R v McCook* [2014] EWCA Crim 734, para. 11. See Chapter 6 for further discussion of the case.

(p)   any previously submitted grounds of appeal;

(q)   any previously submitted Application to Criminal Cases Review Commission;

(r)   prison and probation files, including OASYS reports.

5.14   Building an electronic file makes it easier and quicker to create a chronology of what happened, and who knew what when, as well as an index of appeal issues, with each item linked back to the relevant pages of the file. A similar tagging of witness statements and police interviews is also helpful. There is increasingly sophisticated case analysis software to help with this task.[8]

5.15   In older cases the trial lawyers may no longer be in possession of the case file, as the obligation is only to keep the file for six years.[9] In these circumstances it may be necessary to reconstruct the trial solicitor's files from individual sources such as the Court, the CPS, the police, the defendant and his supporters.

5.16   A complete trial transcript is an invaluable guide to what occurred at trial but the cost of ordering one from the relevant transcription company can be prohibitively high.

Seeking additional material from the prosecution

5.17   Following conviction the prosecution's statutory duty to disclose relevant material ends.[10] There is a continuing common law duty of disclosure when material 'comes to light after the conclusion of the proceedings, which may cast doubt upon the safety of the conviction'.[11]

5.18   In *R (on the application of Nunn) v Chief Constable of Suffolk Constabulary*[12] the Supreme Court held that whilst the prosecution should disclose material that may assist the defence in presenting a ground of appeal 'there is no continuing right to indefinite re-investigation of cases following conviction.' The burden lies on the defence lawyers to make the case for further disclosure of documents in the prosecution or police files.

---

8   Useful software includes DevonThink for Mac, Masterfile for PCs and Casemap for Lexis users, plus various cloud-based offerings.

9   The six-year requirement was originally set out in the Guide to Professional Conduct of Solicitors, Annex 12A, and it is now within the discretion of law firms to decide how long to retain closed cases.

10   Criminal Procedure and Investigations Act 1996, s. 3.

11   Attorney General's Guidelines on Disclosure, Attorney General's Office (2013), s. 72.

12   [2014] UKSC 37.

5.19 *Defence investigations*

5.19 Attempts to obtain new material from the prosecution commence with written requests to the police, the Crown Prosecution Service or other relevant prosecuting authority which should:

(a) specify as clearly as possible what material is sought;

(b) explain why it is sought with reference to any potential grounds of appeal;

(c) state why you believe that they have the material in question; and

(d) ask for full reasons to be given for any refusal to provide disclosure.

5.20 Should relevant material not be provided voluntarily, the Court of Appeal may order its disclosure but it will only consider doing so after an application for leave has been lodged with the Court (see Chapter 6). Therefore, unless and until an application is made the only remedy for the refusal to provide material is an application for judicial review.

Seeking new material

Subject Access Requests under the Data Protection Act 1998

5.21 Material which contains personal information about a particular person may be obtained through a 'Subject Access Request' made under section 7 of the Data Protection Act 1998.[13] Such requests may be made to the agency that holds the information with the written authorisation of the person to whom the data relates, enabling the request to be made on his behalf.

5.22 Personal data processed for the purposes of:

(a) the prevention or detection of crime,

(b) the apprehension or prosecution of offenders,

is exempt from a Subject Access Request to the extent that complying with it might prejudice either of the above.[14] The exemption might apply on appeal when the information sought is still relevant to other investigations or prosecutions.

5.23 If the request is made by someone other than the subject, then a signed authorisation form will also be required which entitles the person making the request to obtain the documents he is requesting on behalf of the subject.

---

13 A Subject Access Request, often abbreviated on agency websites to SAR, is a request made for records that relate to the person making the request, or his representative.
14 Data Protection Act 1998, s. 29.

5.24   Specificity is important to ensuring the success of these requests, which should include the requestor's name and contact details, the data subject's full names and any relevant information that will help the agency concerned to locate the material that is sought.

5.25   Subject Access Requests may involve the payment of an administration fee. The Information Commissioner's Office website provides a useful guide to making them and has examples of pro-forma request letters that can be followed. Some agencies will have their own Subject Access Request application forms available online that they require requests to be made on.

Requests under the Freedom of Information Act 2000

5.26   Applications for data held by public authorities that does not fall under section 7 of the Data Protection Act 1998 can be made under section 1 of the Freedom of Information Act 2000. Again, a clear and detailed guide to making such applications is to be found on the Information Commissioner's website.

5.27   Such applications can be a useful means of obtaining information that is important for understanding the evidence in the case, for example how those with a role in the case are trained to do their jobs and the procedures that are followed by particular institutions. However, freedom of information requests cannot generally be used to bypass the requirements of disclosure in criminal proceedings and obtain material that is held by the prosecution in relation to the case. Material held for the purpose of a criminal investigation or prosecution is exempt from the requirements of section 1 to the extent that the information holder does not regard it as being in the public interest to disclose it.[15]

Records collection generally

5.28

(a)   It is important to follow up on requests sent out. A request may have to be sent several times.

(b)   If the investigator believes that a record exists, but the relevant agency states they cannot find it, or that it has been destroyed, it can be helpful to ask for a sworn statement from a representative of the agency or company attesting to what searches have been made, or to his personal knowledge of the destruction of that particular document.

(c)   It is always necessary (and beneficial) to be polite and courteous to the record holders.

---

15   Freedom of Information Act 2000, s. 30.

(d)   Although it is important to be specific about what records are sought, it is helpful to try to draft a request in such a way as to catch other potentially relevant documents that may be in the possession of the record holder.

(e)   The investigator should personally search any archived files if permitted to do so.

(f)   The investigator should think outside the box ('where else would copies of that missing record end up?').

(g)   Good records should be kept of all requests made.

Visiting and recording the crime scene and other significant locations

5.29   Visiting the crime scene or another location that is significant to the case is something that the defence should consider as part of their preparation for trial. However, it is often overlooked. When investigating a case for a potential appeal one should not assume that site visits have been considered nor that they could not now assist in any appeal. Even if site visits have already taken place, a fresh pair of eyes may notice something that has previously been missed. If a site visit is to take place, the following should be borne in mind:

(a)   It is useful to take cameras with the capacity to shoot both stills and film. One film of a location can then be shot with a voiceover by the film-maker describing what can be seen and its relevance. A second film should be taken without the voiceover, so the ambient sound can be recorded. Stills of the same areas should also be taken.

(b)   Measurements should be taken where possible, using a builder's tape measure or a rolling measuring wheel. This should be done after any film and stills have been taken.

(c)   If access to private property is required to make the recording, the owner should be asked, unless of course the owner or occupier is a complainant, in which case filming will have to be restricted to what can be seen from the street at a time when the complainant is not likely to be disturbed or upset. The relevant privacy, trespass, harassment or data protection laws should be consulted and followed if it appears that filming may give rise to legal issues.

Conducting interviews with potential witnesses

5.30   In addition to the ethical considerations already discussed, following the guidelines will help the investigator obtain useful evidence from potential witnesses:

(a)   Where possible (and where it does not put the investigator at risk) the investigator should seek to conduct the interview in the witness's own home (where they are likely to be more relaxed, less pressed for time and where there is a possibility of meeting other potential witnesses).

(b)   The investigator should be courteous and respectful at all times and dress appropriately for the situation.

(c)   The investigator should prepare for the interview by reviewing all relevant materials in order to understand what the witness has already said. It may be useful for the investigator to take the materials with him but he should only present them to the witness if it is decided that the witness must be confronted with them or reassured by them.

(d)   The investigator should be prepared to explain his role, the status of the case and what may happen next in the case.

(e)   If questioned about his view of the case, the investigator should stay noncommittal, objective and open.

(f)   The questions should generally be open-ended.

(g)   Close attention should be paid to what is said and the witness asked to clarify what he has said, if necessary. Notes should be taken to the extent that is possible without making the witness feel uncomfortable. A record should be typed up as soon as possible afterwards.

(h)   Pregnant pauses should be allowed to deliver. If an uncomfortable silence is allowed to last, the interviewee may fill the silence with exactly what is on his mind.

(i)   The contact details of the interviewee should be confirmed and he should be informed that the defence team may wish to contact him again.

(j)   Notes should be reviewed for coherence. It is important that anyone who reads the notes can understand what was said.

(k)   If the decision is made to take a statement from a witness, it should be done using the format required for admission of the statement under section 9 of the Criminal Justice Act 1967, which allows for the statement to be admitted before the Court without the witness needing to appear.

COOPERATING WITH OTHER INVESTIGATORY BODIES

Investigation by the Criminal Cases Review Commission

5.31   The Commission can deploy powers and call upon expertise to carry out investigations that are unavailable to the defence. However, it faces high demand on its resources. According to 2013/14 figures, the average time a defendant will have to wait while the Commission allocates, reviews and (if it decides to do so) investigates the case is 72.8 weeks.[16] This is a substantial period of imprisonment that a defendant may be able to cut if he or others on his behalf are able to obtain and disclose material to the Commission.

5.32   An application to the Commission which can provide material and give an account of the steps that have already been undertaken and provide the Commission with the responses to any defence enquiry can greatly assist the speed and success of any investigation that the Commission itself decides to carry out and may assist in persuading the Commission that an investigation is necessary.

5.33   For a full considering of making applications to the Commission, see Chapter 9.

Journalistic investigations

5.34   Historically, print and broadcast journalists have done much of the heavy lifting when it comes to righting miscarriages of justice. They can play a vital role in uncovering evidence which the applicant's lawyers can later use in court.

5.35   However, it is necessary to exercise caution when cooperating with or seeking to enlist the help of journalists. Whilst the duties of a lawyer are to his client (subject to his duties to the Court), the journalist's own overriding duty is to tell the truth as he sees it. The interests of a defendant and a journalist's desire to expose the truth may coincide but they may clash.

5.36   Therefore, in those cases where it is believed that cooperating with a journalist may lead to the uncovering of new evidence or may simply raise the profile of a case, it is important to consider the risks and benefits of doing so and ensure that the terms of the relationship are clear at the outset.

SUMMARY OF KEY POINTS

- Defence investigations can uncover vital material for an appeal against conviction or sentence.
- Investigations do not have to be carried out by the defendant's lawyers. However, they should be carried out under their direction.

---

16   Criminal Case Review Commission Annual Report 2013/14 at p. 15.

- Following clear ethical guidelines in conducting any investigation will assist in any application to have evidence that has been obtained received by the Court of Appeal.

- Investigations should be carefully planned. It is first necessary to establish what material the defence already have and what material the prosecution may already have that might be disclosed before considering whether further material should be sought.

- Disclosure requests may be made from the prosecution and, if not complied with, orders for disclosure may be sought from the Court of Appeal when leave has been granted, or judicial review commenced where it has not. However, regard must be had to the limited disclosure duties of the prosecution following a conviction.

- Material may be sought from public authorities under the Data Protection Act 1998 and the Freedom of Information Act 2000.

- Interviewing witnesses, including those who gave evidence for the prosecution in the Crown Court, can be of vital importance but should be done with care, following clear ethical principles.

- Site visits should not be overlooked. It should not be assumed that they took place before trial or, even if they did, that another site visit would not yield further information.

- Informing the Criminal Cases Review Commission of the work that has been undertaken in any defence investigation and providing the Commission with any material obtained may help to persuade the Commission to conduct their own investigation and may assist them in doing so.

Chapter 6

Applying for leave to appeal

INTRODUCTION

6.1   There are two routes of appeal from the Crown Court to the Court of Appeal: application to the Crown Court for a certificate that the case is fit for appeal and application to the Court of Appeal for leave to appeal. It is only in the most exceptional circumstances that it will be appropriate for a judge of the Crown Court to grant a certificate. Therefore, most appeals commence with an application for leave to appeal and most of those applications are decided on the papers by a High Court judge (the 'single judge'). If the application is refused it may then be renewed at a hearing before the full Court.

6.2   For this reason, the main focus of this chapter is on advising on and applying for leave to appeal from the Court of Appeal, advising on and lodging an application that is refused, and on the abandonment of any application for leave or appeal for which leave has been given.

6.3   The preparation and conduct of hearings before the full Court, whether appeals with leave or renewed applications for leave, is considered separately in Chapter 7.

6.4   **Note on terminology:** Unless and until leave is required, anyone applying for leave to appeal is referred to as the 'the applicant'.

ADVICE ON APPEAL

The trial lawyer's duty to advise promptly on appeal

6.5   The duty of lawyers to provide advice on appeal is set out in the Court of Appeal's own Guide:

> 'Provision for advice or assistance on appeal is included in the trial representation order issued by the Crown Court. Solicitors should not wait to be asked for advice by the defendant. Immediately following the conclusion of the case, the legal representatives should see the defendant

and counsel should express orally his final view as to the prospects of a successful appeal (whether against conviction or sentence or both). If there are no reasonable grounds of appeal, that should be confirmed in writing and a copy provided then, or as soon as practicable thereafter, to the defendant by the solicitor. If there are reasonable grounds, grounds of appeal should be drafted, signed and sent to instructing solicitors as soon as possible. Solicitors should immediately send a copy of the documents received from counsel to the defendant.'[1]

6.6   An advocate must only advise in favour of appeal if he concludes that there are arguable grounds that he would be prepared to argue before the Court; this means that the appeal has a real chance of success.

The defendant's right to seek a second opinion

6.7   A defendant should consider carefully the advice that he is given, but he is not bound to accept it. He may ask his solicitors to instruct new counsel to advise on appeal (although whether to do so will be a matter for the solicitor in question). Alternatively, he may wish to seek assistance from new solicitors. Funding may be available under the advice and assistance scheme (see Chapter 8). If he is seeking advice from new lawyers, it is in his interests to do so promptly because of the time limits for lodging an appeal.

Time limits, extensions and the need for expedition

6.8   An application for leave to appeal must be lodged no later than 28 days after the decision which is being appealed.[2] It is a common mistake to assume that the time limit to appeal against a conviction runs from the date of sentence. In fact the period for appeal runs from the date of conviction, the period for appealing sentence runs from the date of sentence and the period for appealing any confiscation order runs from the date on which the confiscation order was made.

6.9   The Court may grant an extension of time in which to appeal, either before or after the 28 days have expired.[3] It will usually only do so if it decides that there is merit in the application for leave itself. Even then, it is not bound to grant the extension but must take an overall view of what justice requires.

6.10   The fact that the Court does generally consider the merits of the application for leave to appeal when deciding whether to grant an extension

---

1   HMCS, *A Guide to Commencing Proceedings in the Court of Appeal (Criminal Division)*, para. AI-I ('the Guide').
2   CAA 1968, s. 18(2).
3   CAA 1968, s.18(3).

should never lead the applicant or his lawyers to be complacent about time limits. If nothing else, it is more difficult for the Court to consider an application in a sympathetic light if the applicant or his legal advisors appear to have done little or nothing for a substantial period of time than one in which they have clearly worked hard to ensure that the application is lodged as soon as possible. The longer the period of time that has elapsed since the 28-day period has expired, the greater the need to show expedition.

6.11   When new lawyers are instructed to advise on appeal, unavoidable delays may arise as a result of the need to obtain transcripts from the trial and contact previous lawyers before advising on the merits. The Court is generally sympathetic to such delays. However, there is always a need to show expedition in the pursuit of such reasonable aims. See **6.32** and **6.33** for consideration of how to make the application for extension.

Obtaining transcripts for the purpose of advising on appeal

6.12   It may occasionally be necessary for the advocate to have access to transcripts in order to advise on whether there are arguable grounds of appeal. In this situation the transcripts of the relevant parts of the trial must be ordered from the transcription company that is used by the particular Crown Court. (The funding for transcripts is considered in Chapter 8.) The Registrar will not obtain transcripts unless and until an application for leave is lodged.

CONTACTING TRIAL LAWYERS

6.13   Until 2014, there was an obligation upon fresh representatives to contact trial lawyers only when they were to be the subject of direct criticism. However, in three cases decided in 2013 and 2014 the Lord Chief Justice made it clear that the Court regarded it as necessary for fresh representatives to seek the views of trial counsel in any case in which there was the risk of the grounds being advanced on the basis of a misunderstanding as to what took place at trial. The principles to be derived from *R v Davis and Thabangu*,[4] *R v Achogbuo*,[5] *R v McCook*,[6] were summarised by the present Registrar, Michael Egan QC, in an article published in *Archbold Review 2014*:[7]

'(1)   The Court of Appeal expects strict compliance with the duties of advocates and solicitors, there is a fundamental duty on them to make applications to the Court only after the exercise of due diligence

---

4   [2013] EWCA Crim 2424.
5   [2014] EWCA Crim 567.
6   [2014] EWCA Crim 734.
7   'Getting an Accurate Picture – A Fresh Look at Fresh Representation' by Master Michael Egan QC, Registrar of Criminal Appeals, *Archbold Review*, Issue 8 (11 September 2014), p 7.

(*Achogbuo*). For fresh lawyers this necessarily entails taking steps to ensure that they are fully apprised of all that occurred whilst the case was in the hands of previous lawyers, insofar as that is relevant to the new proceedings.

(2)   In cases where an application is based upon allegations of actual or implicit incompetence by previous legal advisors, then it is essential that enquiries should be made of those prior lawyers said to have acted improperly and equally important that other objective and independent evidence be sought to substantiate the allegations made (*Achogbuo*).

(3)   These principles apply not only where there is an allegation that previous lawyers have erred or ailed in some way but also in any case where it is essential to ensure that the facts are correct (*McCook*).'

6.14   In the same article the Registrar made the following recommendations to the appropriate procedure to be followed by fresh lawyers:

'i.   When drafting grounds make a sensible decision on whether waiver is required. Any grounds that does to the conduct of the trial is likely to require waive. If so, advise the applicant about the waiver of privilege from the applicant or note that the applicant declines having advised them of the consequences of doing so.

ii.   Send draft grounds to former representatives inviting their comments, particularly on the facts.

iii.   On receiving comments reconsider the draft grounds and include confirmation that trial counsel has seen the grounds or, in cases where there has been no response, that is the position. Should the grounds still be arguable, finalise the same.

iv.   Lodge the grounds. In cases where waiver is judged to be necessary lodge the formal waiver documents with the Grounds or (having confirmed that the applicant does not wish to waive privilege) inform the Court that the applicant is unwilling to do so and has been advised as to the consequences of that decision.'

Whether to apply for a trial judge's certificate

6.15   The alternative to applying for leave is to apply to the Crown Court judge who conducted the trial or imposed the sentence (depending on the nature of the decision being appealed) for a certificate that the conviction or sentence is fit for appeal.[8]

---

8   CAA 1968, s. 1(2)(b) in respect of conviction; s. 11(1A) in respect of sentence.

6.16   However, the circumstances in which the judge should grant a certificate must be very exceptional[9] and only usually arise when the appeal involves a point of law. For those cases where it might be appropriate to apply, the following procedural points must be borne in mind:

(a)   The procedure is governed by section 1(2)(b) of CAA 1968 and rule 68.4 of the CPR.

(b)   Oral application may be made immediately after the relevant decision. Written application must be made within 14 days.

(c)   If the judge decides to issue the certificate he must do so within 28 days of the decision. This statutory time limit may not be extended, with the exception of an appeal concerning insanity or unfitness to stand trial.[10]

(d)   The certificate is issued by the judge completing Form C and sending it to the Registrar.

(e)   The refusal to grant a certificate may not be appealed.

(f)   If the certificate is granted, the Crown Court may also grant bail pending appeal. The procedure for such applications is to be found at paragraph 50.4 of the Criminal Practice Direction.

(g)   If the certificate is granted there is no requirement to lodge grounds. However, a Form NG must still be lodged with the Court.

THE GROUNDS OF APPEAL

Who may draft grounds of appeal

6.17   The grounds may be drafted by the applicant, his solicitor or counsel. The Registrar will not accept grounds drafted by a third party unless they are expressly adopted by the applicant (except in exceptional cases, where the applicant lacks the capacity to do so).

The form and contents of the grounds

6.18   The purpose of the grounds is to convince the High Court judge who will consider them ('the single judge') to grant leave to appeal. They should therefore be drafted with care so as to ensure that they are as clear, concise and persuasive as possible.

---

9   *R v Kalis* [2003] EWCA Crim 1080.
10   CAA 1968, s. 16A.

6.19   The grounds must always be lodged with a Form NG. They should be signed and dated. They should be a single document. The Court has made it clear that traditional practice of submitting short grounds and a separate advice on appeal should no longer be followed.[11] Each ground must be clearly identified and numbered. The arguments in support of the ground should be set out concisely. The relevant facts should be summarised and the supporting authorities cited.[12]

6.20   There is no particular structure which must be followed. However, the following approach is commonly used:

(a)   A paragraph setting out the basic information (the date and place of conviction, the offence and, where relevant, the sentence that was imposed).

(b)   A paragraph summarising the argument, or arguments, being advanced.

(c)   The facts, in as much detail as required, with emphasis on there only being as much detail *as required.*

(d)   The arguments or submissions as to why the conviction is unsafe, or the sentence wrong.

Particular issues

Appeals against conviction

6.21   In an appeal against conviction it is important to identify the particular error at trial or fresh evidence that is relied upon. However, it is just as important to identify how this makes the conviction 'unsafe'. This should not involve a lengthy description of the evidence but it is helpful to set out the context in which the error is said to be significant. A common reason for refusing leave is the single judge's assessment that the evidence was so strong that the error or new evidence would have made no difference to the jury's decision. When the prosecution case was strong, the grounds should anticipate this objection: Was the case truly overwhelming? If not, why not? If it was overwhelming could the new evidence itself have created a doubt where none otherwise existed?

Appeal against sentence (general)

6.22   The grounds should set out the offence, the maximum sentence that was available for the offence, whether the plea was guilty or not guilty, details

---

11   The Guide, para. A2-4.
12   CPR, r. 68.3(2).

of previous convictions and any other order made by the judge when passing sentence. In a case involving several sentences it may be useful to include a table setting out this information in relation to each offence.

Appeal against sentence (assistance provided to the police)

6.23   When a ground of appeal is that insufficient weight was given for assistance that the appellant had provided to the police, there is a particular procedure to be followed.[13] The grounds of appeal and Form NG should be lodged with the Crown Court in the usual way. They should make no mention of the fact that information had been given to the sentencing judge in the form of a 'text' about assistance that the applicant had been provided to the police. This means that if the only ground of appeal is the failure of the Crown Court to make a proper reduction in sentence for such assistance, the grounds will be a very short, bland document. A note should then be lodged with the Criminal Appeal Office, marked for the attention of the Registrar. It should provide the details of the case, alert the Registrar to the existence of the text and might also include any arguments in relation to the text that the applicant wishes the court to consider. The Registrar will ensure that the text is obtained and provided to the single judge.

Citation of authorities

6.24   In *R v Erskine*[14] the Court emphasised that the only authorities that should be cited are those which are strictly necessary to advance the case. Lord Judge CJ said at paragraph 75: 'If it is not necessary to refer to a previous decision of the court, it is necessary not to refer to it.'

6.25   In appeals against conviction the Court emphasised that the authorities relied on should be those which establish a particular proposition and not those which do 'no more than illustrate or restate an established proposition' (para. 78)

6.26   The Court was particularly concerned about unhelpful citation of authorities in sentencing cases:

'Advocates must expect to be required to justify the citation of any authority. In particular where a definitive Sentencing Guidelines Council guideline is available there will rarely be any advantage in citing an authority reached before the issue of the guideline, and authorities after its issue which do not refer to it will rarely be of assistance. In any event, where the authority does no more than uphold a sentence imposed at the Crown Court, the advocate

---

13   The Guide, para. A2-7.3.
14   [2009] EWCA Crim 1425.

must be ready to explain how it can assist the court to decide that a sentence is manifestly excessive or wrong in principle.' (para. 80)

6.27   Whilst it is important to follow this guidance it is also important that it should not cause such anxiety that an authority that is genuinely significant is not drawn to the Court's attention. The golden rule must be that the advocate must be able to justify reference to a particular authority in the light of the approach that *Erskine* requires.

New arguments

6.28   If the appeal is based on a legal argument that was not raised in the Crown Court, the Court of Appeal will want to know why it was not raised. If it is necessary to apologise for failing to spot a legal point, then apologising in the written grounds is more likely to disarm any criticism than having that concession extracted by judicial cross examination at the full hearing.

Failure to object to things said in the summing up

6.29   If there is complaint about the judge's summing up the Court will want to know:

(a)   Did the judge give the advocate the opportunity to address him, before the summing up, on any matters about which the applicant now complains? If so, did the advocate raise the point that is now raised on appeal? If not, why not?

(b)   Did the advocate seek to address the judge at the conclusion of the summing up in relation to the matter? If not, why not?

Criticism of previous lawyers

6.30   See **6.13** above.

Fresh evidence

6.31   In an appeal based on fresh evidence:

(a)   The section 23(2) considerations (as discussed in Chapter 3) need to be addressed.

(b)   If the applicant seeks to call evidence by way of live witnesses, Form W (available on the Ministry of Justice website) must be completed and included. In practice the Court may well hear and decide the appeal without actually hearing any witness. Nonetheless, that is a decision for the Court to take, and the lawyers preparing the appeal need to offer the Court the option of hearing the evidence.

(c)   The Court has the power to order the attendance of a witness.[15] This includes witnesses who would not be compellable to give evidence at trial, such as previous lawyers and jurors.[16] If such an order is required, Form W should make that clear. The granting of such an order does not mean that the Court will hear the evidence. That will be decided by the full Court at the hearing.

(d)   The statements of the witnesses (in section 9 form) or the documents that constitute the fresh evidence, should all be attached.

(e)   In addition, the grounds should attach a '*Gogana*' statement[17] from the applicant's solicitor which explains when the evidence was obtained and why it was not deployed in the Crown Court. In the words of the Guide,[18] 'The Court will require a cogent explanation for the failure to adduce the evidence at trial'.

(f)   Applications for any of the following orders should be made in accordance with the relevant Part of the CPR:[19]

   (i)   measures to assist a witness or defendant to give evidence (CPR Part 29);

   (ii)   hearsay evidence (CPR Part 34);

   (iii)   evidence of bad character (CPR Part 35);

   (iv)   evidence of a complainant's previous sexual behaviour (CPR Part 36).

Applying for extension of time within which to appeal

6.32   For those applications that are lodged after the end of the 28-day period there is a box to be ticked in the Form NG indicating that an application for an extension is being made. However, the reasons for delay should also be clearly explained either in the grounds or as a separate document.

6.33   In a case involving significant delay, particularly where that delay has been brought about by the time that it took fresh solicitors to prepare the appeal, the application should be accompanied by a chronology of the work

---

15   CAA 1968, s. 23(1)(b).
16   The Criminal Justice and Immigration Act 2008, Sch. 8, para. 10 introduced this amendment to s. 23.
17   *R v Gogana*, *Times*, 12 July 1999.
18   The Guide, para. A2-7.1.
19   CPR, r. 68.7(1).

that was undertaken. See **6.8** to **6.11** above, for consideration of time limits, extensions and the need for diligence.

Other documents to be lodged in support of the application

6.34   It is always worth considering what other documents might be needed for the Court to determine the application for leave, for example the written directions handed to the jury in a case where they are the subject of criticism or a witness statement that was admitted in evidence by way of a hearsay ruling which is now the basis of a ground of appeal. It makes sense to copy and attach such documents to avoid any later delay caused by the Registrar later having to obtain them.

OTHER APPLICATIONS WHICH MAY BE MADE ALONG WITH THE APPLICATION FOR LEAVE

Applications for bail

6.35   The single judge does have the power to grant bail pending appeal. However, the Court has held that bail pending appeal should only be granted in those exceptional circumstances in which the Court concludes that it is necessary in order to do justice in the case.[20]

6.36   No application should be made until an application for leave is lodged.[21] If an application is included with the application for leave or lodged before leave is determined, it will normally be considered by the single judge when he considers leave.

6.37   It should be made with Form B, a copy of which should also be served on the CPS (or the prosecuting authority in question). The procedural requirements for making an application for bail are to be found in rule 68.8 of the CPR.

6.38   If there is a reason why bail should be granted urgently, for example the shortness of the sentence or extreme ill-health of the applicant, there should be a note to the Registrar making this clear. The Registrar may then choose to forward the application for bail to the single judge before the application for leave is considered. However, the Court only grants bail in exceptional circumstances and is very unlikely to do so without consideration of the strength of the application for leave itself.

---

20   *R v Watton* (1979) 68 Cr App R 293.
21   *R v Suggett* (1985) 81 Cr App R 243.

6.39   The Court has also emphasised that the granting of bail should not create an expectation that the applicant will not be returned to prison should the appeal fail.[22]

Request for an expedited hearing

6.40   In addition to or as an alternative to applying for bail the applicant can ask for an expedited hearing. There is no form to be submitted but a note attached to the application should make clear the reasons for the request. If the Registrar decides that there should be an expedited hearing he can refer the case to the full court immediately for a hearing at which both the application for leave and, if granted, the final appeal is likely to be determined.

Requests for transcripts

6.41   Once an application for leave is lodged the Registrar will routinely obtain a copy of the summing up (in an appeal against conviction), sentencing remarks (in an appeal on sentence) and prosecution opening facts (in a sentence following a guilty plea).

6.42   If the applicant seeks a transcript of any other part of the trial (whether evidence, ruling or legal argument) in an application for leave to appeal conviction, he should explain why it is necessary for the appeal and identify the date and, insofar as possible, the time at which the relevant part of the trial commenced and concluded.[23] Transcripts can also be requested in application for leave to appeal against sentence.

Applications for funding

6.43   Form NG contains a box which should be ticked if application is made for a representation order. It is likely to be granted if leave to appeal is granted. However, it will usually be granted for counsel alone. Any application for a representation order to extend to solicitors (if the solicitor has a criminal legal aid contract) or more than one counsel (if it is necessary to undertake work in preparation for the appeal) should be supported by a note explaining the additional work that needs to be done in order to prepare the case and why it cannot be carried out by counsel alone.

6.44   In cases in which the representation order in the Crown Court covered representation by junior and leading counsel it is often the practice of the Court to grant a representation order for a single counsel only (on the basis that two

---

22   *R v Kalia* (1974) 60 Cr App R 200.
23   CPR, r. 68.3(2).

counsel will generally be unnecessary for the presentation of the appeal). Therefore, if the applicant's lawyers believe that two counsel are necessary to properly present the case, the reasons should be clearly set out.

Disclosure of third party material

6.45   The full Court, the single judge and Registrar all have the power to order a third party to produce documents or other material. However, this power will only be used in exceptional cases. The burden lies on the applicant to provide a clear and compelling explanation for any failure to obtain the material in the Crown Court.[24]

6.46   An application for third party material should contain:

(a)   a completed Form W;

(b)   details of the material sought;

(c)   its relevance to the appeal;

(d)   details of the party against whom any order for production of the material is to be made;

(e)   details of any refusal of the party to provide the material on a voluntary basis.

6.47   The application should be served on the party in question in order that they can make any representations as to why an order should not be made. In addition, it should be served on the person to whom the material relates, in order that he too may do so.[25] In cases where the Court is considering making such an order but it is opposed, a hearing may be held at which the parties who are directly concerned can be heard.

Request for an oral leave hearing

6.48   It is possible to apply for an oral leave hearing so as to argue the grounds. It is rare that the Registrar will grant a representation order for such a hearing and it is rare to request such a hearing, given that the applicant will have a right to an oral hearing if he renews an application for leave that has been refused on the papers.

---

24   *R v Niwar Doski* [2011] EWCA Crim 987.
25   *R(on the application of TB) v The Combined Courts at Stafford* [2006] EWHC 1645 (Admin).

LODGING THE GROUNDS

6.49   The grounds should be lodged along with all attachments and additional application with the Crown Court at which the decision that is the subject of the appeal is made. The Crown Court is then responsible for checking the accuracy of the case details and sending the paperwork on to the Court of Appeal.

THE ACTIONS OF THE REGISTRAR UPON RECEIPT OF GROUNDS

6.50   Upon receipt of the application the Registrar will:

(a)   check that the application for leave is in valid form;

(b)   if the application is out of time, check an application for extension of time has also been made (although the Registrar has the power to extend time, the practice is for the single judge to determine such an application when considering whether to grant leave);

(c)   contact the Crown Court to ensure that all relevant exhibits are retained until the conclusion of any appeal;

(d)   obtain the transcripts and any other documents that he believes are necessary for the single judge to determine the application;

(e)   where he considers it appropriate, contact previous lawyers for their comments on matters raised in the application;

(f)   where he considers it appropriate, ask the prosecution for their views, before the case is sent to the single judge.[26] The 'respondent's notice' will usually set out reasons why the application for leave should be refused but occasionally the respondent (as the prosecuting authority is now known) indicate that they do not oppose the appeal.

6.51   The Registrar does have the power to refer a case directly to the full court at which leave and appeal can be determined. There are a number of reasons why this might be done: if co-defendants have already been given leave to argue the point; if the need for a hearing is urgent or the question of law is particularly complicated; or if the Registrar is of the view that the application may be considered vexatious. However, referral to the full Court is the exception not the rule.

---

26   Practice Direction 68A concerns notice being given to the prosecution.

FURTHER STEPS BY THE APPLICANT BEFORE THE CASE IS SENT TO THE SINGLE JUDGE

Perfecting the grounds

6.52   Any transcripts that the Registrar obtains will usually be provided to the applicant (or his lawyers, if represented) so that the grounds can be perfected. The perfected grounds should be a new document. It will supersede the original grounds and should contain references to the page and paragraph number of the passages in the transcripts that are relevant to the application.

6.53   The applicant will usually be given 14 days to perfect the grounds. If more time is required it should be requested and reasons for the extension provided.

6.54   The letter from the Registrar sometimes instructs that the transcripts must be returned, unmarked, once they have been used to perfect the grounds. If so, a copy should be made and kept; it has been known for a judge hearing an appeal to ask the advocate to consider a paragraph in the summing up, only to be met with the reply that, following the Registrar's instructions, the summing had been returned after the grounds had been perfected.

Addressing the responses of trial lawyers and the respondent

6.55   The applicant's appeal lawyers will be sent replies by the trial lawyers to questions asked of them by the Registrar and given a period to respond. Any such response can be made by amending the grounds or in a separate document. The opportunity to respond does not involve an obligation to do so and it is unhelpful to simply repeat points that have already been made in the grounds.

6.56   The respondent should serve their notice on the applicant.[27] However, they sometimes fail to do so. It is therefore worth contacting either the CPS Appeals Unit or prosecuting counsel directly in order to obtain a copy.

6.57   The applicant may want to consider responding to any points made in the respondent's notice. However, time will not normally be given for any such response. Therefore it should be drafted swiftly to ensure that it is sent to the single judge with the rest of the papers.

---

27   CPR 2007, r. 68.6(3).

The decision of the single judge

6.58   When the Registrar is satisfied that the Court is in possession of all the necessary paperwork the normal procedure is for the case to be sent to the single judge who may:

(a)   grant leave on some or all of the grounds that he concludes to be arguable;

(b)   refuse leave on all grounds; or

(c)   refer the case to the full Court without granting leave.

6.59   Other subsidiary applications, such as extensions of time, will also be considered. The reasons for the decisions will be set out in the SJ Form which will be sent to the applicant.

6.60   If leave is granted, then a representation order to enable the advocate to prepare and present the case will almost inevitably be granted. However, if leave is limited to certain grounds, the representation order will then be limited to work on the grounds upon which leave was granted.

6.61   Waiting for the decision of the single judge can be frustrating because, once the papers have been sent to the judge, the Criminal Appeal Office cannot tell the applicant how long it will take the judge (who must fit considering applications for leave around normal court work) to make his decision. Often 'the papers are with the judge' is the only information that the applicant will be given until he receives the decision itself.

RENEWING AN APPLICATION FOR LEAVE

6.62   The applicant has the right to renew the application for leave on any of the grounds that have been refused. A renewed application must be lodged within 14 days of receipt of the SJ Form. This is done by completing the SJ Renewal Form that is on the reverse side of the SJ Form and lodging it with the Court. The 14-day period will only be extended in exceptional circumstances. An application for extension is likely to be referred by the Registrar to the full Court.

6.63   If all of the grounds were refused, the application to renew will be decided at a hearing before the Court. If leave has been granted on some grounds, the renewed application for leave for the remaining grounds can be argued at the full appeal hearing.

6.64   Whether to renew the application can be a difficult decision. On the one hand, the advocate will not have drafted grounds unless he thought that they were arguable. On the other hand, if a High Court judge has said the case is not arguable, it is sensible to reflect carefully before renewing.

The risk of loss of time served

6.65   There is a particular risk for the applicant in renewal; the Court has the power to direct that some of the time already served should not count towards sentence.[28] It will only do this if it thinks the case is devoid of merit. This power can in theory be exercised before leave has been refused, but it becomes a more realistic danger after an applicant renews an application for leave.

6.66   The SJ Form contains a box which, if the single judge initials it, indicates that the Court should consider making an order for loss of time if the application for leave is renewed. If the judge does so, there must be a high risk of an order for loss of time being made. If the box is not initialled, then the risk is significantly lower, but it should not be assumed that an order could never be made.[29] Neither should it be assumed that an order would never be made when the applicant's advocate advised that there were grounds of appeal.[30] It is very rare for the Court make an order but the applicant must be advised about the risk before deciding whether to renew. That decision must of course be the applicant's own.

Renewing when considering taking the case to the European Court of Human Rights

6.67   An applicant with ambitions to take his case to the European Court of Human Rights should considering renewing the application.[31] There is a danger that, by not renewing, it could later be said that the domestic remedies had not been exhausted, which can be a bar to the European Court considering an application.

Renewing other applications

6.68   If the applicant decides to renew an application for leave he may also, at the same time, renew other applications, including bail that the single judge has refused. These applications are renewed on the same SJ Renewal Form that is used to renew the application for leave to appeal and are subject to the same time limits. The effect of renewal is that these applications will also be

---

28   CAA 1968, s. 29.
29   Practice Direction 68.E1.
30   *R v Hart* [2006] EWCA Crim 3239.
31   See the discussion in Chapter 11.

considered by the full Court, usually at the same hearing at which the renewed application for leave is determined.

ABANDONING AN APPLICATION FOR LEAVE OR AN APPEAL WITH LEAVE

6.69 Once an application for leave has been lodged it will be considered by the Court unless it is abandoned by the applicant. Similarly, a renewed application for leave or an appeal with leave will be considered by the Court unless it is abandoned. The decision to abandon is communicated when a Form A is signed by or on behalf of the applicant or appellant and lodged with the Court. This can take place at any point before the appeal or renewed application for leave hearing. During the hearing itself the appeal can be abandoned, orally, but only with the leave of the Court.[32]

6.70 Once an appeal is abandoned no new appeal against the same decision may be brought, unless the case is referred to the Court by the Criminal Cases Review Commission. Abandonment cannot be withdrawn. Therefore, by abandoning a case the appellant is effectively signing away his appeal rights.

Abandonment as a nullity

6.71 Abandonment may only be challenged on the basis that an apparent abandonment is a nullity. Abandonment will be regarded as a nullity only when the Court concludes that the mind of the applicant did not go along with the act of abandonment (*R v Medway*).[33] The clearest example of this would be where the applicant signed a notice of abandonment thinking that he was signing a different type of document.[34]

Bad legal advice giving rise to nullity

6.72 The Court may conclude that the abandonment was a nullity if it was based on bad legal advice (*R v L*)[35] but only if that advice was positively wrong, not if it was advice on a difficult point with which some might agree and others disagree (*R v Smith (Paul James)*).[36]

---

32   CPR, r. 65.13(2)(b).
33   (1976) 62 Cr App R 85.
34   As happened in *R v Mohamed* [2010] EWCA Crim 2464.
35   [2013] EWCA Crim 1913.
36   [2013] EWCA Crim 2388.

Making an application for reinstatement

6.73   If the Court concludes that an abandonment was a nullity, it will then reinstate the case, restoring it to the same stage that it has reached before the Form A was lodged. An application to reinstate an appeal or application for leave following abandonment is heard before the full Court. The procedure is contained in rule 65.13 of the CPR.

SUMMARY OF KEY POINTS

- Appeals from the Crown Court against conviction or sentence must, except in rare cases where it might be appropriate to apply to the Crown Court for a certificate of fitness for appeal, commence with an application for leave to appeal being made to the Court.

- Application for leave to appeal must be lodged within 28 days of the decision which is challenged.

- The Court has the power to extend the time either before or after the 28 days expire. However, the application to extend must contain an explanation for the delay.

- The application must be made using Form NG and in accordance with the requirements of rule 68.3(2) of the CPR.

- Other applications, including extension of time, bail and any application for a representation order should be lodged with the grounds.

- The application must be lodged at the Crown Court at which the decision that is subject to challenge was made.

- The Crown Court forwards the application to the Criminal Appeal Office and the Registrar prepares the case in order to either send it to the single judge or refer it directly to the full Court for an application as to whether to grant leave to appeal.

- If leave on any ground is refused by the single judge it may be renewed. The application from renewal must be lodged within 14 days of the decision.

- The Court may consider exercising its power to deduct time that has already been served if an application for leave is renewed that the Court regards as being wholly without merit. If the single judge has indicated on the SJ Form that the Court should consider deducting time, there is a strong chance that it will do so.

- If leave has been granted on some grounds, the renewed application for leave that is pursued in respect of any other ground will be determined at the appeal hearing. When leave has been refused on all grounds but is renewed, it will be considered by the Court at a leave hearing.

- Other applications that were made to the single judge may also be renewed before the Court.

Chapter 7

Preparing for hearings in the Court of Appeal

INTRODUCTION

7.1   Every advocate who has appeared before the Court of Appeal will have had the experience of preparing the case thoroughly and arguing it passionately only to sit down and listen to the Court deliver a judgment that had clearly been written before the hearing commenced. It is tempting to ask what was the point in arguing it at all?

7.2   Before the hearing the Court will often have formed a preliminary view of the case. However, just as every advocate will have had the experience of failing to change the Court's collective mind, judges attest to occasions when the Court was convinced by effective oral advocacy.

7.3   If belief in one's ability to persuade is the first principle of advocacy in the Court of Appeal, the second is that the task of persuading the Court does not begin with the hearing itself. Because the Court often does form a preliminary view of the case, it is important to try to influence its thinking as early as possible by effective drafting, ensuring that important documents are lodged in good time and that the relevant authorities are drawn to the Court's attention.

7.4   This chapter covers the preparation for and presentation of the hearing. The topics covered apply to both appeals with leave and oral applications for leave to appeal. When different considerations apply to each type of hearing, this is made clear.

PREPARING FOR THE HEARING

Considering the Court bundle

7.5   The Registrar (in practice the lawyer at the Criminal Appeal Office who has been assigned to the case) is responsible for compiling the bundle of material that will be considered by the judges. It will be sent to the parties in advance of the hearing. It should be read with care. This is the case that the Court will read. In particular it is necessary to do the following:

Ensure that all the relevant documents are included

7.6 If either of the parties wish the Court to consider any document that is not in the bundle, they should write to the Registrar, enclosing the document, stating its relevance and asking that it be included.

Consider the case summary

7.7 Within the bundle will be the case summary that will have been prepared by the lawyer in the Criminal Appeal Office. It will contain what the writer considers to be the significant information about the facts of the case and its procedural history.

7.8 It should be considered carefully. It is vital that it is accurate and that it refers to the facts that are significant to the appeal. They are usually both accurate and comprehensive but if there is an amendment that should be made, the Registrar should be written to and asked to include it. Whether to make the amendment sought is a matter for the judgment of the summary writer. If it is decided not to include that matter in the case summary, the Court will be provided with the document that requested its inclusion.[1]

7.9 Advocates can (unless the Registrar states otherwise) show the summary to their clients but it should not be copied or reproduced.

Check the time estimate that has been given to the case

7.10 The summary writer's view of the likely time estimate will be on the front page. It will be used to list the case. The Court will expect hearings to be concluded within the time estimate. Therefore, if it is thought that the time estimate is inadequate, the Registrar should be written to and told why.

Skeleton arguments

7.11 The Practice Direction provides:

> '68F.1 Skeleton arguments are not required, but may be provided. Advocates intending to serve a skeleton argument should consider carefully whether a skeleton argument is necessary, or whether the

---

1   Practice Direction 68G.3.

appeal notice or the respondent's notice will suffice. In most cases, if the appeal notice and respondent's notice have been prepared in compliance with Part 68, a skeleton argument will be unnecessary. Advocates should always ensure that the Court, and any other party as appropriate, has a single document containing all of the points that are to be argued.

68F.2 The appellant's skeleton argument, if any, must be served no later than 21 days before the hearing date, and the respondent's skeleton argument, if any, no later than 14 days before the hearing date, unless otherwise directed by the Court.

68F.3 A skeleton argument, if provided, should contain a numbered list of the points the advocate intends to argue, grouped under each ground of appeal, and stated in no more than one or two sentences. It should be as succinct as possible. Advocates should ensure that the correct Criminal Appeal Office number appears at the beginning of the respondent's notice and any skeleton argument and that their names are at the end.'

7.12   It may well be helpful to draft a skeleton in a case that is to be presented in a different way before the full Court to the way in which it was first presented in the grounds (for example, if particular grounds are not going to be advanced before the full Court, or more recent authorities relied on).

New grounds of appeal

7.13   The appellant must obtain leave to advance any new ground that was not in the application for leave. The primary consideration for the Court is likely to be whether the ground is arguable.[2]

Authorities

7.14   Guidance from the Registrar on how authorities should be provided to the Court will be set out in a letter from the Registrar with each case. The general position is that a list of reported cases, with case references, should be supplied to the Criminal Appeal Office (not the head usher) at least two working days in advance of the hearing. The list may be attached to the skeleton argument. If the appellant intends to rely on any unreported cases, three copies should be lodged with the Court.

---

2   *R v Chapman* [2013] EWCA Crim 1370; the Court held that it was implicit in CPR, rr. 68.3(b) and 65.3.

7.15   In deciding what authorities (if any) to rely on, it is important to bear in mind what the Court said in *Erskine* about not placing unnecessary authorities before the Court and, in particular, not relying on sentencing cases that pre-date a sentencing guideline or guideline case, unless there is very good reason to do so. (See **6.24–6.27** for full details.)

LISTING THE HEARING

7.16   The Court of Appeal Listing Office is responsible for fixing a date for hearing, of which the parties are notified. It will consider applications for a hearing to be moved but will generally not move a case because the advocate has another case in a lower Court. Appearances in the Court of Appeal must take precedence.[3]

THE HEARING

Presence of the appellant/applicant

Hearings with leave

7.17   An appellant who is in custody has the right to be produced at his full hearing, unless he suffers from insanity or a disability. There is no right to be present at a preparatory hearing although production can be requested.[4]

7.18   If the appellant does not wish to be produced, the appeal can take place in his absence.[5] For this to take place the Registrar may require his consent to be in writing. The Court, single judge or Registrar may make a direction for a live link to a prison, rather than producing the appellant in person.

Renewed applications for leave

7.19   Applicants have no right to be present at renewed applications for leave. If an application for leave to appeal against conviction is successful then the full hearing will generally take place at a later date at which an appellant who is in custody will then be produced. However, if the application for leave to appear against sentence is successful, the Court will usually proceed to determine the appeal at the same hearing, in the absence of the appellant. If this takes place, the Registrar will then write to the appellant informing him of the result of the hearing and of his right to have a further hearing at which he

---

3   Practice Direction II.2.2.
4   CAA 1968, s. 22.
5   CAA 1968, s. 22(4).

will be present but that the Court will only consider new submissions at such a hearing if the applicant presents new material (*R v Spruce and Anwar*).[6]

7.20   In order to avoid this taking place the applicant's solicitors should, in advance of the hearing, obtain their client's instructions on whether he would wish to be present at the full hearing. In any event, it is often the practice of the Court to produce the applicant from custody in cases where the effect of granting leave and allowing the appeal against sentence would be his immediate release.

When the appellant has absconded

7.21   If the appellant has absconded whilst in custody or on bail, the Court may dismiss the appeal, hear it in the absence of the appellant or adjourn the case pending his being returned to custody. The Court has held that it is only in exceptional cases that the Court will hear the appeal.[7] An important factor will be whether the appellant had given his lawyers instructions that are sufficiently clear and detailed for them to be able to properly advance his case in his absence.[8]

When the appellant has died

7.22   Section 44A of CAA 1968 provides that an appeal can continue when an eligible person can be identified and approved by the Court to take over his case. The categories of eligible persons are:

(a)   the widow or widower of the dead person;

(b)   a person who is the personal representative (within the meaning of section 55(1)(xi) of the Administration of Estates Act 1925) of the dead person; or

(c)   any other person appearing to the Court of Appeal to have, by reason of a family or similar relationship with the dead person, a substantial financial or other interest in the determination of a relevant appeal relating to him.

7.23   Except in the case of an appeal on a reference by the Criminal Cases Review Commission, an application for such approval may not be made after the end of the period of one year beginning with the date of death.

---

6   [2005] EWCA Crim 1090. See also CPR, r. 68.12.
7   *R v Gooch* [1998] 2 Cr App R 130 (CA), confirmed in *R v Salloum* [2010] EWCA Crim 312.
8   *R v Okedare* [2014] EWCA Crim 228.

Whether the prosecution will be represented at the hearing

7.24   The prosecution will be represented in appeals against conviction. They may choose or be asked by the Court to appear in appeals against sentence. They may also choose or be asked by the Court to appear at a renewed application for leave.

Orders restricting public access or reporting of hearings

The public right to attend court hearings

7.25   The general rule is that the Court should hear appeals in public but it may order that a hearing take place in private. The opposite approach applies when the Court is hearing a Public Interest Immunity application which must be held in private, unless the Court decides to hold it in public.[9]

7.26   An order that a hearing take place in private may be made under the Court's inherent power, but only in exceptional circumstances where the Court concludes that a public hearing would frustrate the administration of justice. An order may also be made under the following statutory powers:

(a)   in any appeal against a review of sentence (section 75(1) of the Serious Organised Crime and Police Act 2005 in relation to appeals pursuant to section 74(12));

(b)   where a witness under the age of 18 is giving evidence (Children and Young Person's Act 1933) (note: such an order cannot apply to members of the press);

(c)   where the Court hears evidence from a child or vulnerable adult in relation to a sexual offence (section 25 of the Youth Justice and Criminal Evidence Act 1999).

Reporting restrictions

7.27   The press are entitled to report, in full, the Court's proceedings unless it makes an order placing a restriction upon the reporting of a particular case or unless one of the following three automatic statutory reporting restrictions applies:

(a)   The Sexual Offences (Amendment) Act 1992 gives the victim of a sexual offence lifetime anonymity in respect of their identification. The types of offences covered by this section are set out in section 2 of the Act (as

---

9   CPR, r. 65.6.

amended by subsequent legislation[10]) and includes the majority of sexual offences.

(b)   Section 12 of the Criminal Justice Act 1987 and section 37 of the Criminal Procedure and Investigations Act 1996 provide limitations to the facts that may be reported in an appeal in relation to a preparatory hearing. (See Chapter 12 for consideration of such appeals.)

(c)   Section 71 of the Criminal Justice Act 2003 provides that reporting restrictions apply to prosecution appeals against a preparatory ruling. (See Chapter 13 for consideration of such appeals.)

7.28   The Court may make an order restricting the reporting of a case under its inherent power but it also has a number of statutory powers to do so. Rule 16(1) of the CPR sets out the proper approach to the making of reporting restrictions and also contains a complete schedule of all statutory powers to make such an order.

7.29   In all cases where a reporting restriction might be appropriate, for example one involving children,[11] the parties should check with the Clerk of the Court whether any restrictions are in place. Any application should be made at the commencement of the hearing.

Hearing appeals regarding public immunity applications

7.30   In *R v McDonald, Rafferty and O'Farrell*[12] the Court set out the principles that should govern appeals in which the conduct of a Public Interest Immunity hearing in the Crown Court is the subject of challenge.

Televised Court hearings

7.31   An order has been made which allows television companies to broadcast legal arguments and judgments from the Court of Appeal, for the purpose of news reporting only.[13] Witnesses, victims and appellants must not be shown.

---

10   Criminal Justice and Public Order Act 1994, s. 168(1) and Sch. 9, para. 52(2); Sexual Offences Act 2003, s. 42 and Sch. 6, para. 31; Youth Justice and Criminal Evidence Act 1999, ss. 48(d), 67(3), (4) and Schs 2, paras 6–14, and 6.

11   Children and Young Persons Act 1933, s. 39.

12   [2004] EWCA Crim 2614.

13   The Crime and Courts Act 2013, s. 32, which provides that the Lord Chancellor may, with the concurrence of the Lord Chief Justice, make an order allowing for filming in particular courts. The general ban on filming and recording in court is contained within the Criminal Justice Act 1925, s. 41 and the Contempt of Court Act 1981, s. 9.

The procedure at the hearing

Appeals with leave

7.32   The case commences with the appellant being brought into Court and being identified. The appellant's advocate will make submissions. The advocate for the respondent (if the respondent is represented) will then make submissions. There is a final reply from the appellant. The judges frequently adopt an interventionist approach and will not be slow to ask the advocate about a particular point that concerns or interests them or to indicate that they think that an argument is a bad one.

7.33   If there is evidence to be called, the appellant will generally be expected to call the witness and examine him and the respondent to cross-examine in the normal way. However, when, if at all, that evidence is to be called is a matter to be determined by the Court.

7.34   Unless there is a clear indication, in advance of the hearing, that the Court does not wish to hear from a particular witness, or the prosecution agree the witness, the witness should be at Court and in a position to give evidence if called.

7.35   In most cases the Court gives judgment at the end of the hearing. In more complex cases it may give a reserved judgment and the parties will be informed of the date of a further hearing for judgment to be pronounced.

Renewed applications for leave

7.36   The hearings follow the same procedure as full hearings. Successful renewed applications for leave to appeal against conviction usually result in the Court listing the case for a full hearing on another occasion at which the appellant (if in custody) can be produced and the prosecution can be represented.

7.37   However, if a renewed application for leave to appeal against sentence is successful, the Court will generally proceed to determine the appeal at the same hearing.

Suggestions for advocacy

7.38   When preparing:

(a)   Re-read everything.

(b)   Identify the strongest point (or points) and be prepared to argue it concisely but with conviction. Not to do so is to throw away the opportunity that is presented by oral advocacy.

(c) Search out the difficulties in your case. Every case has them. The Court will identify them and ask the advocate about them.

(d) Clearly tab up the significant parts of the transcript so that they can be found quickly in Court.

(e) If it is intended to rely on authorities that have not been lodged with the Court or that were lodged late (and may not have reached the judges), three additional copies should be brought to court (along with an explanation for not having provided them earlier).

7.39 In Court:

(a) When a judge sits in the Court of Appeal he or she is always addressed as My Lord or My Lady.

(b) The Court will not expect an advocate to introduce his opponent.

(c) The Court will not expect the advocate to tell it about the facts of the case. It should be assumed that the relevant facts are in the papers and that the judges will have read the papers.

(d) It should not be assumed that the Court will be bound by the views of the single judge. Although it is wise to carefully consider the reasons of the single judge for granting or refusing, it is unwise to place reliance on the fact that leave has been given in the submissions themselves.

(e) If there are apologies that may have to be offered (if an argument was missed at trial) or concessions that are going to have to be made (if the judge got the law right once, and the grounds rely on his getting it wrong at some other stage), it is often best to make them immediately. It is more attractive to hear an advocate face up to a problem, admit it and then go straight on to argue why nonetheless the appeal should be allowed, than to witness the Court having to cross examine him into an admission he should have made at once.

(f) When making an application for leave that is out of time the advocate should not forget that the application to extend time must also be made. It is sometimes sensible to mention at the outset when the advocate proposes to deal with it (it usually makes sense to address it at the conclusion of the substantive arguments on the grounds, unless the Court wants it to be addressed immediately) so that the Court is aware that the advocate has not forgotten the need to do so.

APPLICATIONS AT THE CONCLUSION OF THE CASE

Applying for leave to appeal to the Supreme Court

7.40 If the appeal is dismissed, the appellant has 28 days to apply to the Court of Appeal to:

(a)   certify a point of law of general public importance; and

(b)   grant leave to appeal on the point to the Supreme Court.[14]

7.41   The Court of Appeal rarely certifies a point of law and almost never grants permission to appeal.

7.42   If the Court certifies a point and refuses leave to appeal, the appellant then has 28 days to apply to the Supreme Court for permission to appeal. However, if the Court refuses to certify a point of law the appellant cannot apply to the Supreme Court. This is frustrating for appellants and their lawyers who feel there is a good legal argument that deserves further consideration, but both the Court of Appeal and the ECtHR have held that section 33 of CAA 1968, which, in effect, allows the Court of Appeal Criminal Division to terminate any further domestic appeal, is compatible with Article 6 of the Convention.[15]

7.43   A certified point is in the form of a question which should be framed in a way that identifies a particular legal issue that arose in the appeal but also indicates its wider importance.

7.44   If the Court has given judgment on the day of the hearing, the application to certify and for leave to appeal can be made orally, immediately after the judgment. However, it can be useful to reflect and draft a question with some care.

Applying to certification when considering an application to the European Court of Human Rights

7.45   If the appellant wishes to take the case to the ECtHR, it is advisable to make the application to the Court for leave and certification or the appellant may later face a difficulty in satisfying the ECtHR that he has complied with the requirement to exhaust all domestic remedies. (See **11.6** and **11.7** for full discussion.)

Costs

7.46   Orders for costs are not routinely made in the Court of Appeal. Successful appellants cannot usually make a claim for costs because their representation has been paid for by a representation order. If they are unsuccessful, they are often in prison and lack the means to pay an order.

---

14   CAA 1968, s. 34.
15   *R v Dunn* [2010] EWCA Crim 1823 and application 62793/10 (declaration of inadmissibility, by a majority).

Nevertheless, there are a number of orders that the Court may make in appropriate cases. They may be made on application by one of the parties or of the Court's own motion.

7.47   The law in relation to costs is to be found in:

(a)   the Prosecution of Offences Act 1985;

(b)   the Costs in Criminal Cases (General) Regulations 1986 (SI 1986/1335);

(c)   Part 76 of the CPR;

(d)   Practice Direction (Costs in Criminal Proceeding) 2013[16] ('the Costs Practice Direction').

Costs from central funds for the successful applicant/appellant

7.48   A successful appellant can apply for costs from central funds but only to recover the cost of work undertaken on his case that was not covered by a representation order. The Court may make an order that it regards as reasonably sufficient to compensate the appellant for expenses properly incurred in the proceedings.[17] An order can cover proceedings in the Crown Court as well as the Court of Appeal. The Court may decline to make an order, even if it is satisfied that the costs claimed were properly incurred by the appellant. Alternatively, it may make an order for less than was incurred. If it chooses to go down either of these routes, it must give its reasons in open court.

Costs against an unsuccessful appellant or applicant

7.49   The Court may, on its own initiative or following an application from the party who incurred costs (usually but not necessarily the prosecution), make an order requiring an unsuccessful appellant or applicant pay some or all of the costs to that party as the Court finds to be just and reasonable.[18] These costs may include costs of proceedings in the Crown Court. It may include costs met by legal aid.

7.50   The Court should only make an order if it is satisfied that the party has the means and ability to pay. The procedure for making such orders is to be found at paragraph 3.4 of the Costs Practice Direction Part 3 and rule 76.6 of the CPR.

---

16   [2013] EWCA Crim 1632.
17   Prosecution of Offences Act 1985, s. 16(4) and CPR, r. 76.4.
18   Prosecution of Offenders Act 1985, s. 18(2).

Costs for unnecessary or improper expenses

7.51   If the Court is satisfied that a party's unreasonable or improper act or omission has put another party to expense, it may order that party to pay some or all of the other party's costs.[19] The Court may make such an order on the application of a party or on its own initiative. An application should be made in accordance with the requirements of rule 76.8 of the CPR in writing, as soon as practical after becoming aware of the grounds for doing so. A copy should be served on the Registrar and one on the other parties.

Wasted costs orders against representatives

7.52   'Wasted costs' are defined by section 19A(3) of the Prosecution of Offences Act 1985 as any cost incurred:

'(a)   as a result of any improper, unreasonable, or negligent act or omission on the part of any representative or any employee of a representative; or

(b)   which, in the light of any such act or omission occurring after they were incurred, the court considers it is unreasonable to expect that party to pay.'

7.53   The Court may make a wasted costs order against a legal representative or 'other representative', defined in the act as a person who is exercising a right of audience or right to conduct litigation on behalf of any party to the proceedings.

7.54   The guidance for making a wasted costs order is to be found at paragraph 4.2.3. of the Costs Practice Direction. Further guidance is to be found in *Re P (A Barrister)*.[20]

7.55   As an alternative to making a wasted costs order the Court may, when the appellant is funded by a representation or costs are to be paid out of central funds, make adverse observations about the representative's conduct of the case, for use in a costs assessment.[21]

Costs against a third party

7.56   The Court may make an order for costs against a third party when the Court considers that there had been serious misconduct by that party.[22]

---

19   Prosecution of Offenders Act 1985, s. 19(1).
20   [2001] EWCA Crim 1728.
21   CPR, r. 76.9(8).
22   Prosecution of Offences Act 1985, s. 19 B and Criminal Cases (General) Regulations 1986 (SI 1986/1335), reg. 3F(1).

Guidance on the procedure to be followed is at rule 76(10) of the CPR and paragraph 4.7.1 of the Costs Practice Direction.

Applications for a representation order following successful applications for leave

7.57   In successful applications for leave to appeal an application for a representation order may be requested at the conclusion of the hearing. It is a good idea to be specific, so if the preparation *and* presentation of the appeal was all unfunded, asking for 'a representation order for the preparation and presentation of the appeal' will avoid any danger of the Registrar later taking the view that only the work on the day of the hearing was covered by the order obtained.

SUMMARY OF KEY POINTS

- It is important to carefully read the appeal bundle to ensure that:
    - ○   it contains all the documents that are important to the appeal;
    - ○   that the case summary is accurate and covers the points that are important to the appeal;
    - ○   that the time estimate that has been given for the hearing is accurate.
- Whether to lodge a skeleton argument is a matter for the advocate, but the Court does not encourage advocates to provide skeleton arguments when the case is already fully set out in the appeal notice.
- Lists of any reported authorities and bundles of any unreported authorities should be lodged with the Court in good time. The guidance in *Erskine* should be considered when determining what authorities to rely on.
- Leave of the Court will be needed in order to argue any ground that was not contained in the original grounds that were considered by the single judge.
- The appellant has a right to be present at all appeals with leave but not at renewed applications for leave. In those cases which are listed for appeal, leave having been given, the appellant will be produced from prison unless he consents not to be produced. If the Court, having given leave to appeal against sentence, goes on to allow the appeal at the same hearing at which the appellant has not been produced, he will be written to asking if he wishes to have a hearing at which he will be produced.
- When an appellant or applicant has absconded, the Court has a discretion as to whether to hear the case, adjourn or dismiss the appeal.

- If the appellant dies before the hearing, the case may proceed if an approved person can be appointed to continue the case on his behalf.

- The prosecution will be represented at appeals against conviction. They may be represented at appeals against sentence or renewed applications for leave depending on whether the Court requests it or the prosecuting authority themselves decide to be represented.

- The Court's hearings are open to the public unless an order is made that a particular hearing be held in private. Certain reporting restrictions may automatically apply or be made by the Court depending on the nature of the case. In a case in which the parties believe that an order restricting public access of press reporting of the case should be made, it should be applied for at the commencement of the hearing.

- In straightforward appeals the Court will give judgment at the conclusion of the hearing. In complex cases judgment may be reserved to another date.

- At the conclusion the advocate should remember to make any necessary application for costs, representation orders or leave to appeal to the Supreme Court.

Chapter 8

Public funding and pro bono assistance

INTRODUCTION

8.1   When leave to appeal is allowed, a representation order is usually also granted. The Court of Appeal has the power to grant such an order even before leave is considered but a representation order will only be granted once an application for leave to appeal has been lodged.

8.2   The work that is involved in preparing an application for leave or an application to the Criminal Cases Review Commission may be straightforward, but it may often be complex, the work demanding and extensive.

8.3   Public funding is available to enable lawyers to undertake such work. It may be covered by the existing Crown Court representation order or, when a new solicitor is instructed, it may be funded under the 'advice and assistance' scheme in the Appeals and Reviews Class of the 2010 Standard Crime Contract ('SCC').

8.4   However, there are limitations to the work that the Legal Aid Authority ('LAA') will be prepared to fund and there may also be practical difficulties in obtaining assistance because the number of solicitors who are prepared to undertake such work at the rates on offer (which are among the lowest rates for publicly funded work) are threatened by recent cuts to public funding.

8.5   There are also a small number of organisations which may provide free assistance or representation for appeal work. The limitations in the availability of public funding means that these can be a vital backstop for those who seek to challenge their sentence or conviction. The assistance that they may provide is considered at the conclusion of this chapter.

WORK UNDER A CROWN COURT OR COURT OF APPEAL REPRESENTATION ORDER

8.6 A representation order[1] for work in the Crown Court covers advice and assistance on appeal. If there is no application for leave to appeal then there can be no claim as the fixed fee payable under the Litigator Graduated Fee Scheme

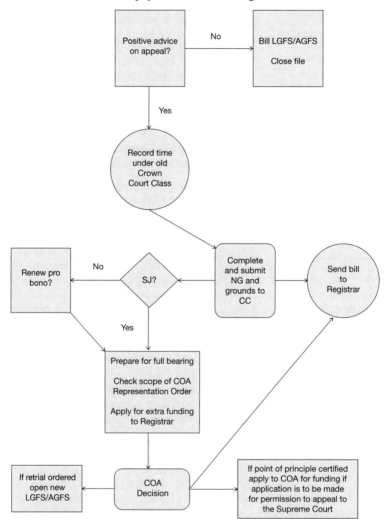

Figure 8.1 Flowchart for appeals under the Crown Court representation order

---

1   Defined as 'a document which records a section 16 determination' by the Criminal Legal Aid (Remuneration) Regulations 2013 (SI 2013/435), reg. 2(1).

will include any time spent providing negative advice. However, if there is a positive advice and a Form NG is submitted, there will be *proceedings* before the Court of Appeal so that a claim can be made in accordance with Schedule 3 of the Criminal Legal Aid (Remuneration) Regulations 2013 (SI 2013/435). In that case the solicitor can make a claim to the Registrar of Criminal Appeals for advice and assistance provided to the client. This will usually involve assisting with the preparation of the grounds and lodging the necessary documents with the Form NG. Any claim must be lodged within three months of the conclusion of the proceedings and can include a claim for work done prior to any determination.[2]

8.7   Where advice and assistance is provided to a client who has been convicted in the Crown Court, the Registrar of Criminal Appeals has issued guidance setting out the (limited) nature of the advice which the Registrar expects to be necessary.[3] It assumes that immediate oral advice is given by the advocate at the conclusion of the relevant hearing which should be confirmed in writing. Usually, the Registrar will expect this advice to be conveyed to the client by way of a letter from the solicitor without the need for an attendance upon the client although it is suggested that where the case is grave, or the issues are complex and, in either event, where the client is vulnerable, by age or otherwise, a face-to-face attendance may be justifiable.

8.8   If the single judge grants leave (or the application is referred by the Registrar to the full court) any advice and assistance under the Crown Court representation order ends and will be superseded by the representation order in the Court of Appeal. That representation order will assign an advocate to conduct the appeal. The Registrar will not usually extend the order to allow litigation work by a solicitor unless persuaded that there is good reason to do so. This is because the Registrar will assume that the appeal will involve solely a point of law which can be dealt with adequately by the advocate without assistance from a litigator. However, the solicitor may need to do work to support the appeal such as instructing an expert or taking statements or indeed other work that the advocate will not be in a position to carry out. Often the representation order will specify the limited purpose(s) for which the solicitor is assigned. Therefore it is important to check and carefully note any such limitations because unauthorised work will be disallowed on assessment of the final bill.

8.9   If there is any doubt about what is allowed, clarification can be obtained from the Criminal Appeal Office and an extension obtained, but this must be done before carrying out the work. There is no set form of application. It can be made by letter and will usually require an advice from the advocate in support of the application.

---

2   Criminal Legal Aid (Remuneration) Regulations 2013 (SI 2013/435), Sch. 3, reg. 3(1)(a).
3   The Guide, para. A1.1.

8.10   Where exceptional work is necessary to investigate or finalise grounds of appeal, provisional grounds can be submitted with a Form NG and a request for a representation order limited to cover that work.[4]

8.11   Where the single judge refuses leave that will usually bring to an end any advice and assistance as no further work will be necessary. However, if the client requires advice on whether to renew the application to the full Court then it is arguable that some limited further advice and assistance may be justified and can be allowed by the Registrar in exceptional cases.[5]

8.12   It is possible to obtain a transfer of the representation order following sentence by applying to the relevant Crown Court. This might be preferable where it is a very serious or complex charge as the rates make allowance for the grade of lawyer employed and can be increased by applying an enhancement. However, it requires a successful application to transfer the representation order and, unless an early Form NG and provisional grounds are submitted, little work can be carried out as the system of payment is based on the expectation that the lawyers will have acted throughout and know the case.

Claiming for work done under a representation order

8.13   The rules for claiming fees for work done in the Court of Appeal are set out in Schedule 3.[6] It should be noted that no claim may be entertained unless made within three months of the conclusion to the proceedings to which it relates. The determining officer must take into account all the relevant circumstances of the case including the nature, importance, complexity or difficulty of the work and the time involved and allow a reasonable amount in respect of all work actually and reasonably done.[7] Schedule 3 of the Criminal Legal Aid (Remuneration) Regulations 2013 (SI 2013/435) prescribes the information to be included in the claim and the matters which the appropriate officer will have regard to in determining the fees and disbursements. The appropriate fees for litigators and advocates are those specified in Schedule 3 but as amended from 20 March 2014 to implement the 8.75% reduction in the Criminal Legal Aid (Remuneration) (Amendment) Regulations 2014 (SI 2014/415).

8.14   The fees for experts are as prescribed in Schedule 5 of the Criminal Legal Aid (Remuneration) Regulations 2013 (SI 2013/435) which, similarly, were reduced by the Criminal Legal Aid (Remuneration) (Amendment)

---

4   The Guide, para. A1.4.
5   *Regina v Gibson (Ivano)* [1983] 1 WLR 1038.
6   Criminal Legal Aid (Remuneration) Regulations 2013 (SI 2013/435).
7   Criminal Legal Aid (Remuneration) Regulations 2013 (SI 2013/435), Sch. 3.

Regulations 2013 (SI 2013/2803). These prescribed rates can be increased if justified in exceptional circumstances.

8.15   The work undertaken is billed on an old style *ex post facto* (or yellow cornered) bill of costs to the Registrar. As practitioners will know, usually Crown Court work is paid in the form of a fixed fee (apart from confiscation proceedings and some other prescribed proceedings) so, unlike fixed fee cases, all actual work which can be shown to be reasonable and necessary to provide advice on appeal should be separately recorded on the file so it can be easily calculated and claimed as an additional amount to the litigator's fee for the Crown Court work. Where it is justified, an enhancement can be applied to the hourly rate in cases requiring exceptional expedition or exceptional competence, skill or expertise (this will normally be vulnerable clients in custody and/or grave offences or complex legal or factual issues).The bill will be assessed by the Registrar's office and it is vital to fully justify the level of fee earner and any enhancement with detailed reference to the circumstances of the case. If reduced, then further representations can be made within 21 days and if they are unsuccessful an application for review can be submitted the Costs Judge at the Senior Courts' Costs Office.

8.16   If any appeal to the Costs Judge is successful (even in part) then usually an order for the reasonable costs of preparing for and attending the appeal hearing (at the solicitor's appropriate private rate) will be made if requested. Similar provisions apply to the advocate's fee where the basic fees would not provide reasonable remuneration for some or all of the work the appropriate officer has allowed.[8] It should also be noted that if the Court makes an adverse observation the appropriate officer may reduce the fees payable, but only after giving the representative an opportunity to make representations as to whether the fee should be reduced and the extent of any reduction.[9] The Practice Direction again discusses these powers in detail.[10]

FUNDING FOR ADVICE AND ASSISTANCE

8.17   Funding for 'advice and assistance' under the Standard Criminal Contract is provided subject to the client's financial eligibility ('the means test') and the merits of the application ('the merits test'). It does not include 'representation', i.e. advocacy. Therefore, funding is limited to:

(a)   providing advice and assistance to the client;

(b)   obtaining the advice of an advocate; and

---

8   Criminal Legal Aid (Remuneration) Regulations 2013 (SI 2013/435), Sch. 3, regs 8, 9.
9   Criminal Legal Aid (Remuneration) Regulations 2013 (SI 2013/435), reg. 28.
10   Practice Direction (Costs in Criminal Proceedings) 2013 [2013] EWCA Crim 1632, paras 4.3.1, 4.3.2.

(c)   any reasonable disbursements (such as transcripts, instruction of expert or counsel).

8.18   Funding is only available when the solicitor's firm that is instructed holds a current contract with the LAA. However, there is a restriction on firms instructing their own in-house advocates to provide advice on appeal:

'a solicitor with higher court advocacy rights instructed by you to give an opinion must be from *a different organisation* from your instructing solicitor unless undertaking advocacy only' [our emphasis][11]

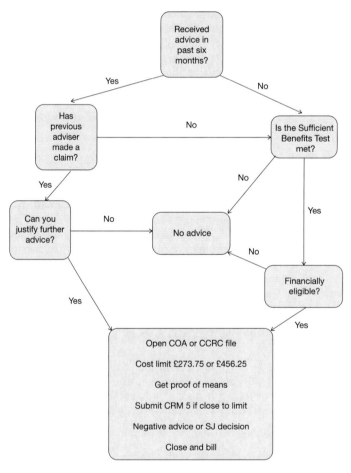

Figure 8.2   Flowchart for advice on appeal to COA or CCRC under SCC 2010 Appeals and Review Class

---

11   SCC Specification, Part A, para. 4.16.

Previous advice and assistance

8.19   Funding for advice and assistance provided to a client who has received advice and assistance for the same matter from another provider within the six months preceding the application may not be claimed except where:

(a)   there is a gap in time and circumstances have changed materially between the first and second occasions when the advice and assistance was sought;

(b)   the client has reasonable cause to transfer from the first provider; or

(c)   the first provider has confirmed that he will be making no claim for the payment for the advice and assistance.[12]

8.20   The effect of this is that if advice has been recently provided and it does not appear to the solicitor who is contemplating applying for funding to have been defective or incomplete, a claim for funding under the advice and assistance scheme should not be made.

Financial eligibility (means)

8.21   Any advice is subject to financial eligibility. Following the enactment of the Legal Aid, Sentencing and Punishment of Offenders Act 2013 ('LASPO 2013'), the assessment of means is now determined in accordance with the Criminal Legal Aid (Financial Resources) Regulations 2013 (SI 2013/471).[13] There is deemed financial eligibility if the individual (or his partner) is in receipt of a 'qualifying benefit': income support; income-based jobseeker's allowance; guaranteed credit; income-related employment and support allowance; and universal credit.[14] In assessing whether to take account of a possible spouse, regard should be had to the definition of a partner in regulation 2:

"'partner" means –

(a)   an individual's spouse or civil partner, from whom the individual is not separated due to a breakdown in the relationship which is likely to be permanent;

(b)   a person with whom the individual lives as a couple; or

(c)   a person with whom the individual ordinarily lives as a couple, from whom they are not separated due to a breakdown in the relationship that is likely to be permanent'

---

12   SCC Specification, Part B, para. 11.26.
13   Subject to minor amendments in the Criminal Legal Aid (Financial Resources)(Amendment) Regulations 2013 (SI 2013/2791).
14   Criminal Legal Aid (Financial Resources) Regulations 2013 (SI 2013/471), reg. 14.

8.22   The financial resources of the individual's partner must be treated as the individual's financial resources unless:

(a)   the individual's partner has a contrary interest in the matter in respect of which the individual is seeking advice and assistance; or

(b)   the Director of Legal Aid Casework considers that, in all the circumstances of the case, it would be inequitable or impractical to do so.

8.23   The period of calculation is defined in regulation 2 as 'the seven days up to and including the date on which the application for a determination under section 15 of LASPO 2013 is made' which is in contrast to the period of one year in the case of a determination of an application under section 16 (representation).

8.24   For those who are not in receipt of a qualifying benefit, Part 2, regulation 8 specifies that for advice and assistance an individual is eligible if disposable income does not exceed £99 and disposable capital does not exceed £1,000. Regulations 11 and 12 apply to the calculation of disposable income and allow for the deduction of:

(a)   income tax;

(b)   estimated National Insurance contributions;

(c)   any attendance allowances;

(d)   disability living allowance and any payments out of the Social Fund;

(e)   any back-to-work bonus treated as jobseeker's allowance;

(f)   any direct payments under the Health and Social Care Act 2001 or section 17A of the Children Act 1989;

(g)   any reasonable living expenses provided as an exception to a restraint order under section 41 of the Proceeds of Crime Act 2002; and

(h)   any personal independent payment paid under Part 4 of the Welfare Reform Act 2012.

8.25   If the individual has dependents then there are fixed deductions of £33.65 for a partner and £47.45 for each child. There is also a list of deductions for maintenance[15] and in assessing disposable capital.[16]

---

15   Criminal Legal Aid (Financial Resources) Regulations 2013 (SI 2013/471), reg. 12.
16   Criminal Legal Aid (Financial Resources) Regulations 2013 (SI 2013/471), reg. 13.

Financial eligibility and children

8.26   Where the applicant is a child (under 18 at the date of the application[17]), a 'maintaining adult's' financial resources are treated as the child's unless it appears to the Director inequitable to do so.[18] This includes consideration of all the circumstances of the case, the age and financial resources of the child (defined as under 18), and any conflict of interest between the child and the maintaining adult. The solicitor should have regard to Part A, paragraphs 4.27 to 4.29 of the SCC, which set out the considerations when deciding whether it is equitable to aggregate the resources of the maintaining adult and the child. However, as advice in the Appeals and Reviews Class will often be provided to a child in custody then arguably his parent or guardian will not be providing maintenance in any event.

The Sufficient Benefits Test (merits)

8.27   This is the test that must be satisfied in order to provide advice and assistance under the SCC:

> 'Advice and Assistance may only be provided on legal issues concerning English (or Welsh) law and where there is sufficient benefit to the Client, having regard to the circumstances of the matter, including the personal circumstances of the Client, to justify work or further work being carried out.'

8.28   The same test applies to any application to any extension of funding under the scheme.

8.29   It is a broad test but includes consideration of not only the importance of the case to the client but the extent to which the advice and assistance can in fact assist. This does not mean that an application must show that there are arguable grounds to appeal. However, it must be shown that there is some good reason to believe that the client would benefit from the assistance of a lawyer. In a case in which trial lawyers have advised negatively, it is not sufficient that the client wishes to obtain a second opinion. The LAA will expect the new solicitors to show that there has been a change of circumstances or grounds for concluding that the advice may have been incorrect or incomplete.

---

17   Criminal Legal Aid (Financial Resources) Regulations 2013 (SI 2013/471), reg. 2.
18   Criminal Legal Aid (Financial Resources) Regulations 2013 (SI 2013/471), reg. 10.

Applying for funding

Completing the CRM 1 and CRM 2

8.30   Care should be exercised in deciding whether there is any 'partner' income or capital to be taken into account as set out above. Prospective clients will often tick 'single' or 'separated' but also supply information that suggests they are married or in a long-term relationship. The fact that they may be separated due to the client's incarceration does not mean the partner's financial resources can be ignored unless that has brought about an end to the emotional relationship. The Director will look at factors such as whether the partner was providing any regular financial support and/or visiting the client on a regular basis. There can also be rare instances when the client still lives with a former partner but as separate households and therefore the former partner's resources can be disregarded. If there is any doubt then it is prudent to address the issue by way of a clear file note supporting your decision.

8.31   Solicitors can accept postal applications where there is good reason (i.e. often the client is in custody – see the note on page 2 of CRM 2). Telephone advice can also be provided to the client before signature (again where the client is in custody and the advice is urgent (which arguably most appeals advice will be) and the client completes the CRM 1 and 2 and qualifies for advice).

8.32   The provider can claim the cost of public transport to visit a client away from their office before the application is signed, provided it is justified and a note made (on page 3 of the CRM 2) and the client meets the qualifying criteria. Indeed, travel time can also be claimed if the client is in detention, prison or hospital.

8.33   If the client has received an adverse advice it is necessary to consider how long it was since the first opinion. If recent, and it appears that all the issues have been considered, no further work may be undertaken.[19] However, in order to provide this screening advice it will usually be necessary to consider some paperwork, including the last written advice. This can be a danger area for unwary solicitors. There is a small cohort of disgruntled convicted prisoners who regularly contact defence firms requesting advice. If a solicitor responds to such a request, he must be very careful not to create, unwittingly, a potential retainer with the client. A clear policy needs to be maintained as to how hopeless requests are rejected and those who may be eligible for advice have their expectations carefully managed. Clear client care letters (with regular updates) must be provided. It cannot be overemphasised that both the

---

19   SCC Specification, Part B, para. 11.5.

Legal Ombudsman and the Court of Appeal require prompt and clear advice to clients.

8.34   In a case where there appears to be further evidence or some defect in the opinion or the proceedings then further work may be justified and the Specification states that up to three hours will be allowed to prepare instructions for counsel or a solicitor with higher rights.[20]

Applications to extend funding

8.35   If the means and merit tests are met and CRM 1 and CRM 2 have been completed, work can be undertaken to the standard upper limit. However, this limit is not high (at time of writing it is £273.75 for normal appeals and £456.25 for CCRC cases). Once the limit has been reached, the solicitor must then apply for extensions in funding using a CRM 5 to carry out further work on the case. The CRM 5 can be completed online and will be considered and determined relatively swiftly by a specialist unit at the LAA. In determining such applications, the LAA will follow its own guidance, which can be found on its website. Refusals may be appealed but this will cause delay. It will often be prudent to attach an advice from the advocate, setting out why the work is necessary in order to advance the case. The greater the expense involved, the more detailed and persuasive this needs to be.

8.36   Applications to extend will be required for the following work:

(a)   Transcripts – it will be necessary to identify and obtain a quote from the transcription company used by the particular Crown Court which heard the case. The application should explain why the transcript of the particular part of the trial that is sought is necessary in order to advise. The LAA regularly provides funding for a transcript of the summing up, the sentencing remarks (when an appeal against sentence is being considered) and any ruling which is relevant to the appeal. However, funding will rarely, if ever, be provided for complete transcripts of the trial.

(b)   Advice from advocates – the LAA will determine the number of hours and the hourly rate at which the advocate will be paid. It is usually no more than £80 for a junior advocate. In exceptional cases it may agree to an increase of up to £125 per hour.

(c)   Expert opinion – strong justification will be generally be needed in order for the LAA to grant funding for an expert. It is advisable for the application to be supported by an advice from an advocate explaining the necessity of the instruction to the proper preparation of the case.

---

20 SCC Specification, Part B, para. 11.6.

(d)   Travel – this is an area that will be carefully scrutinised by the LAA. As a starting point the LAA takes the view that any return travel time over two hours will be disallowed unless justified. If it is a new client this will usually rely on the lack of local solicitors specialising in this area (particularly if your client has made a series of requests for advice from more local providers without any response). Otherwise, if you have significant knowledge of the case or the client you may justify travelling to more distant places of detention. Generally, return travel over four hours will be unlikely to be allowed unless exceptional; however where an existing client has been moved during the course of the case, return travel of up to six hours may be allowed.

Once a representation order is granted by the Court of Appeal

8.37   Once the Court of Appeal has assigned an advocate under a representation order, advice and assistance cannot be used as an alternate or supplement to the Court's powers to grant legal representation, where only counsel has been authorised.[21]

Funding for applications to the Criminal Cases Review Commission

8.38   The Contract Specification makes clear that an application to the Commission is the last resort and can only be made if the client has appealed against the original conviction or leave has been refused.[22]

8.39   A lawyer coming to the case afresh will be unable to decide immediately whether the case is likely to meet the referral criteria so you are allowed to provide 'initial case screening' to an eligible client who it appears may have an application.[23] The LAA expects the lawyer to obtain a statement from the client to carry this out and it suggests that this will 'normally' take two hours.[24] Often it will take longer and, as with all work in this area, file notes should justify the time spent.[25] In making an assessment 'the provider should initially take instructions and ascertain whether the case is both suitable to be heard by the Commission and whether the case meets the referral criteria applied by the Commission'.[26] Often this work will give rise to difficult decisions as to whether the costs of further investigation are justified. The LAA expects the lawyer to make these decisions 'in light of the available information and using

---

21   SCC Specification, Part B, para. 11.7.
22   SCC Specification, Part B, para. 11.19.
23   SCC Specification, Part B, para. 11.21.
24   SCC Specification, Part B, para. 11.22.
25   Criminal Bills Assessment Manual ('CBAM'), Version 1, April 2013, para. 11.2.2.
26   CBAM, Version 1, April 2013, para. 11.3.4.

your professional skill and common sense'.[27] The LAA recognises that it may be necessary to exceed the upper limit in order to do so.[28]

8.40   Indeed, in many cases where there is a real possibility that the Commission will refer the case, the limit may have to be increased. It may be necessary to obtain transcripts of the evidence[29] and the opinion of counsel.[30] The reality is that these cases are often grave and complex. They can involve novel and complex areas of legal interpretation which may require advice from a leading advocate. The LAA will be reluctant to incur the costs of a leading advocate. Therefore, the solicitor must be prepared, perhaps with an advice from a junior advocate, to argue and, if necessary, appeal a refusal.

8.41   It may be necessary to obtain expert evidence where there is an issue that is crucial to the safety of the conviction, prior to the referral, although the LAA expects the defence lawyers to bear in mind that the Commission can obtain or bear the costs of expert reports.[31]

8.42   Once a case is referred back to the Court of Appeal by the Commission the Registrar will usually grant a representation order to include an advocate and litigator.

Claiming for work done under the advice and assistance scheme

8.43   A claim must not be submitted under this part of the contract where representation has been provided for the same client in the proceedings in which the conviction or sentence was imposed in the Magistrates' Court or Crown Court or the Court of Appeal, and advice on appeal or sentence can be claimed under the representation order covering those proceedings (except where the client has changed provider since the original proceedings).

8.44   A claim should only be submitted when:[32]

(a)   the matter has concluded;

(b)   it is known that no further work will be undertaken for the client in the same matter;

(c)   it is unclear whether further work will be undertaken and at least one month has elapsed since the last work was undertaken; or

---

27   SCC Specification, Part B, para. 11.21.
28   SCC Specification, Part B, para. 11.25.
29   SCC Specification, Part B, para. 11.23.
30   SCC Specification, Part B, para. 11.24.
31   CBAM, Version 1, April 2013, para. 11.3.3.
32   SCC Specification, Part B, para. 11.41.

(d)   in the case of a claim for advice and assistance on an appeal against conviction or sentence, including an appeal by way of case stated or an application to vary a sentence, where a determination has been made by the relevant court as soon as the representation order has been issued.

Further instructions after a matter ends or a claim has been submitted

8.45   If a claim for advice and assistance has been submitted, any subsequent advice and assistance in relation to the same matter will require a new application but will be subject to the previous upper limit. This can only be done if there are substantive issues outstanding from the first occasion or there has been a material development or change in the client's circumstances such that further advice and assistance are now required. The client must complete a further CRM 1 and CRM 2 and it is necessary to establish that the qualifying criteria are met. The same reference number must be used and the second file should include a reference to the first and kept together for audit purposes.

ALTERNATIVE SOURCES OF ADVICE AND ASSISTANCE

8.46   There are limitations in the type of work that the LAA may be willing to fund. Funding is rarely extended to complex cases or lengthy investigations. Moreover, the availability of funding does not guarantee that there will be competent lawyers who will be willing to undertake the work in question. Not only are the number of solicitors firms who undertake work in this area threatened by cuts to legal aid, but the limitations in the extent of funding may mean that competent firms who do have LAA contracts may feel that they cannot justify extensive work on complex cases for the limited funding that is available.

8.47   Whilst it is always open to a defendant with means to pay for legal representation, this is not an option for many of those who have been convicted of serious crimes, particularly when the conviction is followed by a substantial custodial sentence. It may, therefore, be necessary for the defendant to consider alternative means of advice or assistance.

Innocence projects

8.48   Innocence projects were first established in the USA. They are university-based projects in which students, under an academic supervisor and often also with the assistance of practising lawyers, investigate potential miscarriages with a view to obtaining evidence that is capable of proving the innocence of the convicted person. In the USA many of the projects have had success in obtaining the evidence that leads to the overturning of convictions.

8.49 The innocence projects that are based in England and Wales have been established more recently than many of their US counterparts and they have yet to achieve the success of which many US projects can boast. The first UK project was established at Bristol University in 2005 and there are now approximately 30 located at various universities.[33] Until 2014 many operated as affiliates to the Innocence Network UK, which was run by the founders of the Bristol University project and provided training and support for other projects.[34] Despite this activity, the work of the UK innocence projects has yet to lead to the overturning of a single conviction. Certain projects, particularly Bristol and Cardiff, have had successes in getting cases are referred back to the Court of Appeal by the CCRC as a result of evidence that they have uncovered. But in 2013 a lawyer from the CCRC remarked in a speech that the number of referrals that they had received from innocence projects was very low (17 in ten years from a total of five universities).[35]

8.50 There a number of limitations to the innocence project model. The fact that they will usually only assist those who proclaim their total non-involvement with their alleged offence (precluding, for example, assistance being given to the defendant convicted of murder who claims to have suffered from provocation or diminished responsibility that would render him guilty of manslaughter) acts as a limit on the number of people that innocence projects can assist. However, it is the experience of lawyers that prisons are not short of prisoners who proclaim their innocence and seek to have their convictions overturned. It seems that there are limitations to what students, who lack legal training and can give neither full-time nor long-term commitment to a particular case can achieve.

8.51 They may be no substitute for qualified legal assistance but innocence projects can supplement the work of lawyers, particularly in undertaking the investigative work for which funding may not be available. For those who seek to prove their innocence and cannot find a lawyer to take on their case, innocence projects may, for months or years, be their sole source of assistance.

---

33 Article by Lee Glendinning, *Guardian*, 3 September 2004. See: www.theguardian.com/uk/2004/sep/03/ukcrime.prisonsandprobation/print.

34 See the Innocence Network UK website at www.innocencenetwork.org.uk for the history of the organisation and its present role.

35 Article by Jon Robbins, *Guardian*, 20 November 2013. See: www.theguardian.com/law/2013/nov/20/appeal-court-innocence-projects-dwaine-george.

The Centre for Criminal Appeals

8.52   The Centre for Criminal Appeals is a not-for-profit organisation that was founded in order to assist those who wish make an application to the Criminal Cases Review Commission and/or appeal a conviction in the Court of Appeal but lack the means to pay for their own representation. As a charity the Centre can raise private funds that will enable its lawyers to focus solely on appeals and overcome the limitations imposed by the public funding regime. At the time of writing, the project is in a pilot phase but is likely in the future to provide valuable advice and assistance, particularly in those cases requiring significant investigation work and a long-term commitment by the legal team.[36]

Bar Pro Bono Unit

8.53   A number of barristers are prepared to provide advice and assistance in particular cases for free. The best chance of obtaining such assistance is through the Bar Pro Bono Unit, which can obtain the details of a particular case and forward it to barristers who may have the experience and willingness to assist. However, it is not altogether clear that a barrister would have the willingness or the best professional expertise to undertake the type of extensive work for which funding would not be available under the advice and assistance scheme.

SUMMARY OF KEY POINTS

- The three regimes for public funding are: representation orders that are granted by the Crown Court; representation orders granted by the Court of Appeal; and funding for advice and assistance under the Standard Crime Contract. These sources of funding are mutually exclusive.

- Positive advice and assistance in lodging an appeal can be claimed under the Crown Court representation order. No claim can be made for a negative advice.

- Funding for advice and assistance under the Standard Crime Contract will enable lawyers who did not represent the defendant at trial to provide advice and assistance (but not representation). It is subject to the criteria of means and merits. An application may not be made until six months have elapsed since the client was last advised under the scheme.

- Application for funding for advice and assistance is by way of CRM 1 and CRM 2. Each application for an extension of funds, including funding to

---

36   See the Centre for Criminal Appeals Project website at www.criminalappeals.org.uk. It should be noted that lawyers from the Centre contributed to Chapter 5 of this book.

cover the advice of an independent advocate, transcript, experts' reports or extensive work by defence solicitors, must be made through CRM 5.

- It will assist an application for extension of funding if it is supported by an advocate's advice that explains why the funding that is sought is necessary to the case.

- The merits criteria must be satisfied in respect of each application for extension of funding. In order to meet the merits criteria the application must provide some reason to show that the work could benefit the client. It is not sufficient simply to suggest that there should be a second opinion.

- For those cases which involve extensive work for which funding may not be granted, the defendant may wish to seek the assistance of an innocence project or the Centre for Criminal Appeals.

Part 3

Applications from the Court of Appeal

Chapter 9

The Criminal Cases Review Commission

INTRODUCTION

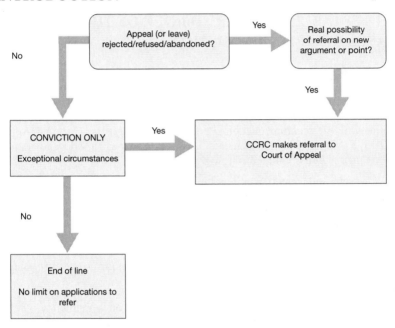

Figure 9.1   Flowchart for referrals by the CCRC

9.1   If an appeal is dismissed or abandoned it may not be resurrected. No new appeal may be brought against the conviction or sentence in question by the defendant himself. The only way in which a new appeal can be brought will be if the Criminal Cases Review Commission refers the case to the Court of Appeal.

9.2   This is a vital mechanism for preventing injustice, particularly in those cases in which new evidence emerges after an appeal has been dismissed. However, the Commission provides more than a referral mechanism. It is also an investigative body and may deploy its powers to uncover evidence that would be out of reach of a defendant and his lawyers. It may use these powers either when considering an application by a defendant to refer a case to the Court of Appeal or when the Court of Appeal at any point in an appeal against conviction or sentence directs it to do so.

9.3   The main focus of this chapter is on making applications to the Commission for a reference, the procedure following a referral and the steps that may be taken if it declines to refer. The Commission's investigatory powers are summarised and the procedure for investigations at the direction of the Court of Appeal is also considered.

THE ESTABLISHMENT AND ROLE OF THE CRIMINAL CASES REVIEW COMMISSION

9.4   In the wake of the exposure of a series of miscarriages of justice which came to light in the late 1980s and early 1990s,[1] a Royal Commission[2] recommended the power to refer possible miscarriages of justice be removed from the Home Secretary and placed in the hands of an independent body. Acting on that recommendation, Parliament, through the Criminal Appeal Act 1995 ('CAA 1995'), established the Commission as an independent, non-governmental body[3] with the following powers:

(a)   to refer any sentence or conviction in the Crown Court to the Court of Appeal if the Commission is of the opinion that there is a real possibility that an appeal will be allowed;

(b)   to conduct any investigation that the Court of Appeal may direct it to undertake in order to assist the Court in the determination of an appeal;

(c)   to refer, on the same basis, any sentence or conviction in the Magistrates Court to the Crown Court;

(d)   to assist the Home Secretary by providing an opinion on whether to recommend the exercise of Her Majesty's prerogative of mercy in relation to a conviction.[4]

---

1   The late 1980s and early 1990s saw the exposure of a series of miscarriages of justice, related to wrongful convictions for terrorist crimes, which culminated with the 'Birmingham Six' appeal in 1991.

2   The Royal Commission on Criminal Justice, commonly referred to as the 'Runciman Commission', was established by the Home Secretary in March 1991 and reported in July 1993.

3   CAA 1995, s. 8 establishes its constitution.

4   CAA 1995, s. 16(1). The Commission has never been called upon to make a recommendation under this section.

THE COMMISSION'S POWER TO REFER TO THE COURT OF APPEAL

9.5   The Commission has a power to refer a conviction or sentence to the Court of Appeal where a person has been convicted of an offence on indictment in England, Wales or Northern Ireland.[5] The power extends to a verdict of not guilty by reason of insanity and a finding that a person was under a disability when he did an act or made an omission.[6]

9.6   It may refer following an application or of its own motion where no application has been made.[7] A referral will be treated as an appeal, with leave, under CAA 1968 and must be heard by the Court.[8]

9.7   Although the Commission only refers a small percentage of applications that it receives, the success rate for those appeals that are referred is around 70%.[9]

THE TEST FOR REFERRAL

9.8   Section 13 of CAA 1995 provides that no reference shall be made unless the Commission considers that there is a 'real possibility' that:

(a)   the conviction, verdict or finding under appeal would not be upheld because of an argument, or evidence, not raised in the proceedings which led to it (or on any appeal or application for leave against it); or

(b)   in the case of a sentence, because of an argument on a point of law or information not so raised; and

(c)   an appeal against the conviction, verdict, finding or sentence has been determined or leave to appeal has been refused.

9.9   However, section 13 gives the Commission the power to refer even when (a) or (c) do not apply if there are 'exceptional circumstances' which justify making it.

---

5   CAA 1995, s. 9. By virtue of s. 12A it has also been extended to include references of convictions and sentences by the Court Martial to the Court Martial Appeal Court and by the Service Civilian Court to the Court Martial.

6   CAA 1995, s. 9(5), (6).

7   CAA 1995, s.14(1).

8   CAA 1995, s. 9(2), (3).

9   Since its inception the Commission has referred on average 32 cases per annum to the Court of Appeal. This works out at a rate of between 2–4% of all applications received. However, if the cases which fail the initial screening were factored out, the referral rate would jump to around 7.5% (CCRC Annual Report and Accounts 2012/2013).

The discretion whether to refer

9.10   It is important to note that the Commission has discretion not to refer even if the test under section 13 is satisfied. For example, if the conviction is likely to be quashed but only to be substituted by an alternative conviction, allowing the original conviction to stand may cause no real injustice to the applicant.[10]

APPLYING TO THE COMMISSION FOR A REFERRAL

Who may apply?

9.11   An application does not have to be made by the defendant himself. This means that a family member with a substantial interest in the outcome of an appeal could make an application on behalf of someone who had died after conviction. However, when a defendant has died, the Commission will only consider the application if an 'approved person'[11] (such as a family member) can be identified in whose name any application for leave might be made.

When to apply

9.12   Normally an application should be made to the Commission only if:

(a)   an appeal has been considered and refused by the Court of Appeal; or

(b)   leave has been refused by the single judge (it need not have been renewed before the full Court); or

(c)   an application for leave or an appeal with leave has been abandoned; and

(d)   there is argument, evidence or information in the terms of section 13(a) or (b) that was not considered by the Court of Appeal in that initial appeal.

9.13   What counts as 'new argument' is a matter to be considered in each case. However, a change in the law will not itself be regarded as giving rise to new argument that raises a real possibility of an appeal being allowed. Section 16C of CAA 1968[12] now provides that the Court may dismiss any reference based solely on the change of law where, had the application for extension of time been made by the defendant, that application would have been refused. The Commission should now only refer cases involving a change in the law

---

10   *Smith (Duncan Wallace)* [2004] EWCA Crim 631.
11   CCA 1968, s. 46A makes the nomination of an approved person following the death of a defendant a pre-condition for a valid appeal.
12   As inserted by the Criminal Justice and Immigration Act 2008, s. 42.

where the test of a change in the law giving rise to 'substantial injustice'(*R v Fletcher; R v Cottrell*)[13] may be said to be met. The Commission has published guidance on this aspect of its discretion.[14]

9.14   There are no time limits for making an application, but this does not mean that the applicant should delay making it. There is no formal restriction on reapplying; indeed a recent successful referral was made at the third time of asking where fresh DNA evidence further undermined questionable identification evidence.[15] However, applications which are substantially the same as those which have already been refused should clearly not be made.

'Exceptional circumstances'

9.15   As indicated, the Commission may, in exceptional circumstances, make a reference to the Court of Appeal even if there was no previous appeal. Whilst there is no statutory definition of 'exceptional circumstances', the Commission's own guidance sets out a number of non-exhaustive situations in which exceptional circumstances may be made out.[16]

9.16   Among them are cases where there may be an arguable appeal but this will depend on further investigations being carried out and third party material being obtained and considered. If the Commission concludes that it is not possible for the applicant and his legal representatives to carry out this investigation but that it might be carried out by the Commission, then this might give rise to exceptional circumstances. However, the Court has stressed that the mere existence of relevant third party material should not necessarily be regarded as giving rise to exceptional circumstances.[17]

Making the application

9.17   The Commission's website contains guidance for the making of an application.[18] In addition, it has published individual memoranda on various aspects of its work describing how it deals with common issues. These can be found in the 'casework' section of the website.

---

13   [2007] EWCA Crim 2016.
14   CCRC Formal Memorandum – Discretion in Referrals (including applications based on a change in the law), Version 1.
15   *Regina v Victor Nealon* [2014] EWCA Crim 574.
16   CCRC Formal Memorandum – Exceptional Circumstances
17   *R v Gerald* [1999] Crim LR 315.
18   www.justice.gov.uk/downloads/about/criminal-cases-review/policies-and-procedures/ccrc-q-and-a.pdf.

9.18 It is advisable, although not necessary, that an application be made with the assistance of a lawyer. Funding may be available for legal representation under the 'Advice and Assistance' scheme (see **8.38–8.42** for details).

9.19 The application should be made using the Commission's application form. However, applicants are likely to benefit by submitting additional grounds which should set out the legal and factual issues that are relevant to the application, address the relevant statutory questions and include all material that may be of assistance to the Commission in making its decision.

Requesting an investigation

9.20 If an applicant wishes the Commission to carry out an investigation, it is important to explain why the material sought is of importance to the application. It is also important to explain what steps the applicant and his lawyers have already taken to obtain the material sought and the outcome of any such enquiries.

9.21 There has been increasing demand for the Commission to use its powers to investigate the adequacy of legal advice given to those who may have been prosecuted in contravention of international conventions or pleaded guilty in ignorance of a defence, in particular section 31 of the Immigration and Asylum Act 1999.[19] The Commission has published specific guidance for potential applicants who may be refugees or the victims of trafficking.[20]

The decision-making process

9.22 An initial screening takes place to ensure that the application is valid. Early steps are taken to secure potentially relevant material that is held by a public body. Certain cases will be given priority.[21] The case will then be allocated to a case review manager who will examine the issues raised in the application to see if there might be anything that could give grounds for referring the case. The Commission is allowed to consider any representations and any matters that appear to be relevant.[22] Investigations are carried out when they are appropriate. Most are carried out by Commission staff. However,

---

19 In *Regina v Mateta* [2013] EWCA Crim 1372 the Commission referred a number of cases to the Court concerning the defence under s. 31.
20 www.justice.gov.uk/downloads/about/criminal-cases-review/policies-and-procedures/ccrc-seeker-refugee-leaflet.pdf.
21 For example, if the applicant is serving a sentence that is soon to expire or is suffering from a potentially fatal illness.
22 CAA 1995, s. 14(2).

investigators may be appointed to assist in carrying out enquiries. If necessary, the Commission can, at any stage, ask the Court of Appeal to provide an opinion on a relevant matter of law.[23]

9.23 When the review is complete it is considered by either a single commissioner or a committee of three commissioners. A single commissioner may decide not to make a referral. However, only a committee of three commissioners can make a referral.[24] If they are of the view that a referral is justified then a final statement of reasons will be completed and sent to the applicant and the Court of Appeal. If it is decided not to refer, a provisional statement of reasons is drafted.

The provisional statement of reasons

9.24 The applicant and his lawyers will be sent a copy of the provisional statement of reasons and be given the opportunity to respond to any points made or to provide further information. The correspondence will usually indicate that any response must be received by a particular date. If more time is needed it should be requested with an explanation.

The final decision

9.25 The final decision will be contained in the 'Final Statement of Reasons' which will be provided to the applicant and his legal representative. The decision must be clear and fully reasoned in order that the applicant can understand how it has been reached. Fairness may require the disclosure of information that the Commission has taken into account when reaching its decision *(R v Secretary of State for the Home Department, ex p. Hickey (No. 2))*.[25]

Likely timeframe for a decision

9.26 In 2013/14 the average time from allocation to a case review manager to a provisional view on a case being taken was 37.8 weeks.[26] However, the length of time can vary from weeks to many months depending on, amongst other things, whether the Commission needs to undertake any investigations.

---

23 CAA 1995, s. 14(3).
24 CAA 1995, Sch. 1, para. 6(3).
25 [1995] 1 WLR 734 (DC).
26 The CCRC Annual Report and Accounts 2013/2014.

CHALLENGING A REFUSAL TO MAKE A REFERENCE

9.27   A decision not to refer the case may be challenged by way of judicial review. As with any judicial review, the Court will not be concerned with whether the decision was right but only whether it was lawful and reasonable (*Ex p. Pearson*).[27] The Administrative Court has indicated that a high threshold will have to be crossed to persuade it that a decision of the Commission not to refer should be quashed (*Cleeland v CCRC*).[28]

THE PROCEDURE FOLLOWING A REFERENCE BEING MADE TO THE COURT OF APPEAL

9.28   The procedure, which is largely governed by section 14 of CAA 1995 and rules 68.2, 68.5 and 68.6 of the CPR, can be summarised as follows:

(a)   If the Commission decides to make a reference to the Court of Appeal it must send that decision to every person who is likely be party to the appeal.[29]

(b)   The decision is also passed to the Registrar of Criminal Appeals who must also serve notice of the decision on the appellant and the respondent.[30]

(c)   The Registrar is likely at this stage to grant representation orders for solicitors and counsel for the purpose of preparing the appeal.

(d)   A Form NG should be served by the legal representatives of the appellant within 28 days of receipt of the Registrar's notice of appeal (application to extend that time can be made) on the Registrar, not the Crown Court.[31]

(e)   Permission of the Court is required if the appellant seeks to advance grounds that are not related to the reasons given in the reference.[32]

(f)   Directions may be made for a particular case. However, the Court in *R v Siddall and Brooke*[33] suggested a timetable that parties should adhere to and indicated delay caused by a failure to adhere to the timetable may give rise to a risk of a wasted costs order being made.

---

27   [2000] 1 Cr App R 141.
28   [2009] EWHC 474 (Admin), para. 48.
29   CAA 1995, s. 14(4)(b).
30   CPR, r. 65.8.
31   CPR, r. 68.2(a)(ii).
32   CAA 1995, s. 14(4A), (4B); and see *Regina v Hallam* [2012] EWCA Crim 1158.
33   [2006] EWCA Crim 1353.

AN OVERVIEW OF THE COMMISSION'S INVESTIGATORY POWERS

9.29   The Commission's investigatory powers are largely contained in sections 17 to 25 of CAA 1995. The law in relation to those powers can be summarised as follows:

(a)   The Commission is authorised to obtain access to (and copy) all documents and material from public bodies if it believes it may assist the investigation. The duty of the public body to comply with a request is not affected by any obligation of secrecy or other limitation on disclosure and therefore will often include material not disclosed or available to the defence at trial,[34] for example social services' files or other sensitive information.

(b)   The power includes a power to direct that such material is preserved in an unaltered state until the Commission further directs.[35] This may be important if there is a risk that efforts may be made to conceal or alter potentially relevant material.

(c)   However, the person providing information to the Commission may withhold consent for it to be disclosed to another party if an obligation of secrecy would otherwise have prevented disclosure to the Commission and it is reasonable to do so.[36]

(d)   Although the public body is required to provide such material to the Commission as it requests, there is no formal sanction for any failure to do so, although the Commission may seek a remedy by way of judicial review.

(e)   In addition to carrying out its own investigations, the Commission may require the appointment of an investigating officer to carry out inquiries on its behalf. Such a person may be from a public body or (more usually) from the police. The Commission can direct that particular individuals are not appointed or that police officers should not be from the police force that carried out the original investigation.[37]

(f)   With the two exceptions set out in (g) and (h) below, the Commission is empowered only to obtain material from public bodies, not from private corporations. The meaning of 'public body' is narrowly defined.[38]

---

34   CAA 1995, s.17(4).
35   CAA 1995, s.17(2).
36   CAA 1995, s. 25.
37   CAA 1995, s. 19. *R v Hallam* [2012] EWCA Crim 1158 is a recent example of the successful use of s. 19 to investigate a police investigation.
38   CAA 1995, s. 22(1).

(g)   As a 'relevant public body'[39] the Commission may, in accordance with the provisions of the Regulation of Investigatory Powers Act 2000, obtain communication data from private individuals and bodies.

(h)   If police officers are appointed to carry out an investigation, they may employ their powers under the Police and Criminal Evidence Act 1984 to obtain material from private individuals or bodies.

(i)   It is a criminal offence under section 23 of CAA 1995 for present or former members or employees of the Commission, or investigating officers appointed by the Commission, to disclose information obtained in the course of the investigation save for one of the purposes contained in section 24 of CAA 1995.

(j)   There is no obligation to disclose all material obtained in an investigation to an applicant or appellant. Indeed, there may be material which should not be disclosed. However, the Commission should provide the applicant with sufficient disclosure to enable him to properly present his best case (*Ex p. Hickey (No. 2)*).[40]

COMMISSION INVESTIGATIONS AT THE DIRECTION OF THE COURT OF APPEAL

9.30   On any appeal against conviction the Court of Appeal may direct the Commission to investigate and report to the Court on any matter, if it appears to the Court that:

(a)   the matter is relevant to the determination of the case and ought, if possible, to be resolved before the case is determined;

(b)   an investigation of the matter by the Commission is likely to result in the Court being able to resolve it; and

(c)   the matter cannot be resolved by the Court without an investigation by the Commission.[41]

9.31   The Court may direct the Commission to carry out such an investigation if any of the potential grounds turn on alleged irregularity in a jury's deliberations.[42] Serious failures by the prosecution in their duties of disclosure have also been the subject of investigations at the direction of the

---

39   By virtue of the Regulation of Investigatory Powers (Communications Data) (Additional Functions and Amendment) Order 2006 (SI 2006/1878).
40   [1995] 1 WLR 734 (DC).
41   CAA 1995, s. 15(1).
42   *Regina v Shabir Ahmed* [2014] EWCA Crim 619; *Regina v Emma Mitchell* [2013] EWCA Crim 1072; *Regina v Ian Lewis* [2013] EWCA Crim 776.

Court.[43] However, the only limits to the type of matter that the Court may ask the Commission to investigate are those in (a) to (c) above.

9.32 The procedure for such investigations is governed by section 23A of CAA 1968 and section 15 of CAA 1995, which provide as follows:

(a) The Court may, at any time, either before leave[44] is considered or after it is granted, make such a direction. However, a direction may not be given by a single judge.[45]

(b) The copies of direction must also be made available to the appellant and respondent.[46]

(c) The investigation must be carried out 'in such manner as the Commission sees fit'.[47]

(d) In doing so it may investigate any related matter that it believes to be relevant to the determination of the case by the Court, which ought to be and can be resolved by the Court.[48]

(e) The Commission must keep the Court informed of the progress of the investigation[49] and must file a report either at the conclusion of the investigation or when directed to do so by the Court.[50] The report should detail the enquiries that were pursued[51] and should be accompanied by any statements and opinions received by the Commission in the investigation.[52]

(f) The Court must notify the appellant and the respondent that the Commission has reported and may make available to them the report of the Commission and any statements, opinions and reports which accompanied it.[53]

SUMMARY OF KEY POINTS

- The Commission has the power to refer appeals against sentence or conviction from the Crown Court to the Court of Appeal or from the

---

43 For example, *R v Joof* [2012] EWCA Crim 1475.
44 CAA 1968, s 23A(1)(aa), inserted by CJA 2003, s. 313.
45 CAA 1968, s. 23A(1A).
46 CAA 1968, s. 23A(5).
47 CAA 1995, s. 15(1).
48 CAA 1995, s. 15(2).
49 CAA 1995, s. 15(3).
50 CAA 1995, s. 15(4).
51 CAA 1995, s. 15(5).
52 CAA 1995, s. 15(6). However, the Commission need not include any reports that were made to the Commission by an investigating officer, pursuant to s. 20(6).
53 CAA 1968, s. 23A(4).

Magistrates' Court to the Crown Court when it is of the view that there is a real possibility that the appeal will be allowed.

- It normally makes referrals following a failed or abandoned appeal if there is new evidence or arguments not originally advanced. However, it has discretion, in exceptional circumstances, to refer even when there was no initial appeal.

- The effect of a referral is that the case will be returned to the Court to be heard as an appeal with leave. However, the Court may dismiss such an appeal when the only ground for a referral is a change in the law.

- In determining whether to refer the Commission may carry out such investigations as it deems necessary.

- It must carry out an investigation when directed to do so by the Court of Appeal in relation to an appeal or an application for leave to appeal against sentence or conviction.

- In carrying out these investigations it has extensive powers to obtain material in the hands of public bodies and, in accordance with the relevant provisions of the Regulation of Investigatory Powers Act 2000, communication data in the hands of private bodies or individuals.

- It may carry out investigations itself or appoint police officers or members of other public bodies to do so.

Chapter 10

Appealing to the Supreme Court

INTRODUCTION

10.1   On 1 October 2009 the Supreme Court was established by the Constitutional Reform Act 2005 ('CRA 2005'). Its jurisdiction corresponds to that of the Appellate Committee of the House of Lords, which it replaced as the final court of appeal.[1]

10.2   The Supreme Court rarely grants leave to appeal from the Court of Appeal (Criminal Division). The effect of this is that when leave is granted the appellant's lawyers may be faced with a procedure that is entirely new to them. Supreme Court procedure has its own terminology and imposes upon the parties a number of exacting procedural requirements. However, there are a number of reasons why case preparation should not be as daunting as it might at first appear:

(a)   The Supreme Court has its own Rules and Practice Directions ('PD') which are clear and detailed.

(b)   The staff of the Registry, which is headed by the Registrar of the Supreme Court, are usually helpful and tend to have more time to devote to a particular case than the staff in lower courts.

(c)   A representation order for a leading advocate is routinely granted, even if there was none in the Court of Appeal. Earlier instruction of an experienced leading advocate should assist.

(d)   The mystery that always surrounded appeals to the House of Lords has not attached itself to the Supreme Court because from the outset its proceedings have been broadcast. An appellant or his lawyers who want to know what to expect can turn on and see the judges who are likely to hear their case at work on another.[2]

---

1   CRA 2005, s. 40, Sch. 9.
2   Hearings are broadcast on Sky supreme-court live.

10.3   Note on terminology: The right of appeal to the Supreme Court exists by virtue of section 33 of CAA 1968 which speaks of 'leave' to appeal. The Court's own Rules and Practice Directions, which apply also to civil appeals, use the term 'permission' to appeal. This chapter follows the statute and uses the term 'leave'.

THE TYPES OF CASES FOR WHICH LEAVE IS GIVEN

10.4   The test set for granting leave to appeal to the Supreme Court is that a point of law of general public importance is involved in the decision and it appears to the Court of Appeal or the Supreme Court (as the case may be) that the point is one which ought to be considered by the Supreme Court.[3]

10.5   Although it is often said that leave is very rarely given in criminal cases, this statement must be qualified. The Court does hear a significant number of appeals that arise out of criminal litigation. From 31 July 2013 to 31 July 2014 it delivered judgment in cases concerning the decisions of the Director of Public Prosecutions to prosecute in assisted suicide cases,[4] disclosure of obligations of the prosecution after conviction,[5] the disclosure of spent convictions in job applications,[6] the right to legal aid in criminal cases in Northern Ireland,[7] and the elements of aggravated trespass,[8] as well as a number of appeals in relation to parole board procedure and extradition. However, the number of appeals from the Court of Appeal Criminal Division is low. In the same 12-month period the Court delivered only three judgments in appeals from the Court of Appeal Criminal Division: *R v O'Brien*[9] concerning contempt of court proceedings following extradition to the UK; *R v Gul*[10] concerning the definition of certain terrorist offences; and *R v Hughes*[11] concerning the elements of the offence of causing death whilst driving without a licence, insurances or whilst disqualified.

10.6   The reason for this low number is not hard to discern. The job of the Court of Appeal is to develop and clarify the criminal law. It is presided over by the Lord Chief Justice, the head of the judiciary, who can and does identify those cases that involve important questions of law and may allocate them to a

---

3   CAA 1968, s. 33.
4   *R (on the application of Nicklinson) v Ministry of Justice* [2014] UKSC 38.
5   *R (Nunn) v Chief Constable of Suffolk Constabulary* [2014] UKSC 37.
6   *R (On the application of T) v Secretary of State for the Home Department* [2014] UKSC 35.
7   *In the matter of an application of Raymond Brownlee for Judicial Review (AP) (Northern Ireland)* [2014] UKSC 4.
8   *Richardson v Director of Public Prosecutions* [2014] UKSC 8.
9   [2014] UKSC 23.
10   [2013] UKSC 64.
11   [2013] UKSC 56.

Court of seven judges. There will be a limited number of cases that then justify further consideration.

10.7   Leave to appeal from the Court of Appeal appears to be given not simply to those cases which involve issues of particular importance but to those cases which involve genuinely difficult points of law and raise wide questions of principle which justify the sustained consideration and analysis that the Supreme Court provides.

10.8   Application for leave should seek to awaken the interest of the justices in the point of public importance which the Court of Appeal has certified, indicating why the point is sufficiently rich in its implications and calls for a depth of analysis that justifies consideration by the Supreme Court.

APPLYING FOR LEAVE

10.9   Before an application for leave to appeal can be made to the Supreme Court, an application for leave and for a certificate of a point of law of public importance must already have been made to the Court of Appeal. As discussed in Chapter 7, the application for leave to appeal will usually be refused. However, it can only be made again before the Supreme Court if the Court of Appeal has certified a point of law of public importance.

10.10   The applicant has 28 days from the refusal of leave by the Court of Appeal to apply to the Supreme Court for leave.[12] The procedure for making such an application is contained in Part 3 of the Practice Direction.

10.11   However, if the applicant wishes to apply for funding to cover the cost of making the application for leave, an application for a representation must be made to the Court of Appeal. If a copy of the application for a representation order and the decision that is being appealed is then sent to the Registry of the Supreme Court, the 28-day time limit will stop running until the application for a representation order is determined.[13] If granted it will usually cover only solicitors and junior advocate at the leave stage and will be extended to cover the instruction of a leading advocate if leave is granted.

10.12   Additional papers can be lodged within seven days of the application for leave. If the respondent wishes to make any objections it must do so within 14 days of the application having been lodged.

---

12   Supreme Court Rules 2009 (SI 2009/1603), r. 11.
13   PD 8.12.6.

10.13   The application is considered by a panel of Supreme Court justices. They may decide to hold an oral hearing but decisions are generally made on the papers.

PREPARING THE CASE FOLLOWING LEAVE

10.14   Once leave has been granted it is necessary to get to grips with the process of preparing the case for hearing. There is no substitute for acquainting oneself with the relevant practice directions that apply at each stage of the case.

10.15   However, the drafting is an exercise in advocacy as much as in rule compliance. Therefore, the leading advocate should be involved at each stage.

The form and content of Supreme Court documents

10.16   The following paragraphs of the Practice Direction provide the guidance as to the form and contents of the significant documents:

- The form of all documents to be presented to the Court: PD 5.1.2.

- The form and content of the statement of facts and issues: PD 5.1.3.

- The form and content of the appendix: PD 5.1.5.

- The form and content of authorities: PD 6.5.2 to 6.5.9.

- The form of core volumes: PD 6.4.

Timetable following the granting of leave by the Supreme Court

10.17   If leave is granted,[14] the timetable for preparation is as follows:

(a)   The appellant must, within 14 days, file a notice of intention to proceed.[15] When the notice is filed, the application for leave to appeal will be re-sealed and the appellant must then serve a copy on each respondent, on any recognised intervener (that is, an intervener whose submissions have been taken into account under rule 15) and on any intervener in the court below; and file seven copies.[16]

---

14   Separate rules apply when permission has already been granted by a lower Court; see Supreme Court Rules 2009 (SI 2009/1603), r. 19.
15   PD 4.1.1.
16   Supreme Court Rules 2009 (SI 2009/1603), r. 18(2).

(b) In a case in which a declaration of incompatibly with the European Convention on Human Rights is sought, Form 1 or 3 must be completed and served and filed along with the notice.

(c) The statement of facts and issues and the appendix must be filed by the appellant within 112 days after the filing of the notice. If the appellant is unable to comply with the relevant time limit, an application for an extension of time must be made.[17]

(d) Within seven days after the filing of the statement of facts and issues and the appendix, the parties must notify the Registrar that the appeal is ready to list and specify the number of hours that their respective counsel estimate to be necessary for their oral submissions.[18]

(e) No later than six weeks before the proposed date of the hearing, the appellants must file at the Registry the original and two copies of their case and serve it on the respondents.[19]

(f) No later than four weeks before the proposed date of the hearing, the respondents must serve on the appellants a copy of their case in response and file at the Registry the original and two copies of their case, as must any other party filing a case (for example, an intervener or advocate to the court). The further copies required by PD 6.4.1 must then be filed.[20]

(g) As soon as the parties' cases have been exchanged, and in any event not later than 14 days before the date fixed for the hearing, the appellant must file ten bound core volumes in accordance with PD 6.4.3 and (if necessary) additional volumes containing further parts of the appendix and ten copies of every case filed by the parties or any intervener. These copies of the cases must contain cross-references (in a footnote or in the body of the text) to the appendix and authorities volumes.

(h) Ten copies of all authorities that may be referred to during the hearing must be filed by the appellant at the same time as the core volumes.[21]

HEARINGS

10.18 Cases are generally heard by a panel of five justices. In particular cases they may sit as a panel of seven. It is only in 'wholly exceptional circumstances'[22] that the Court would sit in private. Most hearings take place in

---

17 Supreme Court Rules 2009 (SI 2009/1603), r. 5 and PD 5.2.3.
18 PD 6.3.8 and Supreme Court Rules 2009 (SI 2009/1603), r. 22(3).
19 PD 6.3.9.
20 PD 6.3.10.
21 PD 6.4.2.
22 PD 6.6.4.

public and are broadcast. The average time for a hearing is two days. Judgments are reserved. PD 6.6.1 to 6.6.10 should be consulted for further details.

PARTICULAR ISSUES

Bail

10.19   Bail is not determined by the Supreme Court but by the Court of Appeal.[23]

Attendance of the appellant

10.20   There is no right for an appellant to be present at the hearing. The effect of this is that whilst an applicant on bail can attend, and is usually required to do so in order to surrender,[24] an appellant who is in custody will not be produced unless the Court deems it necessary.[25]

Costs

10.21   The Court 'may make such orders as it considers just in respect of the costs of any appeal, application for permission to appeal, or other application to or proceeding before the Court'.[26] PD 13.4 gives specific guidance on the making of costs against publically funded parties. PD 13.6 sets out the circumstances in which costs may be claimed against a party who made an unsuccessful application for leave. The subsequent parts of PD 13 provide detailed guidance on costs assessment.

Death of a party

10.22   In the event of the death of a party, the power to appoint an approved person to continue an appeal following the death of the party applies to appeals from the Court of Appeal (Criminal Division) to the Supreme Court.[27]

---

23   CAA 1968, s.36.
24   PD 12.13.2.
25   PD 12.3.2.
26   Supreme Court Rules 2009 (SI 2009/1603), r. 46(1).
27   CAA 1968, s. 44A(2)(b).

SUMMARY OF KEY POINTS

- The Supreme Court is the highest court of the land having been established by the Constitutional Reform Act 2005 to replace the House of Lords.

- It hears appeals from the Court of Appeal (Criminal Division) although permission to appeal from that Court is rarely granted.

- An application for leave can only be made if the Court of Appeal has first certified a point of law of public importance. The applicant then has 28 days to apply to the Supreme Court itself for leave. The time will be extended if application is made to the Court of Appeal for a representation order.

- That application must be made in accordance with the Rules of the Supreme Court.

- If leave is granted there is a particular procedure to be followed for the preparation of the case, which is clearly set out in the Supreme Court Rules and Practice Directions.

- All documents lodged must be in a form that is prescribed by the Rules and Practice Directions.

- A representation order to allow for the instruction of the leading advocate will usually be granted only if leave is granted.

- Bail may be granted by the Court of Appeal.

- Hearings take place in public and may be broadcast live. The average length of a hearing is two days.

- The appellant has no right to be present at the hearing. Therefore, appellants will not generally be produced from custody.

- The Supreme Court has the power to award costs on such terms as it considers just.

Chapter 11

Applications to the European Court of Human Rights

INTRODUCTION

11.1   Making an application to the European Court of Human Rights is for those who are prepared to play a long game in order to keep alive their chances of getting justice through the court system.

11.2   It is not part of the appeal process. The ECtHR cannot quash a conviction or reduce a sentence. However, the impact of a finding by the ECtHR that a conviction or sentence was obtained in a manner that breached an applicant's rights under the European Convention on Human Rights can have a profound impact on the appeal process. It may provide a reason for the Criminal Cases Review Commission to refer the case to the Court of Appeal.

11.3   The fact that the ECtHR has found that there has been a violation of Convention rights does not necessarily require the Commission to make a reference (*Dowsett v Criminal Cases Review Commission*[1]). A violation of a Convention right, even of the right to a fair trial under Article 6, does not necessarily render a conviction unsafe (see Chapter 3). Moreover, the domestic courts are not bound to agree with the ECtHR on what Article 6 requires.

11.4   However, the Convention has proved to be a powerful force in shaping the criminal law in significant and often unpredictable ways. A ruling from the ECtHR may lead the Commission and ultimately the Court of Appeal to consider familiar issues in a new light and so open up the possibility of a successful appeal.

WHETHER TO APPLY

11.5   Before embarking on litigation that may take years to conclude, a potential applicant should consider carefully what he wants to gain from

---

1   [2007] EWHC 1923 (Admin).

the process. Does he want the satisfaction of a finding that his rights were violated? If so, it is necessary to consider the case law of the ECtHR in order to determine the prospects of obtaining such a finding. Does he want to be paid compensation? If so, it is also important to consider the level of compensation that might be awarded (remembering that sometimes the ECtHR decides not to award compensation at all) in the event that the application succeeds. Does he want to challenge the conviction or sentence? If so, it is necessary to consider whether there is a real chance that a finding by the ECtHR that the applicant's rights were violated will lead the Commission to refer the case to the Court of Appeal. This final point must be considered in the light of the time that it is likely to take for an application to be determined. A sentence of two years or less is likely to have been completed by the time that the ECtHR makes a finding that the applicant's rights were violated.

APPLYING TO THE ECtHR

Exhaustion of domestic remedies

11.6   The ECtHR 'may only deal with the matter after all domestic remedies have been exhausted'.[2] However, the domestic remedies must be available and effective. The applicant does not need to exhaust domestic remedies that have no reasonable prospect of success.

11.7   Applying this approach to the criminal appeal process:

(a)   The applicant must have lodged an application for leave to appeal to the Court of Appeal.

(b)   If that application was refused by the single judge and not renewed before the full Court, the ECtHR may well find the applicant had not exhausted his remedies (*Reilly v UK*).[3]

(c)   If a renewed application for leave was refused by the full Court, the domestic remedies will normally have been exhausted (although see (e), below).

(d)   If the Court of Appeal heard and dismissed an appeal, it may be held that domestic remedies would only be exhausted once an application for leave to appeal to the Supreme Court had been sought. In *Selvanayagam v UK*,[4] the ECtHR accepted that domestic remedies had been exhausted when the applicant presented the separate opinions of a number of counsel that appeal to the House of Lords (the predecessor of the

---

2   Convention, Art. 35(1).
3   App. No. 53731/00 (Dec.) 26 June 2003.
4   App. No. 57981/00 (Dec.) 12 December 2002.

Supreme Court) would not have succeeded. However, as is suggested in Chapter 10, it may be better not to take a risk and, in a case in which an application to the ECtHR may be made, apply for leave to appeal to the Supreme Court, notwithstanding the unlikelihood of the application being granted.

(e)   An application to the Commission will not usually be regarded as giving rise to an available remedy but may do in unusual cases where it was highly likely that the Commission would have referred the case to the Court of Appeal. Such a situation might arise where a number of references had been made in similar cases (see *Tucka v UK (No. 1)*[5]).

Time limits for lodging an application

11.8   The current time limit for lodging an application with the ECtHR is six months from the date of the final decision by the UK courts which exhausted the process of seeking domestic remedies.[6] This period is due to be reduced to four months when all member states have ratified Protocol 15.[7] The time limit is strict and there is no discretion to extend it. It stops running when the application is physically received by the Court, with all the required supporting documents. It is therefore important when preparing the application to dispatch it by recorded delivery and to allow time for any potential delays and for the possibility that the Registry of the ECtHR will indicate that a further document is required.

Standing

11.9   Domestic rules on standing will not be decisive.[8] An individual or organisation may bring an action on behalf of another if they have clear written authority to act on their behalf. An application cannot be made on behalf of a deceased person.[9] However, if an applicant dies before the case is determined, the ECtHR usually permits a spouse or close relative to continue the proceedings on his behalf.

Drafting the application

11.10   Rule 47 lists the information that needs to be included with the application. A failure to comply with its requirements will at best add to the delays that are a pronounced feature of proceedings before the ECtHR. At

---

5   App. No. 34566/10 (Dec.) 18 January 2011.
6   Convention, Art. 35.
7   App. No. 53731/00 (Dec.) 26 June 2003.
8   *Scozzai v Italy*, 13 July 2000, ECHR 2000-VIII, paras 138–139.
9   *Dupin v Croatia*, App. No. 363868/03 (Dec.) 7 July 2009.

worst it will lead the Registry to refuse to register the application and, if a second, properly completed, application is then lodged too late, to declare the application inadmissible through being out of time.

11.11   All the documents that are required should be supplied as copies, not originals. The exception is the requirement for an original dated and signed authority from the applicant authorising his lawyer to act on his behalf in the ECtHR proceedings.

11.12   The application form is to be found on the ECtHR website along with the technical requirements, such as page size, font size, spacing, and the like. Three sections of the form require careful drafting:

(a)   the statement of the facts;

(b)   the alleged violation(s) of the Convention and the relevant arguments;

(c)   confirmation of the exhaustion of domestic remedies and that the final domestic decision was made not more than six months before the application was made.

11.13   The statement of facts needs to be concise. It must not mislead or omit crucial unhelpful facts, but it is perfectly proper to focus on matters that support the argument that there has been a violation of the applicant's Convention rights.

11.14   The 'alleged violations' section of the application form allows several pages for submissions. An additional 20 pages can be appended. In drafting this section every lawyer will follow his own style and preferences. However, the following points should be borne in mind:

(a)   The ECtHR is not concerned with whether the UK courts have complied with UK law, practice and precedent, but whether the outcome is such as to breach Convention rights. Therefore, although the domestic law must be accurately stated, it is best to focus on the practical effect of the events in the UK courts and to contrast those effects with the guarantees of the Convention as amplified and explained by decisions of the ECtHR.

(b)   Each of the 47 member states of the Council of Europe has its own legal system, so the enforcement of human rights has to be flexible in its application. The ECtHR is concerned with substance not form. In an Article 6 argument, it is concerned with fairness not with technicalities.

(c)   The judges of the Court will not necessarily speak English as their first language. To allow for this, submissions about violations of Convention rights are best drafted in clear and direct language. An application has to deal with technical legal matters, but the excessive use of legalistic terms or national jargon or idiom may not help the application find favour further down the judicial line.

11.15   For the exhaustion of domestic remedies see **11.6** and **11.7**, above.

11.16   Once the application has been posted and received, the Registry will send the applicant's lawyers a letter giving the application number and, of late, a set of printed bar codes. The number and the bar codes can then be used in all future correspondence.

11.17   Then the applicant has to wait. At the time of writing that wait can be a few months or even a few years. Delay has been a persistent feature of proceedings before the ECtHR, although it is taking significant steps to reduce it.[10]

Progress of the application

11.18   Once they are received by the ECtHR applications may be allocated to a single judge, a committee of three judges or a Chamber.

11.19   The application will be allocated to a single judge if it appears on its face to be inadmissible.[11] The judge may declare it inadmissible, a decision from which there is no appeal. Alternatively he may forward it to a committee of three judges or to a Chamber.

11.20   A committee has the power to declare a case inadmissible or may declare it admissible and go on to deliver judgment on the merits if the underlying question in the case is already the subject of well-established case law.[12]

11.21   A Chamber is composed of seven judges, one of whom must be from the state against whom the application is brought.[13] If a Chamber does not, at the outset, conclude that the case is inadmissible, it will make a 'communication' of the complaint to the government of the state which stands accused of violating the applicant's rights. This is an invitation to the government to answer a series of questions, both about the admissibility and the merits of the application. These will often be directly taken from the application, and will directly address the matter in issue. For example, 'Was the [event at trial that is complained about] a violation of the Applicant's right to a fair trial under Article 6?'

11.22   The fact a communication is made is, of course, an encouraging sign. However, many cases in which a communication takes place are later declared inadmissible or no violation of the Convention is found.

---

10   Both Protocol 14 and 15 introduce measures intended to do so.
11   Convention, Art. 27.
12   Convention, Art. 28.
13   Convention, Art. 29.

11.23   The applicant has a right of reply to any response from the government. In this way, the case is argued on paper and the Chamber will often make final determinations of admissibility and merits on the papers without an oral hearing.

11.24   In a small number of cases Chambers do decide to hold a hearing before determining a case. It will set a date for both sides to travel to the Court and present brief, time-limited, oral arguments, followed by questions from the Court. The Registry supplies full and helpful directions about what is required of the lawyers on these occasions.

11.25   It is the normal practice of Chambers to make a final determination of admissibility and merits in the same judgment, having considered all the representations from the parties.

Referral to a Grand Chamber

11.26   If either party wishes to challenge a judgment they can apply, within three months of judgment being given, for referral to a Grand Chamber, which is composed of 17 judges.[14] A panel of five judges will decide whether to accept the referral. If it is accepted the case will be considered afresh by the Grand Chamber as a complete re-determination. The Grand Chamber almost always holds an oral hearing before reaching its determination. In addition, a Chamber that is hearing the application may transfer it to the Grand Chamber, as long as neither party objects.[15]

A 'friendly settlement' in criminal litigation

11.27   In the course of the correspondence the Registry will offer the two parties the chance to discuss a 'friendly settlement'. Such a settlement involves an agreement by the government to pay compensation and, in some cases, to vary its policies or its actions towards an applicant so as to remove the event or conduct that is claimed to amount to a violation. This mechanism will almost never provide a means of resolving a claim arising out of a sentence or conviction, as the government can obviously not agree to ignore a judicial finding or order, such as a conviction or prison sentence.

11.28   An exception might arise in a case where an applicant has a good claim that the time taken for his trial is too long to comply with Article 6. In such cases, the UK government may sometimes offer to make a payment. It

---

14 Convention, Art. 43.
15 Convention, Art. 30.

may be worth considering accepting such an offer as the chances of such a violation leading to a conviction being quashed may be slim.

Representation

11.29   The ECtHR requires an applicant to be represented by lawyers who are qualified within one of the 47 signatory states.[16] There is no right to self-representation nor is there a right to be represented by a lawyer or another from outside the contracting territories. Any request for self-representation or representation from someone outside the contracting territories must be made in writing to the president of the ECtHR.[17]

Legal aid

11.30   The right to legal aid does not arise unless and until a communication is made to the government of the state which is accused of violating the applicant's Convention rights. At that point means forms may be sent out to the applicant to be completed and returned to the ECtHR. Legal aid is granted only if the ECtHR is satisfied that the applicant does not have the means to pay for all or part of his own representation.[18] Although legal aid is paid by the ECtHR, it asks the domestic legal aid authority to conduct an assessment of means on the basis of the information the applicant provided. It is the practice of the ECtHR to only pay for work undertaken by one lawyer.

THE CONSEQUENCES OF A SUCCESSFUL OUTCOME

The judgment

11.31   For the applicant who wants to return to the domestic courts to appeal his conviction or sentence, the most important outcome is a ruling that contains a finding that his rights have been violated. It will need to be studied with care in order to determine whether it provides the basis for an application to the Commission for a reference.

Compensation

11.32   Even if the ECtHR finds that there has been a violation of the applicant's Convention rights, it will not necessarily order financial compensation. The finding of breach is often considered to be a sufficient remedy. If it does

---

16   Rules of the Court, r. 36(2), (3).
17   *Manoussos v Czech Republic*, App. No. 46488/99 (Dec.) 7 Sept. 2002.
18   Rules of the Court, r. 101(b).

decide to award compensation it may do so on the basis of pecuniary and non-pecuniary loss. However, an application for compensation may be made within two months of the application being declared admissible.

Costs

11.33   There is no provision for the applicant to pay costs to the responding government in the event that the application is withdrawn or dismissed. However, a successful applicant may be awarded his costs, to be paid by the government. It is, therefore, a good idea to keep a record of the tasks completed by solicitors, senior and junior counsel, the hours worked and the hourly rate charged. This should be submitted with the applicant's reply to the government's observations as there is no separate costs stage of proceedings. Although the ECtHR will seek submissions from the government on the applicant's costs, it will generally award what seems to the Court to be a reasonable amount for the work undertaken; often this will be less than claimed, but is always better than nothing. Costs, if awarded, have to be paid within three months of the judgment becoming final.

SUMMARY OF KEY POINTS

- An application to the ECtHR may only be made after domestic remedies have been exhausted.

- It must be received by the Registry within six months of the decision of the domestic courts that exhausted the domestic remedies.

- A finding by the ECtHR that the conviction or sentence gave rise to a breach of Convention rights may lead the Criminal Cases Review Commission to refer the case back to the Court of Appeal, but only if it was capable of leading the Court of Appeal to conclude that a conviction was unsafe or the sentence wrong and should be reduced on appeal.

- The requirement to exhaust domestic remedies does not involve an obligation to pursue those remedies that have no realistic prospect of success. A failure to lodge an application for leave to appeal will be a failure to exhaust domestic remedies, so may a failure to renew an application for leave before the full Court. Whether an application for leave to appeal to the Supreme Court was required, following an unsuccessful appeal in the Court of Appeal, may depend on the facts of the case. The ECtHR would not normally find that the applicant should have made an application to the Criminal Cases Review Commission for a reference, but may do in certain circumstances.

- The application should be made using the forms available on the ECtHR website. Copies of all the documents required by Article 47 of the Convention must be included or the application may not be considered.

- The application will be allocated to a single judge, committee or Chamber, any one of whom may make a declaration of inadmissibility.

- Should the Court not take the view that the application is clearly inadmissible it will issue a communication to the relevant government. It will give the applicant the right of reply to any response from the government.

- Both the final determination of admissibility and the merits of the case are likely to be made on the basis of these documents in a single judgment.

- The Chamber occasionally conducts oral hearings before making its judgment.

- The Chamber can send the case to the Grand Chamber (of 17 judges) for a determination. Alternatively, an unsuccessful party can request a re-hearing before the Grand Chamber (a request that is considered by a panel of five judges).

- Legal aid may be available after a communication has been made to the government of the state that is accused of breaching the applicant's rights.

- A successful applicant may apply for costs and compensation but the Court has no power to order costs to a responding government in the event that the application is withdrawn or dismissed.

Part 4

Other Rights of Appeal

Chapter 12

Appeals against interlocutory rulings

INTRODUCTION

12.1   The right of appeal generally only arises at the conclusion of the case. However, Parliament has created a small number of exceptions in which appeals may be brought against interlocutory rulings. One of those exceptions, the right of prosecution to appeal against certain rulings, is considered in Chapter 13.

12.2   Other exceptions include the following appeals:

(a)   appeals against rulings made at preparatory hearings in serious or complex fraud cases;

(b)   appeals against rulings at preparatory hearings in complex, serious or lengthy cases;

(c)   appeals against a ruling that a case should be tried by a judge alone because of the risk of jury tampering;

(d)   appeals against a decision of the trial judge to discharge a jury and continue to try the case alone;

(e)   appeals against a ruling that certain counts on an indictment should be tried by judge alone, following a conviction by a jury on sample counts.

12.3   The procedures in relation to each appeal are very similar. They follow, in truncated form, the procedures for appealing against conviction and sentence. They are all governed by Part 66 of the CPR as well as their own specific statutory provisions. However, with the exception of appeals against rulings against a decision of the judge to discharge a jury and try the case alone, those statutory provisions replicate or adopt the statutory scheme for appeals from preparatory hearings in complex or lengthy fraud cases that were introduced in the Criminal Justice Act 1987 ('CJA 1987').

APPEALS AGAINST RULINGS MADE AT PREPARATORY HEARINGS IN SERIOUS OR COMPLEX FRAUD CASES

12.4   If a judge has made a wrongful ruling at the beginning of a complex or lengthy case, it would be a waste of time and money for the case to proceed for weeks or months on an incorrect footing when the matter might be immediately appealed and the matter corrected so that the trial can proceed on a correct basis (*R v Hedworth*[1]).

12.5   Such was the thinking behind section 9 of CJA 1987 which established a right of appeal from a ruling of the judge made in serious or complex fraud cases.

The circumstances in which a ruling may be appealed

12.6   Section 7(1) of CJA 1987 provides that:

'Where it appears to a judge of the Crown Court that the evidence on an indictment reveals a case of fraud of such seriousness or complexity that substantial benefits are likely to accrue from a hearing (in this Act referred to as a "preparatory hearing") before the jury are sworn, for the purpose of –

(a)   identifying issues which are likely to be material to the verdict of the jury;

(b)   assisting their comprehension of any such issues;

(c)   expediting the proceedings before the jury; or

(d)   assisting the judge's management of the trial,

he may order that such a hearing shall be held.'

12.7   The right of appeal to the Court of Appeal arises in relation to any ruling made by the judge, in the course of a preparatory hearing on:

(a)   a question arising under section 6 of the Criminal Justice Act 1993 (relevance of external law to certain charges of conspiracy, attempt and incitement);

(b)   any question as to the admissibility of evidence; and

(c)   any other question of law relating to the case.[2]

---

1   [1997] 1 Cr App R 421.
2   CJA 1987, s. 9(3).

12.8   Such a ruling may be appealed to the Court of Appeal.[3]

12.9   In *R v H*[4] the House of Lords held that whilst it was open to a judge to determine disclosure applications at the preparatory hearing, rulings in relation to disclosure were not questions of law within the meaning of section 9(3)(b) of CJA 1987 and could not, therefore, be subject to an interlocutory appeal.

Appealing a ruling

12.10   The procedure for appealing is as follows:

(a)   Leave is needed from the trial judge or the Court of Appeal.[5] Application for leave from the trial judge must be made orally immediately after, or in writing within two days, of the decision having been made.[6]

(b)   Application for leave to the Court of Appeal must be made in writing not more than five business days either after the decision that is the subject of the appeal or after the Crown Court judge refuses to give leave.[7] This time limit may be extended on application to the Court by the Court, single judge or Registrar.[8]

(c)   An application for leave to appeal is made on Form NG.

(d)   The application must be served on the Crown Court, the Registrar and any party directly affected by the application.[9]

(e)   It must be made in the terms prescribed in rule 66.3 of the CPR.

(f)   If the application is opposed, a respondent's notice (Form RN) should be served within five days of the application having been made.[10]

(g)   It is considered by the single judge. If refused it may be renewed before the full court within five days of refusal.[11]

(h)   Once leave is granted the preparatory hearing can continue but trial of facts must not take place until it is determined or abandoned.[12] The party in custody has the right to attend.[13]

---

3   CJA 1987, s. 9(11).
4   [2007] UKHL 7.
5   CJA 1987, s. 9(11); CPIA 1996, s. 35(1).
6   CPR, r. 66.4.1.
7   CPR, r. 66.5.
8   CPR, r. 65.3.
9   CPR, r. 66.2.
10   CPR, r. 66.5.
11   CPR, rr. 66.5, 66.7.
12   CJA 1987, s. 9(13); CPIA 1996, s. 35(2).
13   CPR, r. 66.8.

(i)   The Court can confirm, vary or reverse the decision that is the subject of the appeal.[14] A right of appeal lies from the Court of Appeal to the Supreme Court.[15]

(j)   Funding for the proceedings will generally be covered by the existing Crown Court representation order.[16]

Reporting restrictions on appeals from preparatory hearings

12.11   Section 11(1) of CJA 1987 restricts the reporting of an appeal from a preliminary ruling to those matters contained in section 11(1), which contains lists of the basic information about the case. However, the Court of Appeal may make an order to remove or amend them.[17]

APPEALS UNDER SECTION 35 OF THE CRIMINAL PROCEDURE AND INVESTIGATIONS ACT 1996

12.12   Section 29 of the Criminal Procedure and Investigations Act 1996 ('CPIA 1996') provides that a preparatory hearing may be held where the judge determines that the case is likely to be of such length, seriousness or complexity that there will be significant benefits from holding a hearing in order to:

(a)   identify issues that are likely to be material to the determinations and findings that are likely to be required during the trial;

(b)   if there is to be a jury, assist their comprehension of those issues and expedite the proceedings before them;

(c)   determine an application to which section 45 of the Criminal Justice Act 2003 ('CJA 2003') applies (where the prosecution have applied, under section 43 or 44 of CJA 2003 for the trial to take place without a jury);

(d)   assist the judge's management of the trial;

(e)   consider questions as to the severance or joinder of charges.

12.13   In addition the judge must order a preparatory hearing in a terrorist case.[18]

---

14   CJA 1987, s. 9(14); CPIA 1996, s. 13(3).
15   CAA 1968, s. 33.
16   The Guide, para. D13; Access to Justice Act 1999, Sch. 3, para. 2(2).
17   CJA 1987, s. 11(5).
18   CPIA 1996, s. 29(1B), (1C).

12.14   The right of appeal exists against ruling, made at the preparatory hearing, in relation to:

(i)   any question as to the admissibility of evidence;

(ii)   any other question of law relating to the case;

(iii)   any question as to the severance or joinder of charges.

12.15   In *R v I (C)*[19] the Court of Appeal confirmed that the principles established in *R v H* regarding disclosure rulings (see **12.9**, above) applied to appeals under section 35 of CPIA 1996.

The procedure for appealing

12.16   The procedures for appealing a ruling under section 35 of CPIA 1996 are the same as for the appeals against rulings in serious or complex fraud cases set out in **12.10** and **12.11**, above. The relevant references for appeals under section 35 are contained in the footnotes.

Reporting restrictions

12.17   Section 37(1) of CPIA 1996 mirrors section 11 of CJA 1987 in creating an automatic reporting restriction (which may be removed or varied by the Court of Appeal) that applies to appeals against rulings made under section 35 and restricts reporting to certain basic facts.

APPEALS AGAINST A RULING THAT A CASE SHOULD BE TRIED BY A JUDGE AND NOT A JURY WHEN THERE IS A RISK OF JURY TAMPERING

12.18   A judge may, following an application by the prosecution, order that a trial take place without a jury in a case where there is a risk of jury tampering.[20] If such an application is made, a preparatory hearing must be held at which the application may be determined. The Court must be satisfied to the criminal standard (section 46(3) of CJA 2003) that the following criteria is made out:

'(4)   The first condition is that there is evidence of a real and present danger that jury tampering would take place.

(5)   The second condition is that, notwithstanding any steps (including the provision of police protection) which might reasonably be taken to

---

19   [2009] EWCA Crim 1793.
20   CJA 2003, s. 44.

prevent jury tampering, the likelihood that it would take place would be so substantial as to make it necessary in the interests of justice for the trial to be conducted without a jury.'

The procedure

12.19   Section 45 of CJA 2003 amends the relevant provisions of CJA 1987 and CPIA 1996 so as to ensure that the procedure for preparatory hearings and subsequent appeals applies to the decision of the judge as to whether to order that a trial take place without a jury under section 44. Therefore, the procedure for appeals and powers of the Court and reporting restrictions as set out at **12.10** and **12.11**, above apply to appeals against such an order.

APPEALS AGAINST A DECISION TO ORDER A TRIAL WITHOUT A JURY WHERE JURY TAMPERING HAS TAKEN PLACE

12.20   If, after a trial has commenced, the trial judge is satisfied of the following;

(a)   that jury tampering has taken place, and

(b)   that to continue the trial without a jury would be fair to the defendant or defendants,

the judge may discharge the jury and proceed to try the case alone.[21]

12.21   However, if the judge decides that it is necessary in the interests of justice for the trial to be terminated, he must instead terminate the trial.[22]

12.22   Before determining whether the above test is satisfied, the judge must inform the parties of his grounds for concern and allow them to make representations.

12.23   Such an order may be appealed to the Court of Appeal. The Court may confirm or revoke the order.

12.24   Because such an order does not take place within the context of a preparatory hearing, the relevant powers of the Court of Appeal in relation to appeals from preparatory hearings do not apply to appeals against a decision.

---

21   CJA 2003, s. 47.
22   CJA 2003, s. 47(4).

However, Part 66 of the CPR applies to appeals against a decision under section 46 of CJA 2003 (by virtue of rule 66.1.1(b)).

12.25   For this reason, what is said above about appeals from preparatory hearings applies also to appeals against decisions made under section 46, with the following exceptions:

(a)   Leave may be given by the trial judge or the full court,[23] but because it may not be given by the single judge, there is no procedure for renewing the application for leave.

(b)   The power of the Court is simply to confirm or revoke the order.[24]

(c)   The right to appeal to the Supreme Court against the decision of the Court of Appeal arises under section 47(6), which inserts the right into section 33(1) of CAA 1968.

RULING THAT A JUDGE SHOULD TRY CERTAIN COUNTS ALONE FOLLOWING CONVICTION BY A JURY ON SAMPLE COUNTS

12.26   In a case involving multiple counts the prosecution may apply to the Crown Court for an order that certain counts are to be tried by a judge alone in the absence of a jury. If such an order is made, the trials without jury may only take place if a jury has first tried and convicted the defendant of counts which are to properly be regarded as sample counts of those which may be tried by the judge.

12.27   The conditions of the making of such an order are set out in section 17(3) to (5) of the Domestic Violence, Crime and Victims Act 2004.

12.28   Such an order may only be made at a preparatory hearing and may be appealed to the Court of Appeal. The Domestic Violence, Crime and Victims Act 2004 amends the relevant sections of CJA 1987 and CPIA 1996 so as to ensure that appeals from decisions under section 17 are subject to their statutory regime. Therefore, the powers of the Court of Appeal and the procedure for appealing are as set out at **12.10**, above.

SUMMARY OF KEY POINTS

●   There are a small number of situations in which an appeal against an interlocutory ruling may be brought.

---

23   CJA 2003, s. 47(2).
24   CJA 2003, s. 47(4).

12.28 *Appeals against interlocutory rulings*

- These appeal rights largely follow the procedures set down in relation to appeals against rulings at preparatory hearings that were established by CJA 1987 in relation to appeals against rulings in serious or complex fraud cases.

- The procedure for such appeals is contained in Part 66 of the CPR, which sets out a truncated version of the procedure for appealing against conviction or sentence.

- Applications should be made using the usual forms for appeals against conviction and sentence.

- There are restrictions on the reporting of such appeals, which can, on application, be removed or amended by the Court of Appeal.

Chapter 13

Responding to prosecution appeals

INTRODUCTION

13.1   This chapter sets out the range of the prosecution's right of appeal before focusing on responding to two common prosecution appeals:

(a)   Appeals under section 58 of CJA 2003 against a trial judge's ruling (often misleadingly referred to as appeals against 'terminating rulings').

(b)   Appeals against sentences known as 'Attorney General's References'.

THE PROSECUTION'S RIGHTS OF APPEAL

13.2   The prosecution's rights of appeal are far more restricted than those of the defence. The principle of the finality of the verdict of the jury is respected and there is no general right of appeal against an acquittal. However, Parliament has established the right of prosecution appeal in the following situations:

1   Appeals against rulings

   (a)   The prosecution's rights of appeal against interlocutory rulings are the same as the defence and are considered in Chapter 12.

   (b)   Under section 58 of CJA 2003 the prosecution may, in certain circumstances, appeal against a ruling of the trial judge (see paras **13.3** to **13.18** below).

   (c)   Under section 62 of CJA 2003 the prosecution may appeal against an evidentiary ruling that significantly weakens the prosecution's case. However, this section has never been brought into force. At the time of writing there are no plans to do so.

   (d)   Under section 36 (1) of the Criminal Justice Act 1972 the Attorney General may, following an acquittal on indictment, refer a point of law to the Court of Appeal to be decided for future cases. It is not strictly an appeal since the acquittal will be unaffected by the Court of Appeal's decision.

2   Appeals against acquittals

  (a)   Section 54 of CPIA 1996 gives the prosecution the right to appeal against an acquittal when there has been a conviction for interference or intimidation of a witness or juror in the proceedings that lead to the acquittal and there is a real possibility that the acquittal would not have taken place but for the interference or intimidation.

  (b)   Under Part 10 of CJA 2003 the prosecution may apply to the Court of Appeal to quash an acquittal in England and Wales and apply for a re-trial or apply for a ruling that a foreign acquittal should be no bar to the defendant being tried for the same offence. This is the exception to the double jeopardy rule.

3   Appeals against sentence

  (a)   The prosecution have a right to appeal against a refusal to make a confiscation order under the Proceeds of Crime Act 2002 (see **4.53–4.55**).

  (b)   Under section 14A(5A) of the Football Spectators Act 1989 the prosecution have a right to appeal against the refusal to make a banning order.

  (c)   Under section 36 of the Criminal Justice Act 1988 the Attorney General may refer a sentence to the Court of Appeal on the basis that it is unduly lenient (see paras **13.20** onwards, below).

PROSECUTION APPEALS AGAINST RULINGS UNDER SECTION 58 OF CJA 2003

13.3   Section 58 of CJA 2003 gives the prosecution the right of appeal against a trial judge's ruling. This is often referred to as a right to appeal against a 'terminating' ruling but the Court of Appeal has deprecated the use of the term (*R v Arnold*[1]). It is misleading because the prosecution can appeal against a ruling even when it will not necessarily result in the defendant's acquittal. If, for example, a judge were to exclude a significant part of the evidence, the prosecution could appeal even if there was still some evidence remaining such as might enable the case to continue past a later submission of 'no case to answer'.

13.4   That said, the defining feature of these appeals is that the prosecution may only seek leave to appeal if it is prepared to accept that the defendant will be acquitted of the count that is the subject of the appeal it fails. For this reason

---

1   [2008] EWCA Crim 1034.

it will most usually be deployed where the ruling either does terminate the case on that count, or where it is comes close to doing so.

When an appeal under section 58 may be brought

13.5   Leave to appeal may only be sought if the following conditions are met:

(a)   The appeal must be against a ruling that was made before the summing up.[2]

(b)   It must not be a ruling to discharge the jury.[3]

(c)   There must be no other right of appeal available to the prosecution – this has the effect that rulings made when an appeal might be brought under the regime for interlocutory rulings must be brought under those provisions.[4]

(d)   The prosecution must have given notice of intention to appeal after the ruling was given or have applied for an adjournment in order to consider whether to appeal.[5]

(e)   The prosecution must have given a valid acquittal agreement at the time when the indication of intention to appeal is given (section 58(8)).

13.6   The Court of Appeal has interpreted these preconditions strictly. If they are not met the appeal will be refused (*R v Arnold*[6]).

What is an acquittal agreement?

13.7   Section 58(8) of CJA 2003 requires the prosecution to give the undertaking that in the event of the appeal being refused leave or being abandoned, they will agree to the defendant being acquitted (the undertaking is required in those terms, so as not to include an effective appeal, as if the case actually reaches the Court of Appeal, as the Court itself then acquits the defendant of that charge if the trial judge's ruling is upheld).[7] The undertaking has to be given *at or before* the time that the prosecution tells the Crown Court of its intention to appeal; a failure to give the indication at that time will be fatal to the appeal (R v *Arnold*[8]).

---

2   See s. 74(1) for the broad definition given to ruling; s. 58(13) for the requirement that it be before the summing up.
3   CJA 2003, s. 57(2)(a).
4   CJA 2003, s. 57(2)(b).
5   CJA 2003, s. 58(4).
6   [2008] EWCA Crim 1034.
7   CJA 2003, s. 61(3).
8   [2008] EWCA Crim 1034.

13.8   If the defendant cannot be formally 'acquitted' because of the stage that the case has reached, no such undertaking can be given and therefore the right of appeal does not arise. This has the effect that a ruling that is made before arraignment, following a sending to the Crown Court under section 51 of the Crime and Disorder Act 1998, cannot be appealed because the defendant cannot be formally acquitted; the charge can only be dismissed (*R v Thompson*[9]).

The procedure for appealing

13.9   Appeal is with leave of the trial judge or the Court of Appeal. The Court of Appeal has indicated that it will normally be appropriate to seek leave from the trial judge, seeking leave from the Court only if that application is refused *(R v F*[10]*)*.

13.10   The procedure for applications for leave and subsequent appeals is to be found at Part 67 of the CPR. Part 65 also applies, thereby ensuring the general procedure for applications to the Court of Appeal, extensions of time, renewed applications for leave and abandonment apply with the modifications contained in Part 67.

13.11   The timing of the application for leave and any subsequent appeal will depend on whether the jury in the trial has been discharged or the case has just been adjourned; if the latter, the trial judge, under section 59 of CJA 2003, or the Registrar will very often expedite the case, shortening the time limits for each stage from five days to one. Frequently in an expedited case the Registrar will refer the application for leave to the full Court so that permission and the substantive decision can be determined in a single hearing.

13.12   The procedure commences with the prosecution giving an indication of an intention to appeal. A formal notice of appeal must then be lodged within the time limits contained in rule 67.3.2 of the CPR.

Drafting the respondent's notice

13.13   Once a notice of appeal has been lodged the respondent (as the defendant is now known) must within five days serve a respondent's notice if it wishes to make any representations or if directed to do so by the Court.

13.14   The requirements of service of the respondent's notice are set out in rule 67.7 of the CPR 2013; the notice should be served on the prosecution

---

9   [2006] EWCA Crim 2849.
10   [2009] EWCA Crim 1639.

('the appellant' for these purposes), the Crown Court, the Registrar, and any co-defendants who are also the subject of the application to appeal.

13.15   It must be served not later than the next business day if the appeal is expedited or not later than five business days if it is not. Rule 67.7.5 of the CPR specifies that the respondent's notice must:

'(a)   give the date on which the respondent was served with the appeal notice;

(b)   identify each ground of opposition on which the respondent relies, numbering them consecutively (if there is more than one), concisely outlining each argument in support and identifying the ground of appeal to which each relates;

(c)   summarise any relevant facts not already summarised in the appeal notice;

(d)   identify any relevant authorities;

(e)   include or attach any application for the following, with reasons –

(i)   an extension of time within which to serve the respondent's notice,

(ii)   a direction to attend in person any hearing that the respondent could attend by live link, if the respondent is in custody;

(f)   identify any other document or thing that the respondent thinks the court will need to decide the appeal.'

Arguments to be deployed in responding to an appeal

13.16   Stepping away from the technicalities, the key line for resisting an appeal will often involve persuading the Court to rely on the trial judge's experience and any advantages that the trial had in hearing live evidence in the case. In *R v B*[11] Lord Judge CJ laid emphasis on the trial judge's experience and reputation and indicated that the decision had to be shown to be clearly wrong before the Court of Appeal would think it right to interfere.

13.17   The Court of Appeal's powers in such an appeal are wider than simply to uphold or overturn a trial level ruling. Section 61 of CJA 2003 also permits the Court to vary a ruling, so the arguments mounted can have the fall back position (especially where the ruling by the trial judge is difficult to defend in its precise terms) whereby the respondent can argue that the merits of the law or evidence before the trial court should nonetheless lead the Court to uphold the ruling in modified terms.

---

11   [2008] EWCA Crim 1144.

The hearing

13.18   Rule 67.11 of the CPR makes clear that the defendant has the right to attend the appeal hearing, though the Registrar can direct that this occurs via a video link. There is an automatic restriction on the reporting of appeals which may be lifted or varied by the Court.[12]

13.19   Either party may appeal to the Supreme Court, subject to the Court of Appeal certifying a point of law of general public importance (see Chapter 10).

ATTORNEY GENERAL'S REFERENCES

13.20   Section 36 of the Criminal Justice Act 1988 ('CJA 1988') permits the Attorney General to appeal against unduly lenient sentences in certain serious cases. The types of sentence that are subject to this form of appeal are:

(a)   an offence triable only on indictment;

(b)   an offence specified by the Secretary of State in an order made under CJA 1988[13] or an offence of attempting to commit or inciting the commitment of such an offence;

(c)   a fraud case that was sent to the Crown Court under section 4 of CJA 1987;

(d)   offences that have been tried on a voluntary bill of indictment that has been preferred after a charge has been dismissed under section 6 of CJA 1988.

Grounds for an appeal

13.21   Section 36(1) makes it clear that the overarching basis upon which the Attorney General can appeal is that the sentence passed was 'unduly lenient'. Section 36(2) goes on to specify that the test of undue leniency may be met where a sentencing judge has either erred in law as to his powers of sentencing or failed to pass one of the minimum sentences that must be passed by virtue of:

(a)   section 51A(2) of the Firearms Act 1968;

(b)   section 110(2) or 111(2) of the Powers of Criminal Courts (Sentencing) Act 2000;

(c)   section 225(2) or 226(2) of CJA 2003; or

(d)   section 29(4) or (6) of the Violent Crime Reduction Act 2006.

---

12   CJA 2003, s. 71.
13   Currently the CJA 1988 (Reviews of Sentencing) Order 2006 (SI/2006/1116).

The procedure

13.22   The procedure is governed by Part 70 of the CPR. The general rules contained in Part 65 also apply.

Notification of an appeal and reply

13.23   Schedule 3 to CJA 1988 allows 28 days for the prosecution to lodge an application for leave. In practice the prosecution will usually send out a standard letter with supporting documents within 28 days of the sentence being passed.

13.24   The Registrar will then serve those papers on the respondent who then has 14 days to make representations if he wishes to do so. Most respondents will be keen to do so. There is no specific form or indeed format for the respondent's representations. Any such representations must be served both on the Registrar of the Court of Appeal and on the Attorney General (rule 70.5 of CPR 2013).

Funding for respondent's representation

13.25   The Registrar does not grant representation orders to respondents in Attorney General's References but a defendant who has been represented may be entitled to reasonable costs from central funds. In unusually serious or complicated cases it may be that such costs would cover leading counsel in addition to or instead of junior counsel. If in doubt, the best course is to talk to the case lawyer at the Criminal Appeal Office.

Permission and full hearings

13.26   Attorney General's References require leave from the Court but the practice is to list the case and allow the Court to consider both leave and, if leave is given, to deal with the substantive appeal all in one hearing.

13.27   A respondent who is in custody has the right to attend at the substantive hearing though this may be by video link if the Registrar directs.[14] There is no right to be produced at any permission or other incidental hearings.

The Court's approach to Attorney General's References

13.28   The Court must first decide whether the sentence was unduly lenient. In doing so, it has frequently made clear that sentencing judges are entitled to

---

14   CPR, r. 70.7.

depart from sentencing guidelines provided there is a rational and justifiable basis to do so. Lord Phillips CJ emphasised in *Attorney-General's Reference (No. 8 of 2007)*[15] that a judge who took such a decision should not waver from it for fear of a reference. The power to allow an appeal is for sentences that are *unduly* lenient, not just lenient. The test is a high one and is intend to capture those sentences which cause public concern and affect the confidence in the criminal justice system (*Attorney General's Reference (Nos 3 and 5 of 1989)*).[16]

13.29   In the event that the Court decides that the sentence was unduly lenient, it must then go on to consider whether and to what extent to reduce or vary the sentence. This is a matter that is within the discretion of the Court; there is no statutory guidance on the exercise of that discretion and the Court has been known to take into account a wide range of factors.

13.30   In determining whether the sentence was unduly lenient, the Court considers the facts as they were before the sentencing judge. It will not take account of new material (see *Attorney-General's Reference (No. 19 of 2005)*[17]). The Court has, however, been prepared to look at new material in deciding what the new sentence should be (*Attorney-General's Reference (No. 74 of 2010)*[18]). In both those cases, the new material in question consisted of probation reports but the Court's approach has wider application; in the event that the Court decides that a sentence was unduly lenient it will often consider material in relation to the progress of the respondent from the time when the sentence was passed in order to assist in determining whether to interfere with the sentence.

13.31   Difficulties have occurred where a defendant has been given reasons to expect a certain sentence, most commonly when a *Goodyear*[19] indication has been given. The fact that an indication was given does not necessarily mean that the Court will not interfere with the sentence, nor does the fact that the prosecution at the time raised no objection to the indicated sentence. However, the prosecution's seeming consent may be a powerful reason not to increase a sentence, especially if the offender acted in reliance on the indication that was given (see *Attorney-General's References (Nos 25 and 26 of 2008)*[20]).

Discount for double jeopardy

13.32   Double jeopardy is the term used for the fear and distress that arises from being sentenced a second time. When, following a finding of undue leniency, the Court considers what new sentence to impose, it will often make

---

15   [2007] EWCA Crim 922.
16   (1990) 90 Cr App R 358.
17   [2006] EWCA Crim 785.
18   [2011] EWCA Crim 873.
19   *R v Goodyear* [2005] EWCA Crim 888.
20   [2008] EWCA Crim 2665.

a discount in what would have been the correct sentence, had it been imposed at first instance, to take account of this.

13.33 In *Attorney-General's References (Nos 14 and 15 of 2006)*,[21] the Court reviewed the authorities in relation to double jeopardy. It concluded that deductions at or near the top of the range might be made in the following situations: offenders who faced a custodial sentence when one had not originally been passed; offenders who had committed the offence in question when young and immature; and those offenders who had been about to be released from prison. In relation to those cases where the offender already had a lengthy custodial sentence to serve (and also in relation to discretionary life sentence, see **13.35** below) it was not necessarily wrong to make deductions for double jeopardy. However, those deductions would generally be smaller and in some cases no deduction would need to be made.

13.34 Under section 36A of CJA 1988 the Court should not make any allowance for double jeopardy when the reference relates to a minimum term for a mandatory life sentence under section 269(2) of CJA 2003.

13.35 If and when it comes into force (no date has yet been fixed for it to do so) section 46 of the Criminal Justice and Immigration Act 2008 will amend section 36A of CJA 1988 so as to also include discretionary life sentences in those to which no reductions for double jeopardy should be made.

Responding to the appellant's case

13.36 The respondent may seek to persuade the Court both that the sentence was not unduly lenient and that, even if it was, the Court should exercise its discretion not to increase the sentence. In cases where the correctness of the original sentence is very difficult to justify, the focus of the submissions should often be on the latter point.

13.37 In seeking to persuade the Court that the sentence is not unduly lenient, arguments that are commonly advanced include:

(a)   the high threshold that must be passed for a sentence to be regarded as unduly excessive;

(b)   the fact that the judge was experienced (if true) and the advantage that the judge had of having heard the evidence (if sentence was imposed after trial or *voire dire*);

(c)   the particular facts of the case which justified the judge in departing from the guidelines or the usual sentencing practice.

---

21   [2006] EWCA Crim 1335.

13.38   In certain cases, the problem may be not that the judge passed an unjustifiable sentence but that he failed to justify it in his sentencing remarks. The appellant will seek to set out the facts of the case which justify the sentence that was imposed.

13.39   When seeking to persuade the Court not to increase sentence, the respondent will wish to focus on double jeopardy, any significant progress that the respondent has made in the completion of the sentence or any significant change of circumstances that has occurred since sentence was passed that would make it wrong to now increase it.

Appeal to the Supreme Court

13.40   Either party can appeal to the Supreme Court, subject to the same requirement of certification or permission as in an appellant's appeal to the Supreme Court against conviction, save that the period for applying to the Court of Appeal for certification and permission is 14 days, with the same period for a subsequent application for permission to the Supreme Court.[22]

SUMMARY OF KEY POINTS

- Parliament has established a number of prosecution rights of appeal. The most commonly used are the right to appeal against rulings under section 58 of CJA 2003 and the Attorney General's right to appeal against a sentence that is unduly lenient.

- The procedure for appealing under section 58 of CJA 2003 is governed by Part 67 of the CPR. Attorney General's References are governed by Part 70. Part 65 applies to both.

- There are a number of preconditions on the right to appeal against a ruling, including a requirement that the prosecution provides an agreement that it will seek the acquittal of the defendant if the appeal fails.

- Such an undertaking must be given at the time an indication of an intention to appeal is given.

- Leave to appeal under section 58 may be given by the trial judge or the Court of Appeal.

- In respect of an Attorney General's Reference, leave must be granted by the Court of Appeal. However, it is the normal practice of the Court to hold a single permission/appeal hearing.

---

22   CJA 1988, s. 36 and Sch. 3.

- In these appeals the defendant becomes the respondent who must, if he wishes to be heard, serve and lodge a respondent's notice.

- In both types of appeal either party has the right to appeal to the Supreme Court.

Chapter 14

Appeals in relation to defendants suffering from a mental disorder

INTRODUCTION

14.1 As a matter of principle, once a defendant is found to be suffering either from a disability that makes him unfit to be tried or from insanity, the case is no longer a criminal case. A finding that the defendant committed the act with which he is charged does not amount to a conviction nor should a hospital or supervision order made against such a defendant be regarded as a sentence (*R v H*).[1] However, the procedures for dealing with those suffering from mental disorders who commit criminal acts closely follow criminal law procedures. Appeals are no exception. CAA 1968 establishes the following rights of appeal from decisions of the Crown Court, the procedures for which follow the procedural scheme for appeals against conviction or sentence:

(a) A finding of unfitness to be tried may be appealed under section 15 of CAA 1968.

(b) A defendant who has been found to be unfit to be tried did the act or made the omission with which he is charged may appeal under section 15 of CAA 1968.

(c) A verdict of not guilty by reason of insanity may be appealed under section 12 of CAA 1968.

(d) A hospital or supervision order that was imposed following a finding under (b) or (c), above may be appealed under section 16A of CAA 1968.

14.2 The test to be applied and the powers of disposal which the Court may exercise following a successful appeal differ for appeals under each of the above provisions (and are considered at **14.6–14.19**, below). However, appeals under these provisions share a number of common features. The law in relation to who has the right to appeal, the availability of public funding and the procedures to be followed are the same for each and are considered first.

---

1   [2003] UKHL 1.

14.3 *Appeals in relation to defendants suffering from a mental disorder*

Who may appeal

14.3   These are defence, not prosecution appeals. Given the nature of the disabilities in question, the rights of appeal can be exercised by a defendant's lawyer without the need for the defendant's consent. In *R v Antoine (Pierre Harrison)*[2] the Court held that counsel who had appeared in the Crown Court had the authority to settle grounds, lodge notice of appeal and present the appeal on behalf of a defendant who suffered from a mental disability such that he was incapable of giving instructions.

Funding

14.4   There is no statutory provision for the granting of representation orders in respect of any of these appeals. The successful appellant may apply for a defendant's costs order. Moreover, advocates who are instructed by the Court to represent a defendant who suffers from a mental disorder may claim costs from central funds (see *Antoine,* above).

The appeal process

14.5   The procedure for these appeals follows that for appeals against conviction or sentence. They are contained in the particular provisions of CAA 1968 that apply to each appeal. In addition, Part 65 and 68 of the CPR apply to all of them. The main features of the process are:

(a)   An application for certification of fitness to appeal may be made to the trial judge within 28 days of the decision which is the subject of challenge (but see **14.7** below in relation to when the 28-day period runs in appeals under section 15).

(b)   An application for leave to the Court of Appeal must be made using Form NG within 28 days of the decision but may be extended on application. Leave may be granted by the single judge or the full Court.

(c)   An application for leave that is refused may be renewed orally before the Court.

(d)   The defendant who is in custody as a result of a finding of unfitness to stand trial or insanity does not have a right to be present at the hearing.

(e)   An appeal or application for leave may be abandoned using Form A.

(f)   Under section 33 of CAA 1968 there is a right of appeal from the Court of Appeal to the Supreme Court, which involves the usual requirements of certification and leave.

---

2   [1999] 2 Cr App R 225.

APPEALS AGAINST FINDINGS OF UNFITNESS TO PLEAD AND FINDINGS THAT THE ACCUSED MADE THE ACT OR OMISSION CHARGED

14.6   Sections 4 and 4A of the Criminal Procedure (Insanity) Act 1964 set out a two-stage procedure whereby the Crown Court must first determine whether an accused, who appears to be suffering from some mental illness or disorder, is fit to stand trial and, if found not to be fit, must go on to determine whether he did the acts of which he is accused.

14.7   Under section 15 of CAA 1968 an appeal may be brought against both or either of these findings. The procedural requirements contained in section 15 are as set out at **14.3–14.5**, above. The 28-day period for lodging an appeal is calculated from the date of the decision against which leave is sought. However, the trial judge may only grant a certificate of fitness to appeal within 28 days of the finding that the accused did the act or made the omission charged.[3]

14.8   The test for an appeal under section 15 is whether the finding that is the subject of the appeal is unsafe. If the Court allows an appeal against a finding of disability, it may order that a trial take place and may make orders that are necessary and expedient for custody or release on bail.[4]

14.9   The Court's powers to dispose of an appeal under section 15 are contained in section 16. If the Court allows an appeal against a finding that the defendant committed the act or made the omission in question, it must quash the order and direct that a verdict of acquittal be recorded.

14.10   The Court has no power to order a retrial. However, where the Court finds that there has been a procedural irregularity such as to render the proceedings in the Crown Court a nullity, it may, instead of allowing the appeal, issue a writ of *venire de novo* (discussed more fully in Chapter 3) and order that the case be remitted for fresh proceedings to take place. It did so in *R v D (David Michael)*[5] when it transpired that one of the doctors upon whose opinion the finding of unfitness had been based was not qualified.

14.11   There is no appeal against a finding that the accused is fit to be tried. If such a finding is made and the accused goes on to be convicted, leave to appeal against conviction may be applied for in the usual way. If, in the course of that

---

3   CAA 1968, s.15(2)(b).
4   CAA 1968, s.16(3)(a), (b).
5   [2001] EWCA Crim 911.

appeal, the Court is satisfied on the requisite evidence[6] that the convicted person is not fit but did carry out the acts or make the omission charged, then it may not quash the conviction but must substitute one of the orders under section 5 of the Criminal Procedures (Insanity) Act 1964 (see **14.16**, below) for any sentence that had been imposed.

APPEALS AGAINST A VERDICT OF NOT GUILTY BY REASON OF INSANITY

14.12   Section 2 of the Trial of Lunatics Act 1883 allows a jury to return a special verdict of not guilty by reason of insanity. Appeal against such an order may be brought under section 12 of CAA 1968 and follows the procedures set out at **14.3–14.5**, above. The test is whether the special verdict is unsafe.[7]

14.13   The Court's powers to dispose of an appeal are contained in section 13 of CAA 1968. If the Court finds that the verdict of insanity was unsafe but that the proper verdict would have been guilty of the offence charged or any other offence for which the jury might have found the accused guilty, it may substitute a verdict of guilty of that offence for the verdict of not guilty by reason of insanity.

14.14   If the Court finds that the verdict of insanity is unsafe but that, on the evidence of appropriately qualified and approved practitioners,[8] the accused suffered from a disability within the meaning of sections 4 and 4A of the Criminal Procedure (Insanity) Act 1964 and that he made the act or omission charged, it may make an order under section 5 of the Criminal Procedure (Insanity) Act 1964.

14.15   In all other cases in which an appeal is allowed the Court must substitute a verdict of acquittal.

APPEALS AGAINST AN ORDER MADE UNDER SECTION 5 OF THE CRIMINAL PROCEDURE (INSANITY) ACT 1964

14.16   Following a verdict of insanity or a finding that the defendant did the act or omission with which he is charged, the Crown Court may make one of

---

6   The written or oral evidence of two medical practitioners, one of whom must be duly approved (Criminal Procedure (Insanity) Act 1964, s. 4(5), (6)).

7   CAA 1968, s. 13.

8   See fn 6, above.

the following orders under section 5 of the Criminal Procedure (Insanity) Act 1964. Those orders are:

(a)   a hospital order (with or without a restriction order);

(b)   a supervision order; or

(c)   an absolute discharge.

14.17   Under section 16A of CAA 1968[9] an appeal may be brought against such an order (although it is not clear when a defendant would seek to appeal an order for an absolute discharge). The procedural requirements for such an appeal are as set out at **14.3–14.5**, above. If it allows the appeal, the Court may vary the order or may quash it and substitute it for another order under section 5.

14.18   The test on appeal is simply whether the Court 'considers that the appellant should be dealt with differently to the way in which the Court below dealt with him'.[10]

14.19   If the Court of Appeal disposes of an appeal by making an interim hospital order or a supervision order, that order may be revoked or varied by the Crown Court. The Crown Court also has the power to revoke or vary an interim hospital order or a supervision order when an appeal against that order is still pending.[11]

---

9   As inserted by the Domestic Violence, Crime and Victims Act 2004, s. 25.
10   CAA 1968, s. 16B(1).
11   CAA 1968, s. 16B(2)–(5).

Appendix A

Criminal Practice Direction, Part 68

APPEAL TO THE COURT OF APPEAL ABOUT CONVICTION OR SENTENCE

CPD X Appeal 68A: Appeals Against Conviction and Sentence – the Provision of Notice to the Prosecution

68A.1　When an appeal notice served under Rule 68.2 is received by the Registrar of Criminal Appeals, the Registrar will notify the relevant prosecution authority, giving the case name, reference number and the trial or sentencing court.

68A.2　If the court or the Registrar directs, or invites, the prosecution authority to serve a respondent's notice under Rule 68.6, prior to the consideration of leave, the Registrar will also at that time serve on the prosecution authority the appeal notice containing the grounds of appeal and the transcripts, if available. If the prosecution authority is not directed or invited to serve a respondent's notice but wishes to do so, the authority should request the grounds of appeal and any existing transcript from the Criminal Appeal Office. Any respondent's notice received prior to the consideration of leave will be made available to the single judge.

68A.3　The Registrar of Criminal Appeals will notify the relevant prosecution authority in the event that:

(a)　leave to appeal against conviction or sentence is granted by the single Judge; or

(b)　the single Judge or the Registrar refers an application for leave to appeal against conviction or sentence to the Full Court for determination; or

(c)　there is to be a renewed application for leave to appeal against sentence only.

If the prosecution authority has not yet been served with the appeal notice and transcript, the Registrar will serve these with the notification, and if leave is granted, the Registrar will also serve the authority with the comments of the single judge.

68A.4   The prosecution should notify the Registrar without delay if they wish to be represented at the hearing. The prosecution should note that the Registrar will not delay listing to await a response from the Prosecution as to whether they wish to attend. Prosecutors should note that occasionally, for example, where the single Judge fixes a hearing date at short notice, the case may be listed very quickly.

68A.5   If the prosecution wishes to be represented at any hearing, the notification should include details of Counsel instructed and a time estimate. An application by the prosecution to remove a case from the list for Counsel's convenience, or to allow further preparation time, will rarely be granted.

68A.6   There may be occasions when the Court of Appeal Criminal Division will grant leave to appeal to an unrepresented applicant and proceed forthwith with the appeal in the absence of the appellant and Counsel. The prosecution should not attend any hearing at which the appellant is unrepresented. *Nasteska v. The former Yugoslav Republic of Macedonia (Application No.23152/05)* As a Court of Review, the Court of Appeal Criminal Division would expect the prosecution to have raised any specific matters of relevance with the sentencing Judge in the first instance.

CPD X Appeal 68B: Listing of Appeals Against Conviction and Sentence in the Court of Appeal Criminal Division (CACD)

68B.1   Arrangements for the fixing of dates for the hearing of appeals will be made by the Criminal Appeal Office Listing Officer, under the superintendence of the Registrar of Criminal Appeals who may give such directions as he deems necessary.

68B.2   Where possible, regard will be had to an advocate's existing commitments. However, in relation to the listing of appeals, the Court of Appeal takes precedence over all lower courts, including the Crown Court. Wherever practicable, a lower court will have regard to this principle when making arrangements to release an advocate to appear in the Court of Appeal. In case of difficulty the lower court should communicate with the Registrar. In general an advocate's commitment in a lower court will not be regarded as a good reason for failing to accept a date proposed for a hearing in the Court of Appeal.

68B.3   Similarly when the Registrar directs that an appellant should appear by video link, the prison must give precedence to video-links to the Court of Appeal over video-links to the lower courts, including the Crown Court.

68B.4   The copy of the Criminal Appeal Office summary provided to advocates will contain the summary writer's time estimate for the whole hearing including delivery of judgment. It will also contain a time estimate for the judges' reading time of the core material. The Listing Officer will rely on those estimates, unless the advocate for the appellant or the Crown provides different time estimates to the Listing Officer, in writing, within 7 days of the receipt of the summary by the advocate. Where the time estimates are considered by an advocate to be inadequate, or where the estimates have been altered because, for example, a ground of appeal has been abandoned, it is the duty of the advocate to inform the Court promptly, in which event the Registrar will reconsider the time estimates and inform the parties accordingly.

68B.5   The following target times are set for the hearing of appeals. Target times will run from the receipt of the appeal by the Listing Officer, as being ready for hearing.

68B.6

Nature of Appeal:	*From Receipt by Listing Officer to Fixing of Hearing Date:*	*From Fixing of Hearing Date to Hearing:*	**Total Time from Receipt by Listing Officer to Hearing:**
Sentence Appeal	14 days	14 days	28 days
Conviction Appeal	21 days	42 days	63 days
Conviction Appeal where witness to attend	28 days	52 days	80 days

68B.7   Where legal vacations impinge, these periods may be extended. Where expedition is required, the Registrar may direct that these periods be abridged.

68B.8   "Appeal" includes an application for leave to appeal which requires an oral hearing.

CPD X Appeal 68C: Appeal Notices Containing Grounds OF Appeal

68C.1   The requirements for the service of notices of appeal and the time limits for doing so are as set out in Part 68 of the Criminal Procedure Rules. The Court must be provided with an appeal notice as a single document which sets out the grounds of appeal. Advocates should not provide the Court with an advice addressed to lay or professional clients. Any appeal notice or grounds of appeal served on the Court will usually be provided to the respondent.

68C.2   Advocates should not settle grounds unless they consider that they are properly arguable. Grounds should be carefully drafted; the Court is not assisted by grounds of appeal which are not properly set out and particularised. Should leave to amend the grounds be granted, it is most unlikely that further grounds will be entertained.

CPD X Appeal 68D: Respondents' Notices

68D.1   The requirements for the service of respondents' notices and the time limits for doing so are as set out in Part 68 of the Criminal Procedure Rules. Any respondent's notice served should be in accordance with Rule 68.6. The Court does not require a response to the respondent's notice.

CPD X Appeal 68E: Loss of Time

68E.1   Both the Court and the single judge have power, in their discretion, under the Criminal Appeal Act 1968 sections 29 and 31, to direct that part of the time during which an applicant is in custody after lodging his notice of application for leave to appeal should not count towards sentence. Those contemplating an appeal should seek advice and should remember that a notice of appeal without grounds is ineffective and that grounds should be substantial and particularised and not a mere formula. When leave to appeal has been refused by the single judge, it is often of assistance to consider the reasons given by the single judge before making a decision whether to renew the application. Where an application devoid of merit has been refused by the single judge he may indicate that the Full Court should consider making a direction for loss of time on renewal of the application. However the Full Court may make such a direction whether or not such an indication has been given by the single judge.

68E.2   Applicants and counsel are reminded of the warning given by the Court of Appeal in *R v Hart and Others* [2006] EWCA Crim 3239, [2007] 1 Cr. App. R. 31, [2007] 2 Cr. App. R. (S.) 34 and should 'heed the fact that this court is prepared to exercise its power … The mere fact that counsel has advised that there are grounds of appeal will not always be a sufficient answer to the question as to whether or not an application has indeed been brought which was totally without merit.'

CPD X Appeal 68F: Skeleton Arguments

68F.1   Skeleton arguments are not required, but may be provided. Advocates intending to serve a skeleton argument should consider carefully whether a skeleton argument is necessary, or whether the appeal notice or the respondent's notice will suffice. In most cases, if the appeal notice and respondent's notice have been prepared in compliance with Part 68, a skeleton argument will be unnecessary. Advocates should always ensure that the Court, and any other party as appropriate, has a single document containing all of the points that are to be argued.

68F.2   The appellant's skeleton argument, if any, must be served no later than 21 days before the hearing date, and the respondent's skeleton argument, if any, no later than 14 days before the hearing date, unless otherwise directed by the Court.

68F.3   A skeleton argument, if provided, should contain a numbered list of the points the advocate intends to argue, grouped under each ground of appeal, and stated in no more than one or two sentences. It should be as succinct as possible. Advocates should ensure that the correct Criminal Appeal Office number appears at the beginning of the respondent's notice and any skeleton argument and that their names are at the end.

CPD X Appeal 68G: Criminal Appeal Office Summaries

68G.1   To assist the Court, the Criminal Appeal Office prepares summaries of the cases coming before it. These are entirely objective and do not contain any advice about how the Court should deal with the case or any view about its merits. They consist of two Parts.

68G.2   Part I, which is provided to all of the advocates in the case, generally contains:

(a)   particulars of the proceedings in the Crown Court, including representation and details of any co-accused,

(b)   particulars of the proceedings in the Court of Appeal (Criminal Division),

(c)   the facts of the case, as drawn from the transcripts, appeal notice, respondent's notice, witness statements and / or the exhibits,

(d)   the submissions and rulings, summing up and sentencing remarks.

68G.3   The contents of the summary are a matter for the professional judgment of the writer, but an advocate wishing to suggest any significant alteration to Part I should write to the Registrar of Criminal Appeals. If the Registrar does not agree, the summary and the letter will be put to the Court for decision. The Court will not generally be willing to hear oral argument about the content of the summary.

68G.4   Advocates may show Part I of the summary to their professional or lay clients (but to no one else) if they believe it would help to check facts or formulate arguments, but summaries are not to be copied or reproduced without the permission of the Criminal Appeal Office; permission for this will not normally be given in cases involving children, or sexual offences, or where the Crown Court has made an order restricting reporting.

68G.5   Unless a judge of the High Court or the Registrar of Criminal Appeals gives a direction to the contrary, in any particular case involving material of an explicitly salacious or sadistic nature, Part I will also be supplied to appellants who seek to represent themselves before the Full Court, or who renew to the full court their applications for leave to appeal against conviction or sentence.

68G.6   Part II, which is supplied to the Court alone, contains

(a)   a summary of the grounds of appeal and

(b)   in appeals against sentence (and applications for such leave), summaries of the antecedent histories of the parties and of any relevant pre-sentence, medical or other reports.

68G.7   All of the source material is provided to the Court and advocates are able to draw attention to anything in it which may be of particular relevance.

The Criminal Procedure Rules, Parts 65 to 74

PART 65   APPEAL TO THE COURT OF APPEAL: GENERAL RULES

Contents of this Part

When this Part applies

65.1.—(1) This Part applies to all the applications, appeals and references to the Court of Appeal to which Parts 66, 67, 68, 69, 70 and 74 apply.

(2) In this Part and in those, unless the context makes it clear that something different is meant 'court' means the Court of Appeal or any judge of that court.

[Note. See rule 2.2 for the usual meaning of 'court'.

*Under section 53 of the Senior Courts Act 1981(**a**), the criminal division of the Court of Appeal exercises jurisdiction in the appeals and references to which Parts 66, 67, 68, 69 and 70 apply.*

185

*Under section 55 of that Act(**b**), the Court of Appeal must include at least two judges, and for some purposes at least three.*

*For the powers of the Court of Appeal that may be exercised by one judge of that court or by the Registrar, see sections 31, 31A, 31B, 31C and 44 of the Criminal Appeal Act 1968(**c**); section 49 of the Criminal Justice Act 2003(**a**); The Criminal Justice Act 2003 (Mandatory Life Sentences: Appeals in Transitional Cases) Order 2005(**b**); The Serious Organised Crime and Police Act 2005 (Appeals under section 74) Order 2006(**c**); The Serious Crime Act 2007 (Appeals under Section 24) Order 2008(**d**); and the power conferred by section 53(4) of the 1981 Act.]*

(**a**) 1981 c. 54. The Act's title was amended by section 59(5) of, and paragraph 1 of Schedule 11 to, the Constitutional Reform Act 2005 (c. 4).

(**b**) 1981 c. 54; section 55 was amended by section 170 of, and paragraph 80 of Schedule 15 to, the Criminal Justice Act 1988 (c. 33), section 52 of the Criminal Justice and Public Order Act 1994 (c. 33) and section 58 of the Domestic Violence, Crime and Victims Act 2004 (c. 28). It is further amended by section 40 of, and paragraph 36 of Schedule 9 to, the Constitutional Reform Act 2005 (c. 4).

(**c**) 1968 c. 19; section 31 was amended by section 21 of, and Schedule 2 to, the Costs in Criminal Cases Act 1973 (c. 14), section 24 of, and paragraph 10 of Schedule 6 to, the Road Traffic Act 1974 (c. 50), section 29 of the Criminal Justice Act 1982 (c. 48), section 170 of, and paragraphs 20, 29 and 30 of Schedule 15 to, the Criminal Justice Act 1988 (c. 33), section 4 of, and paragraph 4 of Schedule 3 to, the Road Traffic (Consequential Provisions) Act 1988 (c. 54), section 198 of, and paragraphs 38 and 40 of Schedule 6 to, the Licensing Act 2003 (c. 17), section 87 of the Courts Act 2003 (c. 39), section 331 of, and paragraphs 86, 87 and 88 of Schedule 36 to, the Criminal Justice Act 2003 (c. 44), section 48 of the Police and Justice Act 2006 (c. 48) and section 47 of, and paragraphs 1, 9 and 11 of Schedule 8 to, the Criminal Justice and Immigration Act 2008 (c. 4). It is further amended by section 67 of, and paragraph 4 of Schedule 4 to, the Youth Justice and Criminal Evidence Act 1999 (c. 23), with effect from a date to be appointed. Section 31A was inserted by section 6 of the Criminal Appeal Act 1995 (c. 35) and amended by sections 87 and 109 of, and Schedule 10 to, the Courts Act 2003 (c. 39) and section 331 of, and paragraphs 86 and 88 of Schedule 36 to, the Criminal Justice Act 2003 (c. 44). Section 31B was inserted by section 87 of the Courts Act 2003 (c. 39). Section 31C was inserted by section 87 of the Courts Act 2003 (c. 39) and amended by sections 47 and 149 of, and paragraphs 1 and 12 of Schedule 8 and part 3 of Schedule 28 to, the Criminal Justice and Immigration Act 2008 (c. 4). Section 44 was amended by section 24(2) of, and paragraph 11 of Schedule 6 to, the Road Traffic Act 1974 (c. 50), section 170(1) of, and paragraphs 20 and 31 of the Criminal Justice Act 1988 (c. 33), section 4 of, and paragraph 4(2) of the Road Traffic (Consequential Provisions) Act 1988 (c. 54) and section 198(1), and paragraphs 38 and 41 of Schedule 6 to, the Licensing Act 2003 (c. 17).

Case management in the Court of Appeal

65.2.—(1) The court and the parties have the same duties and powers as under Part 3 (case management).

(2) The Registrar—

(a) must fulfil the duty of active case management under rule 3.2; and

(b) in fulfilling that duty may exercise any of the powers of case management under—

(i)   rule 3.5 (the court's general powers of case management),

(ii)   rule 3.9(3) (requiring a certificate of readiness), and

(iii)   rule 3.10 (requiring a party to identify intentions and anticipated requirements)

subject to the directions of the court.

(3) The Registrar must nominate a case progression officer under rule 3.4.

Power to vary requirements

65.3.   The court or the Registrar may—

(a)   shorten a time limit or extend it (even after it has expired) unless that is inconsistent with other legislation;

(b)   allow a party to vary any notice that that party has served;

(c)   direct that a notice or application be served on any person;

(d)   allow a notice or application to be in a different form, or presented orally.

[Note. The time limit for serving an appeal notice—

*(a)   under section 18 of the Criminal Appeal Act 1968(**e**) on an appeal against conviction or sentence, and*

*(b)   under section 18A of that Act(**f**) on an appeal against a finding of contempt of court may be extended but not shortened: see rule 68.2.*

The time *limit for serving an application for permission to refer a sentencing case under section 36 of the Criminal Justice Act 1988(**g**) may be neither extended nor shortened: see rule 70.2(2).*

The time limits in rule 74.2 for applying to the Court of Appeal for permission to appeal or refer a case to the Supreme Court may be extended or shortened only as explained in the note to that rule.]

(**a**)   2003 c. 44.
(**b**)   S.I. 2005/2798.
(**c**)   S.I. 2006/2135.
(**d**)   S.I. 2008/1863.
(**e**)   1968 c. 19.
(**f**)   1968 c. 19; section 18A was inserted by section 170 of, and paragraphs 20 and 25 of Schedule 15 to, the Criminal Justice Act 1988 (c. 33).
(**g**)   1988 c. 33; section 36 was amended by section 272 of, and paragraphs 45 and 46 of Schedule 32 and paragraph 96 of Schedule 36 to, the Criminal Justice Act 2003 (c. 44), sections 49 and 65 of, and paragraph 3 of Schedule 1 and Schedule 5 to, the Violent Crime Reduction Act 2006 (c. 38), section 40 of, and paragraph 48 of Schedule 9 to, the Constitutional Reform Act 2005 (c. 4), section 149 of, and Part 28 of Schedule 28 to, the Criminal Justice and Immigration Act 2008 (c. 4) and paragraph 2 of Schedule 19 and paragraphs 4 and 5 of Schedule 26 to the Legal Aid, Sentencing and Punishment of Offenders Act 2012 (c. 10). It is further amended by section 46 of the Criminal Justice and Immigration Act 2008 (c. 4), with effect from a date to be appointed.

Application for extension of time

65.4.   A person who wants an extension of time within which to serve a notice or make an application must—

(a)   apply for that extension of time when serving that notice or making that application; and

(b)   give the reasons for the application for an extension of time.

Renewing an application refused by a judge or the Registrar

65.5.—(1) This rule applies where a party with the right to do so wants to renew— (a) to a judge of the Court of Appeal an application refused by the Registrar; or (b) to the Court of Appeal an application refused by a judge of that court.

(2) That party must—

(a)   renew the application in the form set out in the Practice Direction, signed by or on behalf of the applicant;

(b)   serve the renewed application on the Registrar not more than 14 days after—

   (i)   the refusal of the application that the applicant wants to renew; or

   (ii)   the Registrar serves that refusal on the applicant, if the applicant was not present in person or by live link when the original application was refused.

[Note. The time limit of 14 days under this rule is reduced to 5 days where Parts 66, 67 or 69 apply: see rules 66.7, 67.10 and 69.7.

*For the right to renew an application to a judge or to the Court of Appeal, see sections 31(3), 31C and 44 of the Criminal Appeal Act 1968, The Criminal Justice Act 2003 (Mandatory Life Sentences: Appeals in Transitional Cases) Order 2005(**a**), The Serious Organised Crime and Police Act 2005 (Appeals under section 74) Order 2006(**b**) and The Serious Crime Act 2007 (Appeals under Section 24) Order 2008.*

A party has no right under section 31C of the 1968 Act to renew to the Court of Appeal an application for procedural directions refused by a judge, but in some circumstances a case management direction might be varied: see rule 3.6.

If an applicant does not renew an application that a judge has refused, including an application for permission to appeal, the Registrar will treat it as if it had been refused by the Court of Appeal.

*Under section 22 of the Criminal Appeal Act 1968(**c**), the Court of Appeal may direct that an appellant who is in custody is to attend a hearing by live link.]*

(a) S.I. 2005/2798.
(b) S.I. 2006/2135.
(c) 1968 c. 19; section 22 was amended by section 48 of the Police and Justice Act 2006 (c. 48).

Hearings

65.6.—(1) The general rule is that the Court of Appeal must hear in public—

(a)   an application, including an application for permission to appeal; and

(b)   an appeal or reference,

but it may order any hearing to be in private.

(2) Where a hearing is about a public interest ruling, that hearing must be in private unless the court otherwise directs.

(3) Where the appellant wants to appeal against an order restricting public access to a trial, the court—

(a)   may decide without a hearing—

    (i)   an application, including an application for permission to appeal, and

    (ii)   an appeal; but

(b)   must announce its decision on such an appeal at a hearing in public.

(4) Where the appellant wants to appeal or to refer a case to the Supreme Court, the court—

(a)   may decide without a hearing an application—

    (i)   for permission to appeal or to refer a sentencing case, or

    (ii)   to refer a point of law; but

(b)   must announce its decision on such an application at a hearing in public.

(5) A judge of the Court of Appeal and the Registrar may exercise any of their powers—

(a)   at a hearing in public or in private; or

(b)   without a hearing.

[Note. For the procedure on an appeal against an order restricting public access to a trial, see Part 69.]

Notice of hearings and decisions

65.7.—(1) The Registrar must give as much notice as reasonably practicable of every hearing to—

(a)   the parties;

(b)   any party's custodian;

(c)   any other person whom the court requires to be notified; and

(d)   the Crown Court officer, where Parts 66, 67 or 69 apply.

(2) The Registrar must serve every decision on—

(a)   the parties;

(b)   any other person whom the court requires to be served; and

(c)   the Crown Court officer and any party's custodian, where the decision determines an appeal or application for permission to appeal.

(3) But where a hearing or decision is about a public interest ruling, the Registrar must not—

(a)   give notice of that hearing to; or

(b)   serve that decision on,

anyone other than the prosecutor who applied for that ruling, unless the court otherwise directs.

Duty of Crown Court officer

65.8.—(1) The Crown Court officer must provide the Registrar with any document, object or information for which the Registrar asks, within such period as the Registrar may require.

(2) Where someone may appeal to the Court of Appeal, the Crown Court officer must keep any document or object exhibited in the proceedings in the Crown Court, or arrange for it to be kept by some other appropriate person, until—

(a)   6 weeks after the conclusion of those proceedings; or

(b)   the conclusion of any appeal proceedings that begin within that 6 weeks,

unless the court, the Registrar or the Crown Court otherwise directs.

(3) Where Part 66 applies (appeal to the Court of Appeal against ruling at preparatory hearing), the Crown Court officer must as soon as practicable serve on the appellant a transcript or note of—

(a)   each order or ruling against which the appellant wants to appeal; and

(b)   the decision by the Crown Court judge on any application for permission to appeal.

(4) Where Part 67 applies (appeal to the Court of Appeal against ruling adverse to prosecution), the Crown Court officer must as soon as practicable serve on the appellant a transcript or note of—

(a)   each ruling against which the appellant wants to appeal;

(b)   the decision by the Crown Court judge on any application for permission to appeal; and

(c)   the decision by the Crown Court judge on any request to expedite the appeal.

(5) Where Part 68 applies (appeal to the Court of Appeal about conviction or sentence), the Crown Court officer must as soon as practicable serve on the Registrar—

(a)   the appeal notice and any accompanying application that the appellant serves on the Crown Court officer;

(b)   any Crown Court judge's certificate that the case is fit for appeal;

(c)   the decision on any application at the Crown Court centre for bail pending appeal;

(d)   such of the Crown Court case papers as the Registrar requires; and

(e)   such transcript of the Crown Court proceedings as the Registrar requires.

(6) Where Part 69 applies (appeal to the Court of Appeal regarding reporting or public access) and an order is made restricting public access to a trial, the Crown Court officer must—

(a)   immediately notify the Registrar of that order, if the appellant has given advance notice of intention to appeal; and

(b)   as soon as practicable provide the applicant for that order with a transcript or note of the application.

*[Note. See also section 87(4) of the Senior Courts Act 1981(**a**) and rules 5.5 (recording and transcription of proceedings in the Crown Court), 65.9 (duty of person transcribing record of proceedings in the Crown Court) and 65.10 (duty of person keeping exhibit).]*

Duty of person transcribing proceedings in the Crown Court

65.9.   A person who transcribes a recording of proceedings in the Crown Court under arrangements made by the Crown Court officer must provide the Registrar with any transcript for which the Registrar asks, within such period as the Registrar may require.

*[Note. See also section 32 of the Criminal Appeal Act 1968(**b**) and rule 5.5 (recording and transcription of proceedings in the Crown Court).]*

(**a**)   1981 c. 54; section 87(4) was amended by articles 2 and 3 of, and paragraphs 11 and 17 of the Schedule to, S.I. 2004/2035.

(**b**)   1968 c. 19.

Duty of person keeping exhibit

65.10.   A person who under arrangements made by the Crown Court officer keeps a document or object exhibited in the proceedings in the Crown Court must—

(a)   keep that exhibit until—

    (i)   6 weeks after the conclusion of the Crown Court proceedings, or

    (ii)   the conclusion of any appeal proceedings that begin within that 6 weeks,

unless the court, the Registrar or the Crown Court otherwise directs; and

(b) provide the Registrar with any such document or object for which the Registrar asks, within such period as the Registrar may require.

[Note. See also rule 65.8(2) (duty of Crown Court officer).]

Registrar's duty to provide copy documents for appeal or reference

65.11.   Unless the court otherwise directs, for the purposes of an appeal or reference—

(a)   the Registrar must—

    (i)   provide a party with a copy of any document or transcript held by the Registrar for such purposes, or

    (ii)   allow a party to inspect such a document or transcript,

    on payment by that party of any charge fixed by the Treasury; but

(b)   the Registrar must not provide a copy or allow the inspection of—

    (i)   a document provided only for the court and the Registrar, or

    (ii)   a transcript of a public interest ruling or of an application for such a ruling.

[Note. Section 21 of the Criminal Appeal Act 1968 requires the Registrar to collect, prepare and provide documents needed by the court.]

Declaration of incompatibility with a Convention right

65.12.—(1) This rule applies where a party—

(a)   wants the court to make a declaration of incompatibility with a Convention right under section 4 of the Human Rights Act 1998(**a**); or

(b)   raises an issue that the Registrar thinks may lead the court to make such a declaration.

(2) The Registrar must serve notice on—

(a)   the relevant person named in the list published under section 17(1) of the Crown Proceedings Act 1947(**b**); or

(b)   the Treasury Solicitor, if it is not clear who is the relevant person.

(3) That notice must include or attach details of—

(a)   the legislation affected and the Convention right concerned;

(b)   the parties to the appeal; and

(c)   any other information or document that the Registrar thinks relevant.

(4) A person who has a right under the 1998 Act to become a party to the appeal must—

(a)   serve notice on—

    (i)   the Registrar, and

    (ii)   the other parties,

    if that person wants to exercise that right; and

(b)   in that notice—

    (i)   indicate the conclusion that that person invites the court to reach on the question of incompatibility, and

    (ii)   identify each ground for that invitation, concisely outlining the arguments in support.

(5) The court must not make a declaration of incompatibility—

(a)   less than 21 days after the Registrar serves notice under paragraph (2); and

(b)   without giving any person who serves a notice under paragraph (4) an opportunity to make representations at a hearing.

(**a**)   1998 c. 42; section 4 was amended by section 40 of, and paragraph 66 of Schedule 9 to, the Constitutional Reform Act 2005 (c. 4) and section 67 of, and paragraph 43 of Schedule 6 to, the Mental Capacity Act 2005 (c. 9).
(**b**)   1947 c. 44; section 17 was amended by article 3(2) of S.I. 1968/1656.

Abandoning an appeal

65.13.—(1) This rule applies where an appellant wants to—

(a)   abandon—

    (i)   an application to the court for permission to appeal, or

    (ii)   an appeal; or

(b)   reinstate such an application or appeal after abandoning it.

(2) The appellant—

(a)   may abandon such an application or appeal without the court's permission by serving a notice of abandonment on—

    (i)   the Registrar, and

    (ii)   any respondent

    before any hearing of the application or appeal; but

(b)   at any such hearing, may only abandon that application or appeal with the court's permission.

(3) A notice of abandonment must be in the form set out in the Practice Direction, signed by or on behalf of the appellant.

(4) On receiving a notice of abandonment the Registrar must—

(a)   date it;

(b)   serve a dated copy on—

    (i)   the appellant,

    (ii)   the appellant's custodian, if any,

    (iii)   the Crown Court officer, and

    (iv)   any other person on whom the appellant or the Registrar served the appeal notice; and

(c)   treat the application or appeal as if it had been refused or dismissed by the Court of Appeal.

(5) An appellant who wants to reinstate an application or appeal after abandoning it must—

(a)   apply in writing, with reasons; and

(b)   serve the application on the Registrar.

[Note. The Court of Appeal has power only in exceptional circumstances to allow an appellant to reinstate an application or appeal that has been abandoned.]

Abandoning a ground of appeal or opposition

65.14.—(1) This rule applies where a party wants to abandon—

(a)   a ground of appeal identified in an appeal notice; or

(b)   a ground of opposition identified in a respondent's notice.

(2) Such a party must give written notice to—

(a)   the Registrar; and

(b)   every other party,

before any hearing at which that ground will be considered by the court.

PART 66   APPEAL TO THE COURT OF APPEAL AGAINST RULING AT PREPARATORY HEARING

Contents of this Part

When this Part applies

66.1.—(1) This Part applies where a party wants to appeal under—

(a)   section 9(11) of the Criminal Justice Act 1987(**a**) or section 35(1) of the Criminal Procedure and Investigations Act 1996(**b**); or

(b)   section 47(1) of the Criminal Justice Act 2003(**c**).

(2) A reference to an 'appellant' in this Part is a reference to such a party.

[Note. Under section 9(11) of the Criminal Justice Act 1987 (which applies to serious or complex fraud cases) and under section 35(1) of the Criminal Procedure and Investigations Act 1996 (which applies to other complex, serious or long cases) a party may appeal to the Court of Appeal against an order made at a preparatory hearing in the Crown Court.

Under section 47(1) of the Criminal Justice Act 2003 a party may appeal to the Court of Appeal against an order in the Crown Court that because of jury tampering a trial will continue without a jury or that there will be a new trial without a jury.

Part 3 contains rules about preparatory hearings.

The rules in Part 65 also apply where this Part applies.]

(**a**) 1987 c. 38; section 9(11) was amended by sections 45 and 310 of the Criminal Justice Act 2003 (c. 44). The section 45 amendment is in force for certain purposes; for remaining purposes it has effect from a date to be appointed.

(**b**) 1996 c. 25; section 35(1) was amended by section 45 of the Criminal Justice Act 2003 (c. 44). The amendment is in force for certain purposes, for remaining purposes it has effect from a date to be appointed. Section 35 was also amended by paragraphs 65 and 69 of Schedule 36 to the Criminal Justice Act 2003 (c. 44) and section 59 of, and paragraph 1 of Schedule 11 to, the Constitutional Reform Act 2005 (c. 4) and Part 10 of Schedule 10 to the Protection of Freedoms Act 2012 (c. 9).

(c)   2003 c. 44.

Service of appeal notice

66.2.—(1) An appellant must serve an appeal notice on—

(a)   the Crown Court officer;

(b)   the Registrar; and

(c)   every party directly affected by the order or ruling against which the appellant wants to appeal.

(2) The appellant must serve the appeal notice not more than 5 business days after—

(a)   the order or ruling against which the appellant wants to appeal; or

(b)   the Crown Court judge gives or refuses permission to appeal.

Form of appeal notice

66.3.—(1) An appeal notice must be in the form set out in the Practice Direction.

(2) The appeal notice must—

(a)   specify each order or ruling against which the appellant wants to appeal;

(b)   identify each ground of appeal on which the appellant relies, numbering them consecutively (if there is more than one) and concisely outlining each argument in support;

(c)   summarise the relevant facts;

(d)   identify any relevant authorities;

(e)   include or attach any application for the following, with reasons—

    (i)   permission to appeal, if the appellant needs the court's permission,

    (ii)   an extension of time within which to serve the appeal notice,

    (iii) a direction to attend in person a hearing that the appellant could attend by live link, if the appellant is in custody;

(f)   include a list of those on whom the appellant has served the appeal notice; and

(g)   attach—

    (i)   a transcript or note of each order or ruling against which the appellant wants to appeal,

(ii)   all relevant skeleton arguments considered by the Crown Court judge,

(iii)   any written application for permission to appeal that the appellant made to the Crown Court judge,

(iv)   a transcript or note of the decision by the Crown Court judge on any application for permission to appeal, and

(v)   any other document or thing that the appellant thinks the court will need to decide the appeal.

[Note. An appellant needs the court's permission to appeal in every case to which this Part applies unless the Crown Court judge gives permission.]

Crown Court judge's permission to appeal

66.4.—(1) An appellant who wants the Crown Court judge to give permission to appeal must—

(a)   apply orally, with reasons, immediately after the order or ruling against which the appellant wants to appeal; or

(b)   apply in writing and serve the application on—

(i)   the Crown Court officer, and

(ii)   every party directly affected by the order or ruling not more than 2 business days after that order or ruling.

(2) A written application must include the same information (with the necessary adaptations) as an appeal notice.

[Note. For the Crown Court judge's power to give permission to appeal, see section 9(11) of the Criminal Justice Act 1987, section 35(1) of the Criminal Procedure and Investigations Act 1996 and section 47(2) of the Criminal Justice Act 2003.]

Respondent's notice

66.5.—(1) A party on whom an appellant serves an appeal notice may serve a respondent's notice, and must do so if—

(a)   that party wants to make representations to the court; or

(b)   the court so directs.

(2) Such a party must serve the respondent's notice on—

(a)   the appellant;

(b)   the Crown Court officer;

(c)   the Registrar; and

(d)   any other party on whom the appellant served the appeal notice.

(3) Such a party must serve the respondent's notice not more than 5 business days after—

(a)   the appellant serves the appeal notice; or

(b)   a direction to do so.

(4) The respondent's notice must be in the form set out in the Practice Direction.

(5) The respondent's notice must—

(a)   give the date on which the respondent was served with the appeal notice;

(b)   identify each ground of opposition on which the respondent relies, numbering them consecutively (if there is more than one), concisely outlining each argument in support and identifying the ground of appeal to which each relates;

(c)   summarise any relevant facts not already summarised in the appeal notice;

(d)   identify any relevant authorities;

(e)   include or attach any application for the following, with reasons—

   (i)   an extension of time within which to serve the respondent's notice,

   (ii)   a direction to attend in person any hearing that the respondent could attend by live link, if the respondent is in custody;

(f)   identify any other document or thing that the respondent thinks the court will need to decide the appeal.

Powers of Court of Appeal judge

66.6.   A judge of the Court of Appeal may give permission to appeal as well as exercising the powers given by other legislation (including these Rules).

*[Note. See section 31 of the Criminal Appeal Act 1968(**a**) and section 49 of the Criminal Justice Act 2003(**b**).]*

(**a**)   1968 c. 19; section 31 was amended by section 21 of, and Schedule 2 to, the Costs in Criminal Cases Act 1973 (c. 14), section 24 of, and paragraph 10 of Schedule 6 to, the Road Traffic Act 1974 (c. 50), section 29 of the Criminal Justice Act 1982 (c. 48), section 170 of, and paragraphs 20, 29 and 30 of Schedule 15 to, the Criminal Justice Act 1988 (c. 33), section 4 of, and paragraph 4 of Schedule 3 to, the Road Traffic (Consequential Provisions) Act 1988 (c. 54), section 198 of, and paragraphs 38 and 40 of Schedule 6 to, the Licensing Act 2003 (c. 17), section 87 of the Courts Act 2003 (c. 39), section 331 of, and paragraphs 86, 87 and 88 of Schedule 36 to, the Criminal Justice Act 2003 (c. 44), section 48 of the Police and Justice Act 2006 (c. 48) and section 47 of, and paragraphs 1, 9 and 11 of Schedule 8 to, the Criminal Justice and Immigration Act 2008 (c. 4). It is further amended by section 67 of, and paragraph 4 of Schedule 4 to, the Youth Justice and Criminal Evidence Act 1999 (c. 23), with effect a date to be appointed.

(**b**)   2003 c. 44.

Renewing applications

66.7.   Rule 65.5 (renewing an application refused by a judge or the Registrar) applies with a time limit of 5 business days.

Right to attend hearing

66.8.—(1) A party who is in custody has a right to attend a hearing in public.

(2) The court or the Registrar may direct that such a party is to attend a hearing by live link.

[Note. See rule 65.6 (hearings).]

PART 67   APPEAL TO THE COURT OF APPEAL AGAINST RULING ADVERSE TO PROSECUTION

Contents of this Part

When this Part applies

67.1.—(1) This Part applies where a prosecutor wants to appeal under section 58(2) of the Criminal Justice Act 2003(**a**).

(2) A reference to an 'appellant' in this Part is a reference to such a prosecutor.

[Note. Under section 58(2) of the Criminal Justice Act 2003 a prosecutor may appeal to the Court of Appeal against a ruling in the Crown Court. See also sections 57 and 59 to 61 of the 2003 Act.

The rules in Part 65 also apply where this Part applies.]

(**a**)   2003 c. 44.

Decision to appeal

67.2.—(1) An appellant must tell the Crown Court judge of any decision to appeal—

(a)   immediately after the ruling against which the appellant wants to appeal; or

(b)   on the expiry of the time to decide whether to appeal allowed under paragraph (2).

(2) If an appellant wants time to decide whether to appeal—

(a)   the appellant must ask the Crown Court judge immediately after the ruling; and

(b)   the general rule is that the judge must not require the appellant to decide there and then but instead must allow until the next business day.

[Note. If the ruling against which the appellant wants to appeal is a ruling that there is no case to answer, the appellant may appeal against earlier rulings as well: see section 58(7) of the Criminal Justice Act 2003.

Under section 58(8) of the 2003 Act the appellant must agree that a defendant directly affected by the ruling must be acquitted if the appellant (a) does not get permission to appeal or (b) abandons the appeal.

The Crown Court judge may give permission to appeal and may expedite the appeal: see rules 67.5 and 67.6.]

Service of appeal notice

67.3.—(1) An appellant must serve an appeal notice on—

(a)   the Crown Court officer;

(b)   the Registrar; and

(c)   every defendant directly affected by the ruling against which the appellant wants to appeal.

(2) The appellant must serve the appeal notice not later than—

(a)   the next business day after telling the Crown Court judge of the decision to appeal, if the judge expedites the appeal; or

(b)   5 business days after telling the Crown Court judge of that decision, if the judge does not expedite the appeal.

[Note. If the ruling against which the appellant wants to appeal is a public interest ruling, see rule 67.8.]

Form of appeal notice

67.4.—(1) An appeal notice must be in the form set out in the Practice Direction.

(2) The appeal notice must—

(a)   specify each ruling against which the appellant wants to appeal;

(b)   identify each ground of appeal on which the appellant relies, numbering them consecutively (if there is more than one) and concisely outlining each argument in support;

(c)   summarise the relevant facts;

(d)   identify any relevant authorities;

(e)   include or attach any application for the following, with reasons—

    (i)   permission to appeal, if the appellant needs the court's permission,

    (ii)   an extension of time within which to serve the appeal notice,

    (iii)   expedition of the appeal, or revocation of a direction expediting the appeal;

(f)   include a list of those on whom the appellant has served the appeal notice;

(g)   attach—

    (i)   a transcript or note of each ruling against which the appellant wants to appeal,

    (ii)   all relevant skeleton arguments considered by the Crown Court judge,

    (iii)   any written application for permission to appeal that the appellant made to the Crown Court judge,

    (iv)   a transcript or note of the decision by the Crown Court judge on any application for permission to appeal,

    (v)   a transcript or note of the decision by the Crown Court judge on any request to expedite the appeal, and

    (vi)   any other document or thing that the appellant thinks the court will need to decide the appeal; and

(h)   attach a form of respondent's notice for any defendant served with the appeal notice to complete if that defendant wants to do so.

[Note. An appellant needs the court's permission to appeal unless the Crown Court judge gives permission: see section 57(4) of the Criminal Justice Act 2003. For 'respondent's notice' see rule 67.7.]

Crown Court judge's permission to appeal

67.5.—(1) An appellant who wants the Crown Court judge to give permission to appeal must—

(a)   apply orally, with reasons, immediately after the ruling against which the appellant wants to appeal; or

    (b)   apply in writing and serve the application on—

        (i)   the Crown Court officer, and

        (ii)   every defendant directly affected by the ruling on the expiry of the time allowed under rule 67.2 to decide whether to appeal.

(2) A written application must include the same information (with the necessary adaptations) as an appeal notice.

(3) The Crown Court judge must allow every defendant directly affected by the ruling an opportunity to make representations.

(4) The general rule is that the Crown Court judge must decide whether or not to give permission to appeal on the day that the application for permission is made.

[Note. For the Crown Court judge's power to give permission to appeal, see section 57(4) of the Criminal Justice Act 2003.

Rule 67.5(3) does not apply where the appellant wants to appeal against a public interest ruling: see rule 67.8(5).]

Expediting an appeal

67.6.—(1) An appellant who wants the Crown Court judge to expedite an appeal must ask, giving reasons, on telling the judge of the decision to appeal.

(2) The Crown Court judge must allow every defendant directly affected by the ruling an opportunity to make representations.

(3) The Crown Court judge may revoke a direction expediting the appeal unless the appellant has served the appeal notice.

[Note. For the Crown Court judge's power to expedite the appeal, see section 59 of the Criminal Justice Act 2003.

Rule 67.6(2) does not apply where the appellant wants to appeal against a public interest ruling: see rule 67.8(5).]

Respondent's notice

67.7.—(1) A defendant on whom an appellant serves an appeal notice may serve a respondent's notice, and must do so if—

(a)   the defendant wants to make representations to the court; or

(b)   the court so directs.

(2) Such a defendant must serve the respondent's notice on—

(a)   the appellant;

(b)   the Crown Court officer;

(c)   the Registrar; and

(d)   any other defendant on whom the appellant served the appeal notice.

(3) Such a defendant must serve the respondent's notice—

(a)   not later than the next business day after—

    (i)   the appellant serves the appeal notice, or

    (ii)   a direction to do so

    if the Crown Court judge expedites the appeal; or

(b)   not more than 5 business days after—

    (i)   the appellant serves the appeal notice, or

    (ii)   a direction to do so

    if the Crown Court judge does not expedite the appeal.

(4) The respondent's notice must be in the form set out in the Practice Direction.
(5) The respondent's notice must—

(a)   give the date on which the respondent was served with the appeal notice;

(b)   identify each ground of opposition on which the respondent relies, numbering them consecutively (if there is more than one), concisely outlining each argument in support and identifying the ground of appeal to which each relates;

(c)   summarise any relevant facts not already summarised in the appeal notice;

(d)   identify any relevant authorities;

(e)   include or attach any application for the following, with reasons—

    (i)   an extension of time within which to serve the respondent's notice,

    (ii)   a direction to attend in person any hearing that the respondent could attend by live link, if the respondent is in custody;

(f)   identify any other document or thing that the respondent thinks the court will need to decide the appeal.

Public interest ruling

67.8.—(1) This rule applies where the appellant wants to appeal against a public interest ruling.

(2) The appellant must not serve on any defendant directly affected by the ruling—

(a)   any written application to the Crown Court judge for permission to appeal; or

(b)   an appeal notice,

if the appellant thinks that to do so in effect would reveal something that the appellant thinks ought not be disclosed.

(3) The appellant must not include in an appeal notice—

(a)   the material that was the subject of the ruling; or

(b)   any indication of what sort of material it is,

if the appellant thinks that to do so in effect would reveal something that the appellant thinks ought not be disclosed.

(4) The appellant must serve on the Registrar with the appeal notice an annex—

(a)   marked to show that its contents are only for the court and the Registrar;

(b)   containing whatever the appellant has omitted from the appeal notice, with reasons; and

(c)   if relevant, explaining why the appellant has not served the appeal notice.

(5) Rules 67.5(3) and 67.6(2) do not apply.

[Note. Rules 67.5(3) and 67.6(2) require the Crown Court judge to allow a defendant to make representations about (i) giving permission to appeal and (ii) expediting an appeal.]

Powers of Court of Appeal judge

67.9.   A judge of the Court of Appeal may—

(a)   give permission to appeal;

(b)   revoke a Crown Court judge's direction expediting an appeal; and

(c)   where an appellant abandons an appeal, order a defendant's acquittal, his release from custody and the payment of his costs,

as well as exercising the powers given by other legislation (including these Rules).

[Note. See section 73 of the Criminal Justice Act 2003.]

Renewing applications

67.10.   Rule 65.5 (renewing an application refused by a judge or the Registrar) applies with a time limit of 5 business days.

Right to attend hearing

67.11.—(1) A respondent who is in custody has a right to attend a hearing in public.

(2) The court or the Registrar may direct that such a respondent is to attend a hearing by live link.

[Note. See rule 65.6 (hearings).]

PART 68   APPEAL TO THE COURT OF APPEAL ABOUT CONVICTION OR SENTENCE

Contents of this Part

When this Part applies

68.1.—(1) This Part applies where—

(a)   a defendant wants to appeal under—

    (i)   Part 1 of the Criminal Appeal Act 1968(**a**),

    (ii)   section 274(3) of the Criminal Justice Act 2003(**b**),

    (iii)   paragraph 14 of Schedule 22 to the Criminal Justice Act 2003(**c**), or

    (iv)   section 42 of the Counter Terrorism Act 2008(**d**);

(b)   the Criminal Cases Review Commission refers a case to the Court of Appeal under section 9 of the Criminal Appeal Act 1995(**e**);

(c)   a prosecutor wants to appeal to the Court of Appeal under section 14A(5A) of the Football Spectators Act 1989(**f**);

(d)   a party wants to appeal under section 74(8) of the Serious Organised Crime and Police Act 2005(**g**);

(e)   a person found in contempt of court wants to appeal under section 13 of the Administration of Justice Act 1960(**h**) and section 18A of the Criminal Appeal Act 1968(**a**); or

(f)   a person wants to appeal to the Court of Appeal under—

   (i)   section 24 of the Serious Crime Act 2007(**b**), or

   (ii)   regulation 3C or 3H of The Costs in Criminal Cases (General) Regulations 1986(**c**).

(2) A reference to an 'appellant' in this Part is a reference to such a party or person.

[Note. Under Part 1 (sections 1 to 32) of the Criminal Appeal Act 1968, a defendant may appeal against—

*(a)   a conviction (section 1 of the 1968 Act(**d**));*

*(b)   a sentence (sections 9 and 10 of the 1968 Act(**e**));*

*(c)   a verdict of not guilty by reason of insanity (section 12 of the 1968 Act); (d) a finding of disability (section 15 of the 1968 Act(**f**));*

*(e)   a hospital order, interim hospital order or supervision order under section 5 or 5A of the Criminal Procedure (Insanity) Act 1964(**g**) (section 16A of the 1968 Act(**h**)). See section 50 of the 1968 Act(**i**) for the meaning of 'sentence'.*

(**a**)   1968 c. 19.

(**b**)   2003 c. 44; section 274 was amended by section 40 of, and paragraph 82 of Schedule 9 to, the Constitutional Reform Act 2005 (c. 4).

(**c**)   2003 c. 44; paragraph 14 of Schedule 22 was amended by section 40 of, and paragraph 82 of Schedule 9 and paragraph 1 of Schedule 11 to, the Constitutional Reform Act 2005 (c. 4).

(**d**)   2008 c. 28.

(**e**)   1995 c. 35; section 9 was amended by section 58 of, and paragraph 31 of Schedule 10 to, the Domestic Violence, Crime and Victims Act 2004 (c. 28).

(**f**)   1989 c. 37; section 14A(5A) was inserted by section 52 of, and paragraphs 1 and 3 of Schedule 3 to, the Violent Crime Reduction Act 2006 (c. 38).

(**g**)   2005 c. 15.

(**h**)   1960 c. 65; section 13 was amended paragraph 40 of Schedule 8 to, the Courts Act 1971 (c. 23), Schedule 5 to, the Criminal Appeal Act 1968 (c. 19), paragraph 36 of Schedule 7 to, the Magistrates' Courts Act 1980 (c. 43), Schedule 7 to, the Supreme Court Act 1981 (c. 54), paragraph 25 of Schedule 2 to, the County Courts Act 1984 (c. 28), Schedule 15 to, the Access to Justice Act 1999 (c. 22), paragraph 13 of Schedule 9 to the Constitutional Reform Act 2005 (c. 4) and paragraph 45 of Schedule 16 to, the Armed Forces Act 2006 (c. 52).

(**a**)   1968 c. 19; section 18A was inserted by section 170 of, and paragraphs 20 and 25 of Schedule 15 to, the Criminal Justice Act 1988 (c. 33).

(**b**)   2007 c. 27.

(**c**)   S.I. 1986/1335; regulation 3C was inserted by regulation 2 of The Costs in Criminal Cases (General) (Amendment) Regulations 1991 (SI 1991/789) and amended by regulation 5 of The Costs in Criminal Cases (General) (Amendment) Regulations 2004 (SI 2004/2408). Regulation 3H was inserted by regulation 7 of The Costs in Criminal Cases (General) (Amendment) Regulations 2004 (SI 2004/2408).

(**d**)   1968 c. 19; section 1 was amended by section 154 of, and paragraph 71 of Schedule 7 to, the Magistrates' Courts Act 1980 (c. 43), paragraph 44 of Schedule 3 to the Criminal Justice

Act 2003 (c. 44), section 1 of the Criminal Appeal Act 1995 (c. 35) and section 47 of, and paragraphs 1 and 2 of Schedule 8 to, the Criminal Justice and Immigration Act 2008 (c. 4).

(e)   1968 c. 19; section 9 was amended by section 170 of, and paragraph 21 of Schedule 15 to, the Criminal Justice Act 1988 (c. 33), section 119 of, and paragraph 12 of Schedule 8 to, the Crime and Disorder Act 1998 (c. 37), section 58 of the Access to Justice Act 1999 (c. 22) and section 271 of, and paragraph 44 of Schedule 3 and Schedule 37 to, the Criminal Justice Act 2003 (c. 44). Section 10 was amended by section 56 of, and paragraph 57 of Schedule 8 to, the Courts Act 1971 (c. 23), section 77 of, and paragraph 23 of Schedule 14 to, the Criminal Justice Act 1982 (c. 48), section 170 of, and paragraphs 20 and 22 of Schedule 15 and Schedule 16 to, the Criminal Justice Act 1988 (c. 33), section 100 of, and paragraph 3 of Schedule 11 to, the Criminal Justice Act 1991 (c. 53), sections 119 and 120 of, and paragraph 13 of Schedule 8 and Schedule 10 to, the Crime and Disorder Act 1998 (c. 37), section 58 of the Access to Justice Act 1999 (c. 22), section 67 of, and paragraph 4 of Schedule 4 and Schedule 6 to, the Youth Justice and Criminal Evidence Act 1999 (c. 23), section 304 and 319 of, and paragraphs 7 and 8 of Schedule 32 and Schedule 37 to, the Criminal Justice Act 2003 (c. 44) and section 6(2) of, and paragraph 4 of Schedule 4 to, the Criminal Justice and Immigration Act 2008 (c. 4). It is further amended by section 332 of, and Schedule 37 to, the Criminal Justice Act 2003 (c. 44), with effect from a date to be appointed.

(f)   1968 c. 19; section 15 was amended by section 7 of, and paragraph 2 of Schedule 3 to, the Criminal Procedure (Insanity and Unfitness to Plead) Act 1991 (c. 25), section 1 of the Criminal Appeal Act 1995 (c. 35) and section 58 of, and paragraph 4 of Schedule 10 to, the Domestic Violence, Crime and Victims Act 2004 (c. 28) and section 47 of, and paragraphs 1 and 5 of Schedule 8 to, the Criminal Justice and Immigration Act 2008 (c. 4).

(g)   1964 c. 84; section 5 was substituted, and section 5A inserted, by section 24 of the Domestic Violence, Crime and Victims Act 2004 (c. 28). Section 5A was amended by section 15 of the Mental Health Act 2007 (c. 12).

(h)   1968 c. 19; section 16A was inserted by section 25 of the Domestic Violence, Crime and Victims Act 2004 (c. 28).

(i)   1968 c. 19; section 50 was amended by section 66 of the Criminal Justice Act 1982 (c. 48), sections 100 and 101 of, and paragraph 4 of Schedule 11 and Schedule 13 to, the Criminal Justice Act 1991 (c. 53), section 79 of, and Schedule 5 to, the Criminal Justice Act 1993 (c. 36), section 65 of, and Schedule 1 to, the Drug Trafficking Act 1994 (c. 37), section 7 of the Football (Offences and Disorder) Act 1999 (c. 21), section 24 of, and paragraph 3 of Schedule 4 to, the Access to Justice Act 1999 (c. 22), section 165 of, and paragraph 30 of Schedule 9 to, the Powers of Criminal Courts (Sentencing) Act 2000 (c. 6), section 1 of, and Schedule 3 to, the Football (Disorder) Act 2000 (c. 25), section 456 of, and paragraphs 1 and 4 of Schedule 11 to, the Proceeds of Crime Act 2002 (c. 43), section 198 of, and paragraphs 38 and 42 of Schedule 6 to, the Licensing Act 2003 (c. 17), section 52 of, and paragraph 14 of Schedule 3 to, the Violent Crime Reduction Act 2006 (c. 38) and paragraph 3 of Schedule 5 to the Legal Aid, Sentencing and Punishment of Offenders Act 2012 (c. 10). It is further amended by section 55 of, and paragraph 6 of Schedule 4 to, the Crime (Sentences) Act 1997 (c. 43), with effect from a date to be appointed.

Under section 274(3) of the 2003 Act, a defendant sentenced to life imprisonment outside the United Kingdom, and transferred to serve the sentence in England and Wales, may appeal against the minimum term fixed by a High Court judge under section 82A of the Powers of Criminal Courts (Sentencing) Act 2000 or under section 269 of the 2003 Act.

Under paragraph 14 of Schedule 22 to the Criminal Justice Act 2003 a defendant sentenced to life imprisonment may appeal against the minimum term fixed on review by a High Court judge in certain cases.

Under section 42 of the Counter Terrorism Act 2008 a defendant may appeal against a decision of the Crown Court that an offence has a terrorist connection.

207

*See section 13 of the Criminal Appeal Act 1995(**a**) for the circumstances in which the Criminal Cases Review Commission may refer a conviction, sentence, verdict or finding to the Court of Appeal.*

Under section 14A(5A) of the Football Spectators Act 1989 a prosecutor may appeal against a failure by the Crown Court to make a football banning order.

Under section 74(8) of the Serious Organised Crime and Police Act 2005 a prosecutor or defendant may appeal against a review by a Crown Court judge of a sentence that was reduced because the defendant assisted the investigator or prosecutor.

Under section 13 of the Administration of Justice Act 1960 a person in respect of whom an order or decision is made by the Crown Court in the exercise of its jurisdiction to punish for contempt of court may appeal to the Court of Appeal.

Under section 24 of the Serious Crime Act 2007 a person who is the subject of a serious crime prevention order, or the relevant applicant authority, may appeal to the Court of Appeal against a decision of the Crown Court in relation to that order. In addition, any person who was given an opportunity to make representations in the proceedings by virtue of section 9(4) of the Act may appeal to the Court of Appeal against a decision of the Crown Court to make, vary or not vary a serious crime prevention order.

*Under regulation 3C of The Costs in Criminal Cases (General) Regulations 1986, a legal representative against whom the Crown Court makes a wasted costs order under section 19A of the Prosecution of Offences Act 1985(**b**) and regulation 3B may appeal against that order to the Court of Appeal.*

*Under regulation 3H of The Costs in Criminal Cases (General) Regulations 1986, a third party against whom the Crown Court makes a costs order under section 19B of the Prosecution of Offences Act 1985(**c**) and regulation 3F may appeal against that order to the Court of Appeal.*

The rules in Part 65 also apply where this Part applies.]

(**a**)   1995 c. 35; section 13 was amended by section 321 of, and paragraph 3 of Schedule 11 to, the Armed Forces Act 2006 (c. 52).
(**b**)   1985 c. 23; section 19A was inserted by section 111 of the Courts and Legal Services Act 1990 (c. 41).
(**c**)   1985 c. 23; section 19B was inserted by section 93 of the Courts Act 2003 (c. 39).

Service of appeal notice

68.2.—(1) The general rule is that an appellant must serve an appeal notice—

(a)   on the Crown Court officer at the Crown Court centre where there occurred—

   (i)   the conviction, verdict, or finding,

   (ii)   the sentence, or

    (iii)   the order, or the failure to make an order about which the appellant wants to appeal; and

(b)   not more than—

    (i)   28 days after that occurred, or

    (ii)   21 days after the order, in a case in which the appellant appeals against a wasted or third party costs order.

(2) But an appellant must serve an appeal notice—

(a)   on the Registrar instead where—

    (i)   the appeal is against a minimum term review decision under section 274(3) of, or paragraph 14 of Schedule 22 to, the Criminal Justice Act 2003, or

    (ii)   the Criminal Cases Review Commission refers the case to the court; and

(b)   not more than 28 days after—

    (i)   the minimum term review decision about which the appellant wants to appeal, or

    (ii)   the Registrar serves notice that the Commission has referred a conviction.

[Note. The time limit for serving an appeal notice (a) on an appeal under Part 1 of the Criminal Appeal Act 1968 and (b) on an appeal against a finding of contempt of court is prescribed by sections 18 and 18A of the Criminal Appeal Act 1968. It may be extended, but not shortened.

For service of a reference by the Criminal Cases Review Commission, see rule 68.5.]

Form of appeal notice

68.3.—(1) An appeal notice must be in the form set out in the Practice Direction.

(2) The appeal notice must—

(a)   specify—

    (i)   the conviction, verdict, or finding, (ii) the sentence, or

    (iii)   the order, or the failure to make an order about which the appellant wants to appeal;

(b)   identify each ground of appeal on which the appellant relies, numbering them consecutively (if there is more than one) and concisely outlining each argument in support;

(c)   identify the transcript that the appellant thinks the court will need, if the appellant wants to appeal against a conviction;

(d)   identify the relevant sentencing powers of the Crown Court, if sentence is in issue;

(e)   where the Criminal Cases Review Commission refers a case to the court, explain how each ground of appeal relates (if it does) to the reasons for the reference;

(f)   summarise the relevant facts;

(g)   identify any relevant authorities;

(h)   include or attach any application for the following, with reasons—

    (i)   permission to appeal, if the appellant needs the court's permission,

    (ii)   an extension of time within which to serve the appeal notice,

    (iii)   bail pending appeal,

    (iv)   a direction to attend in person a hearing that the appellant could attend by live link, if the appellant is in custody,

    (v)   the introduction of evidence, including hearsay evidence and evidence of bad character,

    (vi)   an order requiring a witness to attend court, (vii) a direction for special measures for a witness,

    (viii)   a direction for special measures for the giving of evidence by the appellant;

(i)   identify any other document or thing that the appellant thinks the court will need to decide the appeal.

[Note. In some legislation, including the Criminal Appeal Act 1968, permission to appeal is described as 'leave to appeal'.

An appellant needs the court's permission to appeal in every case to which this Part applies, except where—

(a)   the Criminal Cases Review Commission refers the case;

(b)   the appellant appeals against—

    (i)   an order or decision made in the exercise of jurisdiction to punish for contempt of court, or

    (ii)   a wasted or third party costs order; or

*(c)   the Crown Court judge certifies under sections 1(2)(a), 11(1A), 12(b), 15(2)(b) or 16A(2)(b) of the Criminal Appeal Act 1968(**a**), under section 81(1B) of the Senior Courts Act 1981(**b**), under section 14A(5B) of the Football Spectators Act 1989(**c**), or under section 24(4) of the Serious Crime Act 2007, that a case is fit for appeal.*

*A judge of the Court of Appeal may give permission to appeal under section 31 of the Criminal Appeal Act 1968(**d**).]*

(a) 1968 c. 19; section 11(1A) was inserted by section 29 of the Criminal Justice Act 1982 (c. 48) and amended by section 47 of, and paragraphs 1 and 3 of Schedule 8 to, the Criminal Justice and Immigration Act 2008 (c. 4).

(b) 1981 c. 54; section 81(1B) was inserted by sections 29 and 60 of the Criminal Justice Act 1982 (c. 48). The Act's title was amended by section 59(5) of, and paragraph 1 of Schedule 11 to, the Constitutional Reform Act 2005 (c. 4).

(c) 1989 c. 37; section 14A(5B) was inserted by section 52 of, and paragraphs 1 and 3 of Schedule 3 to, the Violent Crime Reduction Act 2006 (c. 38).

(d) 1968 c. 19; section 31 was amended by section 21 of, and Schedule 2 to, the Costs in Criminal Cases Act 1973 (c. 14), section 24 of, and paragraph 10 of Schedule 6 to, the Road Traffic Act 1974 (c. 50), section 29 of the Criminal Justice Act 1982 (c. 48), section 170 of, and paragraphs 20, 29 and 30 of Schedule 15 to, the Criminal Justice Act 1988 (c. 33), section 4 of, and paragraph 4 of Schedule 3 to, the Road Traffic (Consequential Provisions) Act 1988 (c. 54), section 198 of, and paragraphs 38 and 40 of Schedule 6 to, the Licensing Act 2003 (c. 17), section 87 of the Courts Act 2003 (c. 39), section 331 of, and paragraphs 86, 87 and 88 of Schedule 36 to, the Criminal Justice Act 2003 (c. 44), section 48 of the Police and Justice Act 2006 (c. 48) and section 47 of, and paragraphs 1, 9 and 11 of Schedule 8 to, the Criminal Justice and Immigration Act 2008 (c. 4). It is further amended by section 67 of, and paragraph 4 of Schedule 4 to, the Youth Justice and Criminal Evidence Act 1999 (c. 23), with effect from a date to be appointed.

Crown Court judge's certificate that case is fit for appeal

68.4.—(1) An appellant who wants the Crown Court judge to certify that a case is fit for appeal must—

(a)   apply orally, with reasons, immediately after there occurs—

    (i)   the conviction, verdict, or finding,

    (ii)   the sentence, or

    (iii)   the order, or the failure to make an order about which the appellant wants to appeal; or

(b)   apply in writing and serve the application on the Crown Court officer not more than 14 days after that occurred.

(2) A written application must include the same information (with the necessary adaptations) as an appeal notice.

[Note. The Crown Court judge may certify that a case is fit for appeal under sections 1(2)(b), 11(1A), 12(b), 15(2)(b) or 16A(2)(b) of the Criminal Appeal Act 1968, under section 81(1B) of the Senior Courts Act 1981, under section 14A(5B) of the Football Spectators Act 1989 or under section 24(4) of the Serious Crime Act 2007.

See also rule 68.2 (service of appeal notice in all cases).]

Reference by Criminal Cases Review Commission

68.5.—(1) The Registrar must serve on the appellant a reference by the Criminal Cases Review Commission.

(2) The court must treat that reference as the appeal notice if the appellant does not serve such a notice under rule 68.2.

Respondent's notice

68.6.—(1) The Registrar—

(a)   may serve an appeal notice on any party directly affected by the appeal; and

(b)   must do so if the Criminal Cases Review Commission refers a conviction, verdict, finding or sentence to the court.

(2) Such a party may serve a respondent's notice, and must do so if—

(a)   that party wants to make representations to the court; or

(b)   the court or the Registrar so directs.

(3) Such a party must serve the respondent's notice on—

(a)   the appellant;

(b)   the Registrar; and

(c)   any other party on whom the Registrar served the appeal notice.

(4) Such a party must serve the respondent's notice—

(a)   not more than 14 days after the Registrar serves—

   (i)   the appeal notice, or

   (ii)   a direction to do so; or

(b)   not more than 28 days after the Registrar serves notice that the Commission has referred a conviction.

(5) The respondent's notice must be in the form set out in the Practice Direction.

(6) The respondent's notice must—

(a)   give the date on which the respondent was served with the appeal notice;

(b)   identify each ground of opposition on which the respondent relies, numbering them consecutively (if there is more than one), concisely outlining each argument in support and identifying the ground of appeal to which each relates;

(c)   identify the relevant sentencing powers of the Crown Court, if sentence is in issue;

(d)   summarise any relevant facts not already summarised in the appeal notice;

(e)   identify any relevant authorities;

(f)   include or attach any application for the following, with reasons—

    (i)   an extension of time within which to serve the respondent's notice,

    (ii)   bail pending appeal,

    (iii)   a direction to attend in person a hearing that the respondent could attend by live link, if the respondent is in custody,

    (iv)   the introduction of evidence, including hearsay evidence and evidence of bad character,

    (v)   an order requiring a witness to attend court,

    (vi)   a direction for special measures for a witness; and

(g)   identify any other document or thing that the respondent thinks the court will need to decide the appeal.

[Note. Part II of the Practice Direction sets out the circumstances in which the Registrar usually will serve a defendant's appeal notice on the prosecutor.]

Adaptation of rules about introducing evidence

68.7.—(1) The following Parts apply with such adaptations as the court or the Registrar may direct—

(a)   Part 29 (measures to assist a witness or defendant to give evidence);

(b)   Part 34 (hearsay evidence);

(c)   Part 35 (evidence of bad character); and

(d)   Part 36 (evidence of a complainant's previous sexual behaviour).

(2) But the general rule is that—

(a)   a respondent who opposes an appellant's application to which one of those Parts applies must do so in the respondent's notice, with reasons;

(b)   an appellant who opposes a respondent's application to which one of those Parts applies must serve notice, with reasons, on—

    (i)   the Registrar, and

    (ii)   the respondent

    not more than 14 days after service of the respondent's notice; and

(c)   the court or the Registrar may give directions with or without a hearing.

[Note. An application to introduce evidence or for directions about evidence must be included in, or attached to, an appeal notice or a respondent's notice: see rule 68.3 and 68.6(6).]

*Under section 23 of the Criminal Appeal Act 1968(**a**), the Court of Appeal may allow the introduction of evidence that was not introduced at trial.*

See also Part 27 (witness statements) and Part 33 (expert evidence).]

Application for bail pending appeal or retrial

68.8.—(1) This rule applies where a party wants to make an application to the court about bail pending appeal or retrial.

(2) That party must serve an application in the form set out in the Practice Direction on—

(a)   the Registrar, unless the application is with the appeal notice; and

(b)   the other party.

(3) The court must not decide such an application without giving the other party an opportunity to make representations, including representations about any condition or surety proposed by the applicant.

*[Note. See section 19 of the Criminal Appeal Act 1968(**b**) and section 3(8) of the Bail Act 1976(**c**). An application about bail or about the conditions of bail may be made either by an appellant or respondent.*

*Under section 81(1) of the Senior Courts Act 1981(**a**), a Crown Court judge may grant bail pending appeal only (a) if that judge gives a certificate that the case is fit for appeal (see rule 68.4) and (b) not more than 28 days after the conviction or sentence against which the appellant wants to appeal.]*

(**a**)   1968 c. 19; section 23 was amended by sections 4 and 29 of, and paragraph 4 of Schedule 2 to, the Criminal Appeal Act 1995 (c. 35), section 48 of the Police and Justice Act 2006 (c. 48) and section 47 of, and paragraphs 1 and 10 of Schedule 8 to, the Criminal Justice and Immigration Act 2008 (c. 4).

(**b**)   1968 c. 19; section 19 was substituted by section 29 of the Criminal Justice Act 1982 (c. 48) and was amended by section 170 of, and paragraphs 20 and 26 of Schedule 15 to, the Criminal Justice Act 1988 (c. 33), section 168 of, and paragraph 22 of Schedule 10 to, the Criminal Justice and Public Order Act 1994 (c. 33) and section 59 of, and paragraph 1 of Schedule 11 to, the Constitutional Reform Act 2005 (c. 4).

(**c**)   1976 c. 63; section 3(8) was amended by section 65 of, and Schedule 12 to, the Criminal Law Act 1977 (c. 45) and paragraph 48 of Schedule 3 to the Criminal Justice Act 2003 (c. 44).

Conditions of bail pending appeal or retrial

68.9.—(1) This rule applies where the court grants a party bail pending appeal or retrial subject to any condition that must be met before that party is released.

(2) The court may direct how such a condition must be met.

(3) The Registrar must serve a certificate in the form set out in the Practice Direction recording any such condition and direction on—

(a)   that party;

(b)   that party's custodian; and

(c)   any other person directly affected by any such direction.

(4) A person directly affected by any such direction need not comply with it until the Registrar serves that person with that certificate.

(5) Unless the court otherwise directs, if any such condition or direction requires someone to enter into a recognizance it must be—

(a)   in the form set out in the Practice Direction and signed before—

    (i)   the Registrar,

    (ii)   the custodian, or

    (iii)   someone acting with the authority of the Registrar or custodian;

(b)   copied immediately to the person who enters into it; and

(c)   served immediately by the Registrar on the appellant's custodian or vice versa, as appropriate.

(6) Unless the court otherwise directs, if any such condition or direction requires someone to make a payment, surrender a document or take some other step—

(a) that payment, document or step must be made, surrendered or taken to or before—

    (i)   the Registrar,

    (ii)   the custodian, or

    (iii)   someone acting with the authority of the Registrar or custodian;

(b)   the Registrar or the custodian, as appropriate, must serve immediately on the other a statement that the payment, document or step has been made, surrendered or taken, as appropriate.

(7) The custodian must release the appellant where it appears that any condition ordered by the court has been met.

(8) For the purposes of section 5 of the Bail Act 1976(**b**) (record of decision about bail), the Registrar must keep a copy of—

(a)   any certificate served under paragraph (3);

(b)   a notice of hearing given under rule 65.7(1); and

(c)   a notice of the court's decision served under rule 65.7(2).

(9) Where the court grants bail pending retrial the Registrar must serve on the Crown Court officer copies of the documents kept under paragraph (8).

(**a**) 1981 c. 54; section 81(1) was amended by sections 29 and 60 of the Criminal Justice Act 1982 (c. 48), section 15 of, and paragraph 2 of Schedule 12 to, the Criminal Justice Act 1987 (c. 38), section 168 of, and paragraph 19 of Schedule 9 and paragraph 48 of Schedule 10 to, the Criminal Justice and Public Order Act 1994 (c. 33), section 119 of, and paragraph 48 of Schedule 8 and Schedule 10 to, the Crime and Disorder Act 1998 (c. 37), section 165 of, and paragraph 87 of Schedule 9 and Schedule 12 to, the Powers of Criminal Courts (Sentencing) Act 2000 (c. 6), paragraph 54 of Schedule 3, paragraph 4 of Schedule 36 and Part 4 of Schedule 37 to the Criminal Justice Act 2003 (c. 44), articles 2 and 6 of S.I. 2004/1033 and section 177(1) of, and paragraph 76 of Schedule 21 to, the Coroners and Justice Act 2009 (c. 25).

(**b**) 1976 c. 63; section 5 was amended by section 65 of, and Schedule 12 to, the Criminal Law Act 1977 (c. 45), section 60 of the Criminal Justice Act 1982 (c. 48), paragraph 1 of Schedule 3 to the Criminal Justice and Public Order Act 1994 (c. 33), paragraph 53 of Schedule 9 to the Powers of Criminal Courts (Sentencing) Act 2000 (c. 6), section 129(1) of the Criminal Justice and Police Act 2001 (c. 16), paragraph 182 of Schedule 8 to the Courts Act 2003 (c. 39), paragraph 48 of Schedule 3, paragraphs 1 and 2 of Schedule 36, and Parts 2, 4 and 12 of Schedule 37 to the Criminal Justice Act 2003 (c. 44) and section 208 of, and paragraphs 33 and 35 of Schedule 21 to, the Legal Services Act 2007 (c. 27).

Forfeiture of a recognizance given as a condition of bail

68.10.—(1) This rule applies where—

(a)   the court grants a party bail pending appeal or retrial; and

(b)   the bail is subject to a condition that that party provides a surety to guarantee that he will surrender to custody as required; but

(c)   that party does not surrender to custody as required.

(2) The Registrar must serve notice on—

(a) the surety; and

(b) the prosecutor,

of the hearing at which the court may order the forfeiture of the recognizance given by that surety.

(3) The court must not forfeit a surety's recognizance—

(a)   less than 7 days after the Registrar serves notice under paragraph (2); and

(b)   without giving the surety an opportunity to make representations at a hearing.

[Note. If the purpose for which a recognizance is entered is not fulfilled, that recognizance may be forfeited by the court. If the court forfeits a surety's recognizance, the sum promised by that person is then payable to the Crown.]

Right to attend hearing

68.11.   A party who is in custody has a right to attend a hearing in public unless—

(a)   it is a hearing preliminary or incidental to an appeal, including the hearing of an application for permission to appeal; or

(b)   that party is in custody in consequence of—

    (i)   a verdict of not guilty by reason of insanity, or

    (ii)   a finding of disability.

[Note. See rule 65.6 (hearings) and section 22 of the Criminal Appeal Act 1968(a). There are corresponding provisions in The Criminal Justice Act 2003 (Mandatory Life Sentences: Appeals in Transitional Cases) Order 2005(b), The Serious Organised Crime and Police Act 2005 (Appeals under section 74) Order 2006(c) and The Serious Crime Act 2007 (Appeals under Section 24) Order 2008(d). Under section 22 of the 1968 Act and corresponding provisions in those Orders, the court may direct that an appellant who is in custody is to attend a hearing by live link.]

(**a**)   1968 c. 19; section 22 was amended by section 48 of the Police and Justice Act 2006 (c. 48).
(**b**)   S.I. 2005/2798.
(**c**)   S.I. 2006/2135.
(**d**)   S.I. 2008/1863.

Power to vary determination of appeal against sentence

68.12.—(1) This rule applies where the court decides an appeal affecting sentence in a party's absence.

(2) The court may vary such a decision if it did not take account of something relevant because that party was absent.

(3) A party who wants the court to vary such a decision must—

(a)   apply in writing, with reasons;

(b)   serve the application on the Registrar not more than 7 days after—

    (i)   the decision, if that party was represented at the appeal hearing, or

    (ii)   the Registrar serves the decision, if that party was not represented at that hearing.

[Note. Section 22(3) of the Criminal Appeal Act 1968 allows the court to sentence in an appellant's absence. There are corresponding provisions in The Criminal Justice Act 2003 (Mandatory Life Sentences: Appeals in Transitional Cases) Order 2005 and in The Serious Organised Crime and Police Act 2005 (Appeals under Section 74) Order 2006.]

Directions about re-admission to hospital on dismissal of appeal

68.13.—(1) This rule applies where—

(a)   an appellant subject to—

    (i)   an order under section 37(1) of the Mental Health Act 1983(**a**) (detention in hospital on conviction), or

    (ii)   an order under section 5(2) of the Criminal Procedure (Insanity) Act 1964(**b**) (detention in hospital on finding of insanity or disability)

has been released on bail pending appeal; and

(b)   the court—

    (i)   refuses permission to appeal,

    (ii)   dismisses the appeal, or

    (iii) affirms the order under appeal.

(2) The court must give appropriate directions for the appellant's—

(a)   re-admission to hospital; and

(b)   if necessary, temporary detention pending re-admission.

Renewal or setting aside of order for retrial

68.14.—(1) This rule applies where—

(a)   a prosecutor wants a defendant to be arraigned more than 2 months after the court ordered a retrial under section 7 of the Criminal Appeal Act 1968(**c**); or

(b)   a defendant wants such an order set aside after 2 months have passed since it was made.

(2) That party must apply in writing, with reasons, and serve the application on—

(a)   the Registrar;

(b)   the other party.

*[Note. Section 8(1) and (1A) of the Criminal Appeal Act 1968(**d**) set out the criteria for making an order on an application to which this rule applies.]*

(**a**) 1983 c. 20; section 37(1) was amended by section 55 of, and paragraph 12 of Schedule 4 to, the Crime (Sentences) Act 1997 (c. 43) and section 304 of, and paragraphs 37 and 38 of Schedule 32 to, the Criminal Justice Act 2003 (c. 44).

(**b**) 1964 c. 84.

(**c**) 1968 c.19; section 7 was amended by sections 43 and 170 of, and Schedule 16 to, the Criminal Justice Act 1988 (c. 33) and section 331 of, and paragraph 44 of Schedule 36 to, the Criminal Justice Act 2003 (c. 44).

(**d**) 1968 c.19; section 8(1) was amended by section 56 of, and Part IV of Schedule 11 to, the Courts Act 1971 (c. 23) and section 43 of the Criminal Justice Act 1988 (c. 33). Section 8(1A) was inserted by section 43(4) of the Criminal Justice Act 1988 (c. 33).

PART 69   APPEAL TO THE COURT OF APPEAL REGARDING REPORTING OR PUBLIC ACCESS RESTRICTION

Contents of this Part

When this Part applies

69.1.—(1) This Part applies where a person directly affected by an order to which section 159(1) of the Criminal Justice Act 1988(**a**) applies wants to appeal against that order.

(2) A reference to an 'appellant' in this Part is a reference to such a party.

[Note. Section 159(1) of the Criminal Justice Act 1988 gives a 'person aggrieved' (in this Part described as a person directly affected) a right of appeal to the Court of Appeal against a Crown Court judge's order—

*(a)   under section 4 or 11 of the Contempt of Court Act 1981(**b**);*

*(b)   under section 58(7) of the Criminal Procedure and Investigations Act 1996(**c**);*

(c)   restricting public access to any part of a trial for reasons of national security or for the protection of a witness or other person; or

(d)   restricting the reporting of any part of a trial.

See also Part 16 (Reporting, etc. restrictions) and Part 29 (Measures to assist a witness or defendant to give evidence).

The rules in Part 65 also apply where this Part applies.]

(**a**) 1988 c. 33; section 159(1) was amended by section 61 of the Criminal Procedure and Investigations Act 1996 (c. 25).
(**b**) 1981 c. 49; section 4 was amended by section 57 of the Criminal Procedure and Investigations Act 1996 (c. 25), section 16 of, and Schedule 2 to, the Defamation Act 1996 (c. 31), paragraph 53 of Schedule 3 to the Criminal Justice Act 2003 (c. 44) and the Statute Law (Repeals) Act 2004 (c. 14).
(**c**) 1996 c. 25.

Service of appeal notice

69.2.—(1) An appellant must serve an appeal notice on—

(a)   the Crown Court officer;

(b)   the Registrar;

(c)   the parties; and

(d)   any other person directly affected by the order against which the appellant wants to appeal.

(2) The appellant must serve the appeal notice not later than—

(a)   the next business day after an order restricting public access to the trial;

(b)   10 business days after an order restricting reporting of the trial.

Form of appeal notice

69.3.—(1) An appeal notice must be in the form set out in the Practice Direction.

(2) The appeal notice must—

(a)   specify the order against which the appellant wants to appeal;

(b)   identify each ground of appeal on which the appellant relies, numbering them consecutively (if there is more than one) and concisely outlining each argument in support;

(c)   summarise the relevant facts;

(d)   identify any relevant authorities;

(e)   include or attach, with reasons—

   (i)   an application for permission to appeal,

   (ii)   any application for an extension of time within which to serve the appeal notice,

   (iii) any application for a direction to attend in person a hearing that the appellant could attend by live link, if the appellant is in custody,

   (iv) any application for permission to introduce evidence, and

   (v)   a list of those on whom the appellant has served the appeal notice; and

(f)   attach any document or thing that the appellant thinks the court will need to decide the appeal.

[Note. An appellant needs the court's permission to appeal in every case to which this Part applies.

220

*A Court of Appeal judge may give permission to appeal under section 31(2B)
of the Criminal Appeal Act 1968(a).]*

(a) 1968 c. 19; section 31(2B) was inserted by section 170 of, and paragraphs 20 and 30 of
Schedule 15 to, the Criminal Justice Act 1988 (c. 33).

Advance notice of appeal against order restricting public access

69.4.—(1) This rule applies where the appellant wants to appeal against an
order restricting public access to a trial.

(2) The appellant may serve advance written notice of intention to appeal
against any such order that may be made.

(3) The appellant must serve any such advance notice—

(a)   on—

    (i)   the Crown Court officer,

    (ii)   the Registrar,

    (iii)   the parties, and

    (iv)   any other person who will be directly affected by the order against
which the appellant intends to appeal, if it is made; and

(b)   not more than 5 business days after the Crown Court officer displays
notice of the application for the order.

(4) The advance notice must include the same information (with the necessary
adaptations) as an appeal notice.

(5) The court must treat that advance notice as the appeal notice if the order is
made.

Duty of applicant for order restricting public access

69.5.—(1) This rule applies where the appellant wants to appeal against an
order restricting public access to a trial.

(2) The party who applied for the order must serve on the Registrar—

(a)   a transcript or note of the application for the order; and

(b)   any other document or thing that that party thinks the court will need to
decide the appeal.

(3) That party must serve that transcript or note and any such other document
or thing as soon as practicable after—

(a)   the appellant serves the appeal notice; or

(b)   the order, where the appellant served advance notice of intention to appeal.

Respondent's notice on appeal against reporting restriction

69.6.—(1) This rule applies where the appellant wants to appeal against an order restricting the reporting of a trial.

(2) A person on whom an appellant serves an appeal notice may serve a respondent's notice, and must do so if—

(a)   that person wants to make representations to the court; or

(b)   the court so directs.

(3) Such a person must serve the respondent's notice on—

(a)   the appellant;

(b)   the Crown Court officer;

(c)   the Registrar;

(d)   the parties; and

(e)   any other person on whom the appellant served the appeal notice.

(4) Such a person must serve the respondent's notice not more than 3 business days after—

(a)   the appellant serves the appeal notice; or

(b)   a direction to do so.

(5) The respondent's notice must be in the form set out in the Practice Direction.

(6) The respondent's notice must—

(a)   give the date on which the respondent was served with the appeal notice;

(b)   identify each ground of opposition on which the respondent relies, numbering them consecutively (if there is more than one), concisely outlining each argument in support and identifying the ground of appeal to which each relates;

(c)   summarise any relevant facts not already summarised in the appeal notice;

(d)   identify any relevant authorities;

(e)   include or attach any application for the following, with reasons—

(i)   an extension of time within which to serve the respondent's notice,

(ii)   a direction to attend in person any hearing that the respondent could attend by live link, if the respondent is in custody,

(iii) permission to introduce evidence; and

(f)   identify any other document or thing that the respondent thinks the court will need to decide the appeal.

Renewing applications

69.7.   Rule 65.5 (renewing an application refused by a judge or the Registrar) applies with a time limit of 5 business days.

Right to introduce evidence

69.8.   No person may introduce evidence without the court's permission.

[Note. Section 159(4) of the Criminal Justice Act 1988 entitles the parties to give evidence, subject to procedure rules.]

Right to attend hearing

69.9.—(1) A party who is in custody has a right to attend a hearing in public of an appeal against an order restricting the reporting of a trial.

(2) The court or the Registrar may direct that such a party is to attend a hearing by live link.

[Note. See rule 65.6 (hearings). The court must decide an application and an appeal without a hearing where the appellant wants to appeal against an order restricting public access to a trial: rule 65.6(3).]

PART 70   REFERENCE TO THE COURT OF APPEAL OF POINT OF LAW OR UNDULY LENIENT SENTENCING

Contents of this Part

When this Part applies

70.1.   This Part applies where the Attorney General wants to—

(a)   refer a point of law to the Court of Appeal under section 36 of the Criminal Justice Act 1972(**a**); or

(b)   refer a sentencing case to the Court of Appeal under section 36 of the Criminal Justice Act 1988(**b**).

[Note. Under section 36 of the Criminal Justice Act 1972, where a defendant is acquitted in the Crown Court the Attorney General may refer to the Court of Appeal a point of law in the case.

*Under section 36 of the Criminal Justice Act 1988, if the Attorney General thinks the sentencing of a defendant in the Crown Court is unduly lenient he may refer the case to the Court of Appeal: but only if the sentence is one to which Part IV of the 1988 Act applies, and only if the Court of Appeal gives permission. See also section 35 of the 1988 Act(**c**) and the Criminal Justice Act 1988 (Reviews of Sentencing) Order 2006(**d**).*

The rules in Part 65 also apply where this Part applies.]

(**a**)   1972 c. 71; section 36 was amended by section 31 of, and paragraph 8 of Schedule 1 to, the Prosecution of Offences Act 1985 (c. 23) and section 40 of, and paragraph 23 of Schedule 9 to, the Constitutional Reform Act 2005 (c. 4).

(**b**)   1988 c. 33; section 36 was amended by section 272 of, and paragraphs 45 and 46 of Schedule 32 and paragraph 96 of Schedule 36 to, the Criminal Justice Act 2003 (c. 44), sections 49 and 65 of, and paragraph 3 of Schedule 1 and Schedule 5 to, the Violent Crime Reduction Act 2006 (c. 38), section 40 of, and paragraph 48 of Schedule 9 to, the Constitutional Reform Act 2005 (c. 4), section 149 of, and Part 28 of Schedule 28 to, the Criminal Justice and Immigration Act 2008 (c. 4) and paragraph 2 of Schedule 19 and paragraphs 4 and 5 of Schedule 26 to the Legal Aid, Sentencing and Punishment of Offenders Act 2012 (c. 10). It is further amended by section 46 of the Criminal Justice and Immigration Act 2008 (c. 4), with effect from a date to be appointed.

(**c**)   1988 c. 33; section 35(3) was amended by section 168 of, and paragraph 34 of Schedule 9 to, the Criminal Justice and Public Order Act 1994 (c. 33).

(**d**)   S.I. 2006/1116.

Service of notice of reference and application for permission

70.2.—(1) The Attorney General must—

(a)   serve on the Registrar—

    (i)   any notice of reference, and

    (ii)   any application for permission to refer a sentencing case; and

(b)   with a notice of reference of a point of law, give the Registrar details of—

    (i)   the defendant affected,

    (ii)   the date and place of the relevant Crown Court decision, and

    (iii)   the relevant verdict and sentencing.

(2) The Attorney General must serve an application for permission to refer a sentencing case not more than 28 days after the last of the sentences in that case.

[Note. The time limit for serving an application for permission to refer a sentencing case is prescribed by paragraph 1 of Schedule 3 to the Criminal Justice Act 1988. It may be neither extended nor shortened.]

Form of notice of reference and application for permission

70.3.—(1) A notice of reference and an application for permission to refer a sentencing case must be in the appropriate form set out in the Practice Direction, giving the year and number.

(2) A notice of reference of a point of law must—

(a)   specify the point of law in issue and indicate the opinion that the Attorney General invites the court to give;

(b)   identify each ground for that invitation, numbering them consecutively (if there is more than one) and concisely outlining each argument in support;

(c)   exclude any reference to the defendant's name and any other reference that may identify the defendant;

(d)   summarise the relevant facts; and

(e)   identify any relevant authorities.

(3) An application for permission to refer a sentencing case must—

(a)   give details of—

(i)   the defendant affected,

(ii)   the date and place of the relevant Crown Court decision, and

(iii) the relevant verdict and sentencing;

(b)   explain why that sentencing appears to the Attorney General unduly lenient, concisely outlining each argument in support; and

(c)   include the application for permission to refer the case to the court.

(4) A notice of reference of a sentencing case must—

(a)   include the same details and explanation as the application for permission to refer the case;

(b)   summarise the relevant facts; and

(c)   identify any relevant authorities.

(5) Where the court gives the Attorney General permission to refer a sentencing case, it may treat the application for permission as the notice of reference.

Registrar's notice to defendant

70.4.—(1) The Registrar must serve on the defendant—

(a)   a notice of reference;

(b)   an application for permission to refer a sentencing case.

(2) Where the Attorney General refers a point of law, the Registrar must give the defendant notice that—

(a)   the outcome of the reference will not make any difference to the outcome of the trial; and

(b)   the defendant may serve a respondent's notice.

(3) Where the Attorney General applies for permission to refer a sentencing case, the Registrar must give the defendant notice that—

(a)   the outcome of the reference may make a difference to that sentencing, and in particular may result in a more severe sentence; and

(b)   the defendant may serve a respondent's notice.

Respondent's notice

70.5.—(1) A defendant on whom the Registrar serves a reference or an application for permission to refer a sentencing case may serve a respondent's notice, and must do so if—

(a)   the defendant wants to make representations to the court; or

(b)   the court so directs.

(2) Such a defendant must serve the respondent's notice on—

(a)   the Attorney General; and

(b)   the Registrar.

(3) Such a defendant must serve the respondent's notice—

(a)   where the Attorney General refers a point of law, not more than 28 days after—

    (i)   the Registrar serves the reference, or

    (ii)   a direction to do so;

(b)   where the Attorney General applies for permission to refer a sentencing case, not more than 14 days after—

    (i)   the Registrar serves the application, or

    (ii)   a direction to do so.

(4) Where the Attorney General refers a point of law, the respondent's notice must—

(a)   identify each ground of opposition on which the respondent relies, numbering them consecutively (if there is more than one), concisely outlining each argument in support and identifying the Attorney General's ground or reason to which each relates;

(b)   summarise any relevant facts not already summarised in the reference;

(c)   identify any relevant authorities; and

(d)   include or attach any application for the following, with reasons—

    (i)   an extension of time within which to serve the respondent's notice,

    (ii)   permission to attend a hearing that the respondent does not have a right to attend,

    (iii)   a direction to attend in person a hearing that the respondent could attend by live link, if the respondent is in custody.

(5) Where the Attorney General applies for permission to refer a sentencing case, the respondent's notice must—

(a)   say if the respondent wants to make representations at the hearing of the application or reference; and

(b)   include or attach any application for the following, with reasons—

    (i)   an extension of time within which to serve the respondent's notice,

    (ii)   permission to attend a hearing that the respondent does not have a right to attend,

    (iii)   a direction to attend in person a hearing that the respondent could attend by live link, if the respondent is in custody.

Variation or withdrawal of notice of reference or application for permission

70.6.—(1) This rule applies where the Attorney General wants to vary or withdraw—

(a)   a notice of reference; or

(b)   an application for permission to refer a sentencing case.

(2) The Attorney General—

(a)   may vary or withdraw the notice or application without the court's permission by serving notice on—

    (i)   the Registrar, and

    (ii)   the defendant

before any hearing of the reference or application; but

(b)   at any such hearing, may only vary or withdraw that notice or application with the court's permission.

Right to attend hearing

70.7.—(1) A respondent who is in custody has a right to attend a hearing in public unless it is a hearing preliminary or incidental to a reference, including the hearing of an application for permission to refer a sentencing case.

(2) The court or the Registrar may direct that such a respondent is to attend a hearing by live link.

[Note. See rule 65.6 (hearings) and paragraphs 6 and 7 of Schedule 3 to the Criminal Justice Act 1988. Under paragraph 8 of that Schedule, the Court of Appeal may sentence in the absence of a defendant whose sentencing is referred.]

Anonymity of defendant on reference of point of law

70.8.   Where the Attorney General refers a point of law, the court must not allow anyone to identify the defendant during the proceedings unless the defendant gives permission.

PART 71   APPEAL TO THE COURT OF APPEAL UNDER THE PROCEEDS OF CRIME ACT 2002: GENERAL RULES

Contents of this Part

Extension of time

71.1.—(1) An application to extend the time limit for giving notice of application for leave to appeal under Part 2 of the Proceeds of Crime Act 2002(**a**) must—

(a)   be included in the notice of appeal; and

(b)   state the grounds for the application.

(2) The parties may not agree to extend any date or time limit set by this Part, Part 72 or Part 73, or by The Proceeds of Crime Act 2002 (Appeals under Part 2) Order 2003(**b**).

Other applications

71.2.   Rule 68.3(2)(h) (form of appeal notice) applies in relation to an application—

(a)   by a party to an appeal under Part 2 of the Proceeds of Crime Act 2002 that, under article 7 of The Proceeds of Crime Act 2002 (Appeals under Part 2) Order 2003, a witness be ordered to attend or that the evidence of a witness be received by the Court of Appeal; or

(b)   by the defendant to be given leave by the court to be present at proceedings for which leave is required under article 6 of the 2003 Order,

as it applies in relation to applications under Part I of the Criminal Appeal Act 1968(**c**) and the form in which rule 68.3 requires notice to be given may be modified as necessary.

(**a**)   2002 c. 29.
(**b**)   S.I. 2003/82.
(**c**)   1968 c. 19.

Examination of witness by court

71.3.   Rule 65.7 (notice of hearings and decisions) applies in relation to an order of the court under article 7 of the Proceeds of Crime Act 2002 (Appeals under Part 2) Order 2003 to require a person to attend for examination as it applies in relation to such an order of the court under Part I of the Criminal Appeal Act 1968.

Supply of documentary and other exhibits

71.4. Rule 65.11 (Registrar's duty to provide copy documents for appeal or reference) applies in relation to an appellant or respondent under Part 2 of the Proceeds of Crime Act 2002 as it applies in relation to an appellant and respondent under Part I of the Criminal Appeal Act 1968.

Registrar's power to require information from court of trial

71.5.   The Registrar may require the Crown Court to provide the Court of Appeal with any assistance or information which they may require for the purposes of exercising their jurisdiction under Part 2 of the Proceeds of Crime Act 2002, The Proceeds of Crime Act 2002 (Appeals under Part 2) Order 2003, this Part or Parts 72 and 73.

Hearing by single judge

71.6.   Rule 65.6(5) (hearings) applies in relation to a judge exercising any of the powers referred to in article 8 of The Proceeds of Crime Act 2002 (Appeals under Part 2) Order 2003(**a**) or the powers in rules 72.2(3) and (4) (respondent's notice), 73.2(2) (notice of appeal) and 73.3(6) (respondent's notice), as it applies in relation to a judge exercising the powers referred to in section 31(2) of the Criminal Appeal Act 1968(**b**).

Determination by full court

71.7.   Rule 65.5 (renewing an application refused by a judge or the registrar) shall apply where a single judge has refused an application by a party to exercise in his favour any of the powers listed in article 8 of The Proceeds of Crime Act 2002 (Appeals under Part 2) Order 2003, or the power in rule 72.2(3) or (4) as it applies where the judge has refused to exercise the powers referred to in section 31(2) of the Criminal Appeal Act 1968.

Notice of determination

71.8.—(1) This rule applies where a single judge or the Court of Appeal has determined an application or appeal under The Proceeds of Crime Act 2002 (Appeals under Part 2) Order 2003 or under Part 2 of the Proceeds of Crime Act 2002.

(2) The Registrar must, as soon as practicable, serve notice of the determination on all of the parties to the proceedings.

(3) Where a single judge or the Court of Appeal has disposed of an application for leave to appeal or an appeal under section 31 of the 2002 Act(**c**), the registrar must also, as soon as practicable, serve the order on a court officer of the court of trial and any magistrates' court responsible for enforcing any confiscation order which the Crown Court has made.

(**a**)   S.I. 2003/82.
(**b**)   1968 c. 19; section 31(2) was amended by section 21 of, and Schedule 2 to, the Costs in Criminal Cases Act 1973 (c. 14), section 29 of the Criminal Justice Act 1982 (c. 48), section 170 of, and paragraphs 20 and 29 of Schedule 15 to, the Criminal Justice Act 1988 (c. 33), section 87 of the Courts Act 2003 (c. 39) and section 48 of the Police and Justice Act 2006 (c. 48).
(**c**)   2002 c. 29; section 31 was amended by section 74 of, and paragraphs 1 and 16 of Schedule 8 to, the Serious Crime Act 2007 (c. 27).

Record of proceedings and transcripts

71.9.   Rule 65.8(2)(a) and (b) (duty of Crown Court officer – arranging recording of proceedings in Crown Court and arranging transcription) and rule 65.9 (duty of person transcribing proceedings in the Crown Court) apply in relation to proceedings in respect of which an appeal lies to the Court of Appeal under Part 2 of the Proceeds of Crime Act 2002 as they apply in relation to proceedings in respect of which an appeal lies to the Court of Appeal under Part I of the Criminal Appeal Act 1968.

Appeal to the Supreme Court

71.10.—(1) An application to the Court of Appeal for leave to appeal to the Supreme Court under Part 2 of the Proceeds of Crime Act 2002 must be made—

(a)   orally after the decision of the Court of Appeal from which an appeal lies to the Supreme Court; or

(b)   in the form set out in the Practice Direction, in accordance with article 12 of The Proceeds of Crime Act 2002 (Appeals under Part 2) Order 2003 and served on the Registrar.

(2) The application may be abandoned at any time before it is heard by the Court of Appeal by serving notice in writing on the Registrar.

(3) Rule 65.6(5) (hearings) applies in relation to a single judge exercising any of the powers referred to in article 15 of the 2003 Order, as it applies in relation to a single judge exercising the powers referred to in section 31(2) of the Criminal Appeal Act 1968.

(4) Rule 65.5 (renewing an application refused by a judge or the Registrar) applies where a single judge has refused an application by a party to exercise in his favour any of the powers listed in article 15 of the 2003 Order as they apply where the judge has refused to exercise the powers referred to in section 31(2) of the 1968 Act.

(5) The form in which rule 65.5(2) requires an application to be made may be modified as necessary.

PART 72   APPEAL TO THE COURT OF APPEAL UNDER THE PROCEEDS OF CRIME ACT 2002: PROSECUTOR'S APPEAL REGARDING CONFISCATION

Contents of this Part

Notice of appeal

72.1.—(1) Where an appellant wishes to apply to the Court of Appeal for leave to appeal under section 31 of the Proceeds of Crime Act 2002(**a**), he must serve a notice of appeal in the form set out in the Practice Direction on—

(a)   the Crown Court officer; and

(b)   the defendant.

(2) When the notice of the appeal is served on the defendant, it must be accompanied by a respondent's notice in the form set out in the Practice Direction for the defendant to complete and a notice which—

(a)   informs the defendant that the result of an appeal could be that the Court of Appeal would increase a confiscation order already imposed on him, make a confiscation order itself or direct the Crown Court to hold another confiscation hearing;

(b)   informs the defendant of any right he has under article 6 of the Proceeds of Crime Act 2002 (Appeals under Part 2) Order 2003(**b**) to be present at the hearing of the appeal, although he may be in custody;

(c)   invites the defendant to serve notice on the registrar if he wishes—

     (i)   to apply to the Court of Appeal for leave to be present at proceedings for which leave is required under article 6 of the 2003 Order, or

     (ii)   to present any argument to the Court of Appeal on the hearing of the application or, if leave is given, the appeal, and whether he wishes to present it in person or by means of a legal representative;

(d)   draws to the defendant's attention the effect of rule 71.4 (supply of documentary and other exhibits); and

(e)   advises the defendant to consult a solicitor as soon as possible.

(3) The appellant must provide a Crown Court officer with a certificate of service stating that he has served the notice of appeal on the defendant in accordance with paragraph (1) or explaining why he has been unable to effect service.

(**a**) 2002 c. 29; section 31 was amended by section 74 of, and paragraphs 1 and 16 of Schedule 8 to, the Serious Crime Act 2007 (c. 27).
(**b**) S.I. 2003/ 82.

Respondent's notice

72.2.—(1) This rule applies where a defendant is served with a notice of appeal under rule 72.1. (2) If the defendant wishes to oppose the application for leave to appeal, he must, not later than 14 days after the date on which he received the notice of appeal, serve on the Registrar and on the appellant a notice in the form set out in the Practice Direction—

(a)   stating the date on which he received the notice of appeal;

(b)   summarising his response to the arguments of the appellant; and

(c)   specifying the authorities which he intends to cite.

(3) The time for giving notice under this rule may be extended by the Registrar, a single judge or by the Court of Appeal.

(4) Where the Registrar refuses an application under paragraph (3) for the extension of time, the defendant shall be entitled to have his application determined by a single judge.

(5) Where a single judge refuses an application under paragraph (3) or (4) for the extension of time, the defendant shall be entitled to have his application determined by the Court of Appeal.

Amendment and abandonment of appeal

72.3.—(1) The appellant may amend a notice of appeal served under rule 72.1 or abandon an appeal under section 31 of the Proceeds of Crime Act 2002—

(a)   without the permission of the Court at any time before the Court of Appeal have begun hearing the appeal; and

(b)   with the permission of the Court after the Court of Appeal have begun hearing the appeal, by serving notice in writing on the Registrar.

(2) Where the appellant serves a notice abandoning an appeal under paragraph (1), he must send a copy of it to—

(a)   the defendant;

(b)   a court officer of the court of trial; and

(c)   the magistrates' court responsible for enforcing any confiscation order which the Crown Court has made.

(3) Where the appellant serves a notice amending a notice of appeal under paragraph (1), he must send a copy of it to the defendant.

(4) Where an appeal is abandoned under paragraph (1), the application for leave to appeal or appeal shall be treated, for the purposes of section 85 of the 2002 Act (conclusion of proceedings), as having been refused or dismissed by the Court of Appeal.

PART 73   APPEAL TO THE COURT OF APPEAL UNDER POCA 2002: RESTRAINT OR RECEIVERSHIP ORDERS

Contents of this Part

Leave to appeal

73.1.—(1) Leave to appeal to the Court of Appeal under section 43 or section 65 of the Proceeds of Crime Act 2002(**a**) will only be given where—

(a)   the Court of Appeal considers that the appeal would have a real prospect of success; or

(b)   there is some other compelling reason why the appeal should be heard.

(2) An order giving leave may limit the issues to be heard and be made subject to conditions.

(**a**)   2002 c. 29; section 65 was amended by section 74 of, and paragraphs 1 and 32 of Schedule 8 to, the Serious Crime Act 2007 (c. 27).

Notice of appeal

73.2.—(1) Where an appellant wishes to apply to the Court of Appeal for leave to appeal under section 43 or 65 of the Proceeds of Crime Act 2002 Act, he must serve a notice of appeal in the form set out in the Practice Direction on the Crown Court officer.

(2) Unless the Registrar, a single judge or the Court of Appeal directs otherwise, the appellant must serve the notice of appeal, accompanied by a respondent's notice in the form set out in the Practice Direction for the respondent to complete, on—

(a)   each respondent;

(b)   any person who holds realisable property to which the appeal relates; and

(c)   any other person affected by the appeal,

as soon as practicable and in any event not later than 7 days after the notice of appeal is served on a Crown Court officer.

(3) The appellant must serve the following documents with his notice of appeal—

(a)   four additional copies of the notice of appeal for the Court of Appeal;

(b)   four copies of any skeleton argument;

(c)   one sealed copy and four unsealed copies of any order being appealed;

(d)   four copies of any witness statement or affidavit in support of the application for leave to appeal;

(e)   four copies of a suitable record of the reasons for judgment of the Crown Court; and

(f)   four copies of the bundle of documents used in the Crown Court proceedings from which the appeal lies.

(4) Where it is not possible to serve all of the documents referred to in paragraph (3), the appellant must indicate which documents have not yet been served and the reasons why they are not currently available.

(5) The appellant must provide a Crown Court officer with a certificate of service stating that he has served the notice of appeal on each respondent in accordance with paragraph (2) and including full details of each respondent or explaining why he has been unable to effect service.

Respondent's notice

73.3.—(1) This rule applies to an appeal under section 43 or 65 of the Proceeds of Crime Act 2002.

(2) A respondent may serve a respondent's notice on the Registrar.

(3) A respondent who—

(a)   is seeking leave to appeal from the Court of Appeal; or

(b)   wishes to ask the Court of Appeal to uphold the decision of the Crown Court for reasons different from or additional to those given by the Crown Court,

must serve a respondent's notice on the Registrar.

(4) A respondent's notice must be in the form set out in the Practice Direction and where the respondent seeks leave to appeal to the Court of Appeal it must be requested in the respondent's notice.

(5) A respondent's notice must be served on the Registrar not later than 14 days after—

(a)   the date the respondent is served with notification that the Court of Appeal has given the appellant leave to appeal; or

(b)   the date the respondent is served with notification that the application for leave to appeal and the appeal itself are to be heard together.

(6) Unless the Registrar, a single judge or the Court of Appeal directs otherwise, the respondent serving a respondent's notice must serve the notice on the appellant and any other respondent—

(a)   as soon as practicable; and

(b)   in any event not later than seven days, after it is served on the Registrar.

Amendment and abandonment of appeal

73.4.—(1) The appellant may amend a notice of appeal served under rule 73.2 or abandon an appeal under section 43 or 65 of the Proceeds of Crime Act 2002—

(a)   without the permission of the Court at any time before the Court of Appeal have begun hearing the appeal; and

(b)   with the permission of the Court after the Court of Appeal have begun hearing the appeal, by serving notice in writing on the Registrar.

(2) Where the appellant serves a notice under paragraph (1), he must send a copy of it to each respondent.

Stay

73.5.   Unless the Court of Appeal or the Crown Court orders otherwise, an appeal under section

43 or 65 of the Proceeds of Crime Act 2002 shall not operate as a stay of any order or decision of the Crown Court.

Striking out appeal notices and setting aside or imposing conditions on leave to appeal

73.6.—(1) The Court of Appeal may—

(a)   strike out the whole or part of a notice of appeal served under rule 73.2; or

(b)   impose or vary conditions upon which an appeal under section 43 or 65 of the Proceeds of Crime Act 2002 may be brought.

(2) The Court of Appeal will only exercise its powers under paragraph (1) where there is a compelling reason for doing so.

(3) Where a party is present at the hearing at which leave to appeal was given, he may not subsequently apply for an order that the Court of Appeal exercise its powers under paragraph (1)(b).

Hearing of appeals

73.7.—(1) This rule applies to appeals under section 43 or 65 of the Proceeds of Crime Act 2002.

(2) Every appeal will be limited to a review of the decision of the Crown Court unless the Court of Appeal considers that in the circumstances of an individual appeal it would be in the interests of justice to hold a re-hearing.

(3) The Court of Appeal will allow an appeal where the decision of the Crown Court was—

(a)   wrong; or

(b)   unjust because of a serious procedural or other irregularity in the proceedings in the Crown Court.

(4) The Court of Appeal may draw any inference of fact which it considers justified on the evidence.

(5) At the hearing of the appeal a party may not rely on a matter not contained in his notice of appeal unless the Court of Appeal gives permission.

PART 74   APPEAL OR REFERENCE TO THE SUPREME COURT

Contents of this Part

When this Part applies

74.1.—(1) This Part applies where—

(a)   a party wants to appeal to the Supreme Court after—

    (i)   an application to the Court of Appeal to which Part 41 applies (retrial following acquittal for serious offence), or

    (ii)   an appeal to the Court of Appeal to which applies Part 66 (appeal to the Court of Appeal against ruling at preparatory hearing), Part 67 (appeal to the Court of Appeal against ruling adverse to prosecution), or Part 68 (appeal to the Court of Appeal about conviction or sentence); or

(b)   a party wants to refer a case to the Supreme Court after a reference to the Court of Appeal to which Part 70 applies (reference to the Court of Appeal of point of law or unduly lenient sentencing).

(2) A reference to an 'appellant' in this Part is a reference to such a party.

*[Note. Under section 33 of the Criminal Appeal Act 1968(**a**), a party may appeal to the Supreme Court from a decision of the Court of Appeal on—*

*(a) an application to the court under section 76 of the Criminal Justice Act 2003(**b**) (prosecutor's application for retrial after acquittal for serious offence). See also Part 41. (b) an appeal to the court under—*

237

*(i)   section 9 of the Criminal Justice Act 1987(**c**) or section 35 of the Criminal Procedure and Investigations Act 1996(**d**) (appeal against order at preparatory hearing). See also Part 66.*

(**a**) 1968 c. 19; section 33 was amended by section 152 of, and Schedule 5 to, the Supreme Court Act 1981 (c. 54), section 15 of, and paragraph 3 of Schedule 2 to, the Criminal Justice Act 1987 (c. 38), section 36(1)(a) of the Criminal Procedure and Investigations Act 1996 (c. 25), section 456 of, and paragraphs 1 and 4 of Schedule 11 to, the Proceeds of Crime Act 2002 (c. 29), sections 47, 68 and 81 of the Criminal Justice Act 2003 (c. 44), by section 40 of, and paragraph 16 of Schedule 9 to, the Constitutional Reform Act 2005 (c. 4) and sections 74 and 92 of, and paragraph 144 of Schedule 8, and Schedule 14 to, the Serious Crime Act 2007 (c. 27).

(**b**) 2003 c. 44.

(**c**) 1987 c. 38; section 9 was amended by section 170 of, and Schedule 16 to, the Criminal Justice Act 1988 (c. 33), section 6 of the Criminal Justice Act 1993 (c. 36), sections 72, 74 and 80 of, and paragraph 3 of Schedule 3 and Schedule 5 to, Criminal Procedure and Investigations Act 1996 (c. 25), sections 45 and 310 of, and paragraphs 18, 52 and 54 of Schedule 36 and Part 3 of Schedule 37 to, the Criminal Justice Act 2003 (c. 44), article 3 of, and paragraphs 21 and 23 of S.I. 2004/2035, section 59 of, and paragraph 1 of Schedule 11 to, the Constitutional Reform Act 2005 (c. 4) and Part 10 of Schedule 10 to the Protection of Freedoms Act 2012 (c. 9). The amendment made by section 45 of the Criminal Justice Act 2003 (c. 44) is in force for certain purposes; for remaining purposes it has effect from a date to be appointed.

(**d**) 1996 c. 25; section 35(1) was amended by section 45 of the Criminal Justice Act 2003 (c. 44). The amendment is in force for certain purposes, for remaining purposes it has effect from a date to be appointed. Section 35 was also amended by paragraphs 65 and 69 of Schedule 36 to the Criminal Justice Act 2003 (c. 44) and section 59 of, and paragraph 1 of Schedule 11 to, the Constitutional Reform Act 2005 (c. 4) and Part 10 of Schedule 10 to the Protection of Freedoms Act 2012 (c. 9).

*(ii)   section 47 of the Criminal Justice Act 2003(**a**) (appeal against order for non-jury trial after jury tampering.) See also Part 66.*

*(iii)   Part 9 of the Criminal Justice Act 2003(**b**) (prosecutor's appeal against adverse ruling). See also Part 67.*

*(iv)   Part 1 of the Criminal Appeal Act 1968(**c**) (defendant's appeal against conviction, sentence, etc.). See also Part 68.*

*Under section 13 of the Administration of Justice Act 1960(**d**), a person found to be in contempt of court may appeal to the Supreme Court from a decision of the Court of Appeal on an appeal to the court under that section. See also Part 68.*

*Under article 12 of the Criminal Justice Act 2003 (Mandatory Life Sentence: Appeals in Transitional Cases) Order 2005(**e**), a party may appeal to the Supreme Court from a decision of the Court of Appeal on an appeal to the court under paragraph 14 of Schedule 22 to the Criminal Justice Act 2003(**f**) (appeal against minimum term review decision). See also Part 68.*

*Under article 15 of the Serious Organised Crime and Police Act 2005 (Appeals under Section 74) Order 2006(**g**), a party may appeal to the Supreme Court from a decision of the Court of Appeal on an appeal to the court under section 74 of the Serious Organised Crime and Police Act 2005(**h**) (appeal against sentence review decision). See also Part 68.*

*Under section 24 of the Serious Crime Act 2007(**i**), a party may appeal to the Supreme Court from a decision of the Court of Appeal on an appeal to that court under that section (appeal about a serious crime prevention order). See also Part 68.*

*Under section 36(3) of the Criminal Justice Act 1972(**j**), the Court of Appeal may refer to the Supreme Court a point of law referred by the Attorney General to the court. See also Part 70.*

*Under section 36(5) of the Criminal Justice Act 1988(**k**), a party may refer to the Supreme Court a sentencing decision referred by the Attorney General to the court. See also Part 70.*

*Under section 33(3) of the Criminal Appeal Act 1968, there is no appeal to the Supreme Court— (a) from a decision of the Court of Appeal on an appeal under section 14A(5A) of the Football Spectators Act 1989(**l**) (prosecutor's appeal against failure to make football banning order). See Part 68.*

*(b) from a decision of the Court of Appeal on an appeal under section 159(1) of the Criminal Justice Act 1988(**m**) (appeal about reporting or public access restriction). See Part 69.*

The rules in Part 65 also apply where this Part applies.]

(**a**) 2003 c. 44; section 47 was amended by section 59(5) of, and paragraph 1(2) of Schedule 11 to, the Constitutional Reform Act 2005 (c. 4).

(**b**) 2003 c. 44.

(**c**) 1968 c. 19.

(**d**) 1960 c. 65; section 13 was amended paragraph 40 of Schedule 8 to, the Courts Act 1971 (c. 23), Schedule 5 to, the Criminal Appeal Act 1968 (c. 19), paragraph 36 of Schedule 7 to, the Magistrates' Courts Act 1980 (c. 43), Schedule 7 to, the Supreme Court Act 1981 (c. 54), paragraph 25 of Schedule 2 to, the County Courts Act 1984 (c. 28), Schedule 15 to, the Access to Justice Act 1999 (c. 22), paragraph 13 of Schedule 9 to the Constitutional Reform Act 2005 (c. 4) and paragraph 45 of Schedule 16 to, the Armed Forces Act 2006 (c. 52).

(**e**) S.I. 2005/2798.

(**f**) 2003 c. 44; paragraph 14 of Schedule 22 was amended by section 40 of, and paragraph 82 of Schedule 9 and paragraph 1 of Schedule 11 to, the Constitutional Reform Act 2005 (c. 4).

(**g**) S.I. 2006/2135.

(**h**) 2005 c. 15. (**i**) 2007 c. 27.

(**j**) 1972 c. 71; section 36(3) was amended by section 40 of, and paragraph 23 of Schedule 9 to, the Constitutional Reform Act 2005 (c. 4).

(**k**) 1988 c. 33; section 36(5) was amended by section 40(4) of, and paragraph 48(1) and (2) of Schedule 9 to, the Constitutional Reform Act 2005 (c. 4).

(**l**) 1989 c. 37; section 14A(5A) was inserted by section 52 of, and paragraphs 1 and 3 of Schedule 3 to, the Violent Crime Reduction Act 2006 (c. 38).

(**m**) 1988 c. 33; section 159(1) was amended by section 61 of the Criminal Procedure and Investigations Act 1996 (c. 25).

Application for permission or reference

74.2.—(1) An appellant must—

(a)   apply orally to the Court of Appeal—

      (i)   for permission to appeal or to refer a sentencing case, or

      (ii)   to refer a point of law

      immediately after the court gives the reasons for its decision; or

(b)   apply in writing and serve the application on the Registrar and every other party not more than—

      (i)   14 days after the court gives the reasons for its decision if that decision was on a sentencing reference to which Part 70 applies (Attorney General's reference of sentencing case), or

      (ii)   28 days after the court gives those reasons in any other case.

(2) An application for permission to appeal or to refer a sentencing case must—

(a)   identify the point of law of general public importance that the appellant wants the court to certify is involved in the decision; and

(b)   give reasons why—

      (i)   that point of law ought to be considered by the Supreme Court, and

      (ii)   the court ought to give permission to appeal.

(3) An application to refer a point of law must give reasons why that point ought to be considered by the Supreme Court.

(4) An application must include or attach any application for the following, with reasons—

(a)   an extension of time within which to make the application for permission or for a reference;

(b)   bail pending appeal;

(c)   permission to attend any hearing in the Supreme Court, if the appellant is in custody.

(5) A written application must be in the form set out in the Practice Direction.

[Note. In some legislation, including the Criminal Appeal Act 1968, permission to appeal is described as 'leave to appeal'.

Under the provisions listed in the note to rule 74.1, except section 36(3) of the Criminal Justice Act 1972 (Attorney General's reference of point of law), an appellant needs permission to appeal or to refer a sentencing case. Under those provisions, the Court of Appeal must not give permission unless it first certifies that—

(a)   a point of law of general public importance is involved in the decision, and

(b)   it appears to the court that the point is one which the Supreme Court ought to consider.

If the Court of Appeal gives such a certificate but refuses permission, an appellant may apply for such permission to the Supreme Court.

Under section 36(3) of the Criminal Justice Act 1972 an appellant needs no such permission. The Court of Appeal may refer the point of law to the Supreme Court, or may refuse to do so.

For the power of the court or the Registrar to shorten or extend a time limit, see rule 65.3. The time limit in this rule—

(a)   *for applying for permission to appeal under section 33 of the Criminal Appeal Act 1968 (28 days) is prescribed by section 34 of that Act(**a**). That time limit may be extended but not shortened by the court. But it may be extended on an application by a prosecutor only after an application to which Part 41 applies (retrial after acquittal for serious offence).*

(b)   *for applying for permission to refer a case under section 36(5) of the Criminal Justice Act 1988 (Attorney General's reference of sentencing decision: 14 days) is prescribed by paragraph 4 of Schedule 3 to that Act. That time limit may be neither extended nor shortened.*

(c)   *for applying for permission to appeal under article 12 of the Criminal Justice Act 2003 (Mandatory Life Sentence: Appeals in Transitional Cases) Order 2005 (28 days) is prescribed by article 13 of that Order. That time limit may be extended but not shortened.*

(d)   *for applying for permission to appeal under article 15 of the Serious Organised Crime and Police Act 2005 (Appeals under Section 74) Order 2006 (28 days) is prescribed by article 16 of that Order. That time limit may be extended but not shortened.*

(**a**)   1968 c. 19; section 34 was amended by section 88 of the Courts Act 2003 (c. 39), section 81 of the Criminal Justice Act 2003 (c. 44), and section 40(4) of, and paragraph 16 of Schedule 9 to, the Constitutional Reform Act 2005 (c. 4).

For the power of the Court of Appeal to grant bail pending appeal to the Supreme Court, see—

(a)   *section 36 of the Criminal Appeal Act 1968(**a**);*

(b)   *article 18 of the Serious Organised Crime and Police Act 2005 (Appeals under Section 74) Order 2006(**b**).*

For the right of an appellant in custody to attend a hearing in the Supreme Court, see—

(a)   *section 38 of the Criminal Appeal Act 1968(**c**).*

(b)   *paragraph 9 of Schedule 3 to the Criminal Justice Act 1988(**d**).*

(c)   *article 15 of the Criminal Justice Act 2003 (Mandatory Life Sentences: Appeals in Transitional Cases) Order 2005(**e**).*

(d)   *article 20 of the Serious Organised Crime and Police Act 2005 (Appeals under Section 74) Order 2006(**f**).]*

Determination of detention pending appeal, etc.

74.3.   On an application for permission to appeal, the Court of Appeal must—

(a)   decide whether to order the detention of a defendant who would have been liable to be detained but for the decision of the court; and

(b)   determine any application for—

   (i)   bail pending appeal,

   (ii)   permission to attend any hearing in the Supreme Court, or

   (iii)   a representation order.

[Note. For the liability of a defendant to be detained pending a prosecutor's appeal to the Supreme Court and afterwards, see—

*(a)   section 37 of the Criminal Appeal Act 1968(**g**).*

*(b)   article 19 of the Serious Organised Crime and Police Act 2005 (Appeals under Section 74) Order 2006(**a**).*

*For the grant of legal aid for proceedings in the Supreme Court, see sections 14, 16 and 19 of the Legal Aid, Sentencing and Punishment of Offenders Act 2012(**b**).]*

(**a**)   1968 c. 19; section 36 was amended by section 12 of, and paragraph 43 of Schedule 2 to, the Bail Act 1976 (c. 63), section 15 of, and paragraph 4 of Schedule 2 to, the Criminal Justice Act 1987 (c. 38), section 168 of, and paragraph 23 of Schedule 10 to, the Criminal Justice and Public Order Act 1994 (c. 33), section 36 of the Criminal Procedure and Investigations Act 1996 (c. 25), sections 47 and 68 of the Criminal Justice Act 2003 (c. 44) and section 40 of, and paragraph 16 of Schedule 9 to, the Constitutional Reform Act 2005 (c. 4).

(**b**)   S.I. 2006/2135.

(**c**)   1968 c. 19; section 38 was amended by section 81 of the Criminal Justice Act 2003 (c. 44), and section 40(4) of, and paragraph 16 of Schedule 9 to, the Constitutional Reform Act 2005 (c. 4).

(**d**)   1988 c. 33; paragraph 9 of Schedule 3 was amended by section 40 of, and paragraph 48 of Schedule 9 to, the Constitutional Reform Act 2005 (c. 4).

(**e**)   S.I. 2005/2798.

(**f**)   S.I. 2006/2135.

(**g**)   1968 c. 19; section 37 was amended by section 65(1) of, and paragraph 39 of Schedule 3 to, the Mental Health (Amendment) Act 1982 (c. 51), section 148 of, and paragraph 23 of Schedule 4 to, the Mental Health Act 1983 (c. 20), section 58(1) of, and paragraph 5 of Schedule 10 to, the Domestic Violence, Crime and Victims Act 2004 (c. 28), section 40 of, and paragraph 16 of Schedule 9 to, the Constitutional Reform Act 2005 (c. 4) and section 47 of, and paragraphs 1 and 13 of Schedule 8 to, the Criminal Justice and Immigration Act 2008 (c. 4).

(**a**)   S.I. 2006/2135.

(**b**)   2012 c. 10.

Bail pending appeal

74.4.   Rules 68.8 (Application for bail pending appeal or retrial), 68.9 (Conditions of bail pending appeal or re-trial) and 68.10 (Forfeiture of a recognizance given as a condition of bail) apply.

A Guide to Commencing Proceedings in the Court of Appeal (Criminal Division)

FOREWORD BY THE LORD CHIEF JUSTICE OF ENGLAND AND WALES

In recent years the Court of Appeal Criminal Division has faced increased complexity in appeals, not only against conviction but also against sentence, particularly in the light of the plethora of recent sentencing legislation. Additionally, the jurisdiction of the Court has expanded to encompass a variety of diverse applications and appeals by the defence, the Crown and other interested parties.

This guide provides invaluable advice as to the initial steps for commencing proceedings in the Court of Appeal Criminal Division generally and in relation to perhaps unfamiliar provisions.

The first and most important step is, of course, the preparation of the grounds of appeal. The Rules prescribe the form and content of the Notice and Grounds of Appeal. Practitioners are also required to summarise the facts and outline their arguments concisely. Well drafted grounds of appeal assist the single Judge when considering leave and serve to shorten any hearing before the full Court. Ill prepared and prolix documents necessarily lead to wasted time spent on preparation and unnecessarily protracted hearings.

It is important that we all take seriously our responsibility to ensure the effective progression of cases and keep delay to a minimum. Once an application or appeal is commenced, the responsible officer at the Criminal Appeal Office will be available to assist with any queries on practice or procedure.

The Court could not deal with this volume of work efficiently without the support of the Registrar and his staff in the Criminal Appeal Office. Their experience and expertise is invaluable and can always be relied on by those who use the Court, not least those who are unfamiliar with its practice and procedures.

Judge C.J.
October 2008

CONTENTS

INTRODUCTION

Since the publication of the last Guide to Proceedings in the Court of Appeal (Criminal Division), the court's jurisdiction has increased. It hears appeals not only against conviction and sentence, but also against various interlocutory rulings, as well as other appeals and applications.

This guide provides practical information about how to commence and conduct proceedings before the court. Once proceedings are commenced, an application will have its own unique reference number and a case progression officer who can help with any difficulties or queries about procedure.

The guide is set out as follows:

A.   General principles of practice and procedure when applying for leave to appeal conviction and sentence.

B.   Guidance on appeals against rulings made in preparatory hearings.

C.   Guidance on prosecution appeals against 'terminating' rulings.

D.   Brief guidance on other appeals in bullet point form showing:

- the type of appeal,
- the relevant section of the statute
- the relevant Criminal Procedure Rules
- who can apply
- the forms to be used and time limits
- respondents' notices,
- whether representation orders are available
- whether leave to appeal is required

245

E.   Guidance on applications for a retrial for a serious offence.

A list of all up to date forms referred to in this guide may be accessed from the HMCS website at www.hmcourts-service.gov.uk or the Criminal Procedure Rules Committee website at www.justice.gov.uk/criminal/procrules. Where the Criminal Procedure Rules do not provide for a specific form, this guide indicates the appropriate form to be used.

This guide was prepared under my direction by the staff of the Criminal Appeal Office, but principally by Ms Alix Beldam and Ms Susan Holdham. It describes the law and practice of the Court as at 1st October 2008.

Master Venne
Registrar of Criminal Appeals

TERMINOLOGY

The Criminal Appeal Act 1968 refers to 'leave to appeal'. This is now referred to as 'permission to appeal' in the Criminal Procedure Rules 2007. This guide keeps to the terminology used by the Act.

Also consistently with the Act, an 'appellant' is referred to without distinction, but it should be borne in mind that it is the accepted practice of the Criminal Appeal Office (CAO) to refer to a person who has served notice of appeal but not been granted leave to appeal as an 'applicant' and use the term 'appellant' to refer to a person who has been granted leave to appeal.

Any reference to Counsel should be read as including a Solicitor Advocate as appropriate.

A   GENERAL PRINCIPLES OF PRACTICE AND PROCEDURE WHEN APPLYING FOR LEAVE TO APPEAL CONVICTION AND SENTENCE

A1   Advice and Assistance

A1-1   Provision for advice or assistance on appeal is included in the trial representation order issued by the Crown Court. Solicitors should not wait to be asked for advice by the defendant. Immediately following the conclusion of the case, the legal representatives should see the defendant and counsel should express orally his final view as to the prospects of a successful appeal (whether against conviction or sentence or both). If there are no reasonable grounds of appeal, that should be confirmed in writing and a copy provided then, or as soon as practicable thereafter, to the defendant by the solicitor. If there are reasonable grounds, grounds of appeal should be drafted, signed and sent to instructing solicitors as soon as possible. Solicitors should immediately send a copy of the documents received from counsel to the defendant.

A1-2   Prior to the lodging of the notice and grounds of appeal by service of Form NG, the Registrar has no power to grant a representation order. Also, the Crown Court can only amend a representation order in favour of fresh legal representatives if advice on appeal has not been given by trial legal representatives and it is necessary and reasonable for another legal representative to be instructed. Where advice on appeal has been given by trial legal representatives, application for funding may only be made to the Legal Services Commission (LSC).

A1-3   Once the Form NG has been lodged, the Registrar is the authority for decisions about representation orders, in accordance with the principle that the Court before which there are proceedings is the Court with power to grant a right to representation (Schedule 3 of the Access to Justice Act 1999 affirmed by Regulation 10 of the Criminal Defence Service (General) (No2) Regs 2001).

A1-4   Where, in order to settle grounds of appeal, work of an exceptional nature is contemplated or where the expense will be great, legal representatives should submit a Form NG with provisional grounds of appeal and with a note to the Registrar requesting a representation order to cover the specific work considered necessary to enable proper grounds of appeal to be settled.

A2   Form NG and Grounds of Appeal

A2-1   Where counsel has advised an appeal, solicitors should forward the signed grounds of appeal to the Crown Court accompanied by Form NG and such other forms as may be appropriate. It should be noted that Form NG and grounds of appeal are required to be served within the relevant time limit in all cases, whether or not leave to appeal is required (e.g. where a trial Judge's certificate has been granted). However, on a reference by the Criminal Cases Review Commission (CCRC), if no Form NG and grounds are served within the required period, then the reference shall be treated as the appeal notice: Rule 68.5(2).

A2-2   Grounds must be settled with sufficient particularity to enable the Registrar, and subsequently the Court, to identify clearly the matters relied upon. A mere formula such as 'the conviction is unsafe' or 'the sentence is in all the circumstances too severe' will be ineffective as grounds and time will continue to run against the defendant.

A2-3   Rule 68.3(1) sets out the information that must be contained in the appeal notice. The notice must:

(a)   specify:

    (i)   the conviction, verdict, or finding,

    (ii)   the sentence, or

      (iii)   the order, or the failure to make an order about which the appellant wants to appeal;

(b)   identify each ground of appeal on which the appellant relies, numbering them consecutively (if there is more than one) and concisely outlining each argument in support;

(c)   identify the transcript that the appellant thinks the court will need, if the appellant wants to appeal against a conviction;

(d)   identify the relevant sentencing powers of the Crown Court, if sentence is in issue;

(e)   where the Criminal Cases Review Commission refers a case to the court, explain how each ground of appeal relates (if it does) to the reasons for the reference;

(f)   summarise the relevant facts;

(g)   identify any relevant authorities;

(h)   include or attach any application for the following, with reasons

      (i)   permission to appeal, if the appellant needs the court's permission,

      (ii)   an extension of time within which to serve the appeal notice,

      (iii) bail pending appeal,

      (iv)   a direction to attend in person a hearing that the appellant could attend by live link, if the appellant is in custody,

      (v)   the introduction of evidence, including hearsay evidence and evidence of bad character,

      (vi)   an order requiring a witness to attend court, (vii) a direction for special measures for a witness,

      (viii) a direction for special measures for the giving of evidence by the appellant;

(i)   identify any other document or thing that the appellant thinks the court will need to decide the appeal.

A2-4   There is now a requirement for the grounds of appeal to set out the relevant facts and nature of the proceedings <u>concisely</u> in one all encompassing document, not separate grounds and advice. The intended readership of this document is the Court and not the lay or professional client. Its purpose is to enable the single Judge to grasp quickly the facts and issues in the case. In appropriate cases, draft grounds of appeal may be perfected before submission to the single Judge (*see further below para A5*).

A2-5   Any document mentioned in the grounds should be identified clearly, by exhibit number or otherwise. Similarly, if counsel requires an original exhibit or shorthand writer's tape recording, he should say so well in advance of any determination or hearing.

A2-6   Counsel should not settle or sign grounds unless they are reasonable, have some real prospect of success and are such that he is prepared to argue them before the Court. Counsel should not settle grounds he cannot support because he is 'instructed' to do so by a defendant.

A2-7   Procedure in relation to particular grounds of appeal

A2-7.1   Applications to call Fresh Evidence

A Form W and a statement from the witness in the form prescribed by s.9 of the Criminal Justice Act 1967 should be lodged in respect of each witness it is proposed to call. The Form W should indicate whether there is an application for a witness order. The Registrar or the single Judge may direct the issue of a witness order, but only the Court hearing the appeal may give leave for a witness to be called.

The Court will require a cogent explanation for the failure to adduce the evidence at trial. A supporting witness statement or affidavit from the appellant's solicitor should be lodged in this regard. (*Gogana* (The Times 12/07/1999))

If there is to be an application to adduce hearsay and/or evidence of bad character or for special measures, then the appropriate forms should be lodged: Rule 68.7(1).

A2-7.2   Complaints against trial counsel as a ground of appeal

Where a ground of appeal explicitly criticises trial counsel and/or trial solicitors, the Registrar will institute the 'waiver of privilege' procedure. The appellant will be asked to 'waive privilege' in respect of instructions to and advice at trial from legal representatives. If he does waive privilege, the grounds of appeal are sent to the appropriate trial representative(s) and they are invited to respond. Any response will be sent to the appellant or his fresh legal representatives for comment. All these documents will be sent to the single Judge when considering the application for leave. The single Judge may draw inferences from any failure to participate in the process. 'Waiver of privilege' is a procedure that should be instigated by the Registrar and not by fresh legal representatives, who should go no further than obtaining a waiver of privilege from the appellant: Doherty and McGregor [1997] 2 Cr.App.R. 218.

A2-7.3   Insufficient weight given to assistance to prosecution authorities

Where a ground of appeal against sentence is that the Judge has given insufficient weight to the assistance given to the prosecution authorities, the 'text' which had been prepared for the sentencing Judge is obtained by the Registrar. Grounds of appeal should be drafted in an anodyne form with a note to the Registrar alerting him to the existence of a 'text'. The single Judge will have seen the 'text' when considering leave as will the full Court before the appeal hearing and it need not be alluded to in open court.

A3   Time Limits

A3-1   Notice and grounds should reach the Crown Court within 28 days from the date of the conviction in the case of an application for leave to appeal against conviction and within 28 days from the date of sentence in the case of an application for leave to appeal against sentence [s.18 Criminal Appeal Act 1968 & Rule 68.2(1)]. On a reference by the CCRC, Form NG and grounds should be served on the Registrar not more than 56 days after the Registrar has served notice that the CCRC has referred a conviction and not more than 28 days in the case of a sentence referral: Rule 68.2(2).

A3-2   A confiscation order (whether made under the Criminal Justice Act 1988, the Drug Trafficking Act 1994 or the Proceeds of Crime Act 2002) is a sentence [s.50 Criminal Appeal Act 1968]. Where sentences are passed in separate proceedings on different dates there may be two appeals against sentence. Thus, there may be an appeal against the custodial part of a sentence and an appeal against a confiscation order. (Neal [1999] 2 Cr.App.R. (S) 352)

A3-3   An application for extension of the 28 day period in which to give notice of application for leave to appeal or notice of appeal must always be supported by reasons why the application for leave was not submitted in time. It is not enough merely to tick the relevant box on Form NG.

A3-4   Such an application should be submitted when the application for leave to appeal against either conviction or sentence is made and not in advance. Notwithstanding the terms of s.18(3) Criminal Appeal Act 1968, it has long been the practice of the Registrar to require the extension of time application to be made at the time of service of the notice and grounds of appeal. This practice is now reflected by Criminal Procedure Rule 65.4.

A4   Transcript and notes of evidence

A4-1   In conviction cases, transcripts of the summing up and proceedings up to and including verdict are obtained as a matter of course. Similarly, the transcript of the prosecution opening of facts on a guilty plea and the judge's observations on passing sentence are usually obtained in sentence cases. There is now an obligation under Rule 68.3(2) for counsel to identify any further transcript which counsel considers the court will need and to provide a note of names, dates and times to enable an order to be placed with the shorthand writers. Whether or not any further transcript is required is a matter for the judgment of the Registrar or his staff.

A4-2   Transcript should only be requested if it is essential for the proper conduct of the appeal in the light of the grounds. If the Registrar and counsel are unable to agree the extent of the transcript to be obtained, the Registrar may refer that matter to a Judge. In some cases the Registrar may propose that counsel agree a note in place of transcript.

A4-3   In certain circumstances the costs of unnecessary transcript could be ordered to be paid by the appellant. Where transcript is obtained otherwise than through the Registrar, he may disallow the cost on taxation of public funding.

A5   Perfection of grounds of appeal

A5-1   The purpose of perfection is (a) to save valuable judicial time by enabling the Court to identify at once the relevant parts of the transcript and (b) to give counsel the opportunity to reconsider his original grounds in the light of the transcript. Perfected grounds should consist of a fresh document which supersedes the original grounds of appeal and contains *inter alia* references by page number and letter (or paragraph number) to all relevant passages in the transcript.

A5-2   In conviction or confiscation cases, the Registrar will almost certainly invite counsel to perfect grounds in the light of the transcript obtained, to assist the single Judge or full Court. Where counsel indicates a wish to perfect grounds of appeal against sentence, the Registrar will consider the request and will only invite perfection where he considers it necessary for the assistance of the single Judge or full Court.

A5-3   If perfection is appropriate, counsel will be sent a copy of the transcript and asked to perfect his grounds within 14 days. In the absence of any response from counsel, the existing notice and grounds of appeal will be placed before the single Judge or the Court without further notice. If counsel does not wish to perfect his grounds, the transcript should be returned with a note to that effect.

A5-4   If, having considered the transcript, counsel is of opinion that there are no valid grounds, he should set out his reasons in a further advice and send it to his instructing solicitors. He should inform the Registrar that he has done so, but should not send him a copy of that advice. Solicitors should send a copy to the appellant and obtain instructions, at the same time explaining that if the appellant persists with his application the Court may consider whether to make a loss of time order. (see further below A-13)

A6 Respondent's Notice

A6-1   The Criminal Procedure Rules 2007 provide for the service of a respondent's notice. Under Rule 68.6(1) the Registrar may serve the appeal notice on any party directly affected by the appeal (usually the prosecution) and must do so in a CCRC case. That party may then serve a respondent's notice if it wishes to make representations and must do so if the Registrar so directs: Rule 68.6(2). The respondent's notice should be served within 14 days (Rule 68.6(4)) on the appellant, the Registrar and any other party on whom the Registrar served the appeal notice (Rule 68.6(3)). The respondent's notice must be in the specified form [Form RN], in which a respondent should set out the grounds of opposition (Rule 68.6(5)) and which must include the information set out in Rule 68.6(6).

A6-2   In practice, this procedure primarily applies prior to consideration of leave by the single Judge in both conviction and sentence cases. The Attorney General and the Registrar, following consultation with representatives from the Crown Prosecution Service (CPS) and the Revenue and Customs Prosecution Office (RCPO), have agreed guidance on types of cases and/or issues where the Registrar should consider whether to serve an appeal notice and direct or invite a party to serve a respondent's notice before the consideration of leave by the single Judge. Examples of when the Registrar might **direct** a respondent's notice include where the grounds concern matters which were the subject of public interest immunity (PII), allegations of jury irregularity, criticism of the conduct of the judge and complex frauds. Cases where it might be appropriate for the Registrar to **invite** a respondent's notice include, for example, homicide offences, serious sexual offences, cases with national profile or high media interest, cases of violence or domestic violence.

A6-3   In conviction cases where leave has been granted or where the application for leave has been referred to the full Court, the Crown is briefed to attend the hearing and required to submit a respondent's notice/skeleton argument. In relation to sentence cases where leave has been granted, referred or an appellant is represented on a renewed application, the sentence protocol set out in para.II.1 of the Consolidated Criminal Practice Direction will apply. In those cases, a respondent's notice/skeleton argument will have to be served when the Crown indicates a wish to attend or when the Registrar invites or directs the Crown to attend.

A7 Referral by the Registrar

A7-1   Leave to appeal is required in all cases except where the trial Judge or sentencing Judge has certified that the case is fit for appeal (ss.1(2) and 11(1A) Criminal Appeal Act 1968 as amended) or where the case has been referred by the CCRC. The appellant must obtain leave to pursue grounds not related to the Commission's reasons for referral: s.14(4B) Criminal Appeal Act 1995 amended by s.315 Criminal Justice Act 2003.

A7-2   Where leave to appeal is required and the Registrar has obtained the necessary documents, he will refer the application(s) either (a) to a single Judge for decision under s. 31 Criminal Appeal Act 1968 or (b) directly to the full Court, in which case a representation order is usually granted for the hearing. However, the Registrar will not grant a representation order when the presence of counsel is not required, e.g. where the application refers solely to an amendment of the number of days to be credited as 'remand time' and the figure is agreed by the parties. Where an application is referred to the full Court by the Registrar because an unlawful sentence has been passed or other procedural error identified, a representation order will ordinarily be granted, but counsel should be aware that the Court may make observations for the attention of the determining officer that a full fee should not be allowed on taxation.

A7-3   Where leave to appeal is not required, e.g. on appeal by certificate of the trial Judge, the Registrar will usually grant a representation order for the hearing. On a reference from the CCRC, it is the Registrar's usual practice to grant a representation order in the first instance, to solicitors for them to nominate and instruct counsel to settle grounds of appeal. Once counsel's details are known, a further representation order will be granted to cover the preparation (including settling grounds) and presentation of the appeal by counsel and further work by solicitors, as necessary in light of the grounds.

A8   Bail pending appeal

A8-1   Bail may be granted (a) by a single Judge or the full Court or (b) by a trial or sentencing Judge who has certified the case fit for appeal. In the latter case, bail can only be granted within 28 days of the conviction or sentence which is the subject of the appeal and may not be granted if an application for bail has already been made to the Court of Appeal.

A8-2   An application to the Court of Appeal for bail must be supported by a completed Form B, whether or not the application is made at the same time as the notice and grounds are served. The completed Form B must be served on the Registrar <u>and the prosecution</u> at least 24 hours before any application is made to enable the Crown to make representations (either written or oral) about the application and any conditions.

A8-3   An application for bail will not be considered by a single Judge or the Court until notice of application for leave to appeal or notice of appeal has first been given. In practice, Judges will also require the relevant transcripts to be available so they may take a view as to the merits of the substantive application.

A8-4   It is the practice of the Court, if bail is granted, to require a condition of residence. An application for variation of conditions of bail may be determined by the Registrar (if unopposed) or a single Judge.

A9   Consideration of the applications by single Judge

A9-1   Normally a single Judge will consider the application for leave to appeal together with any ancillary applications, e.g. for bail or representation order, without hearing oral argument. Counsel may request an oral hearing, but it is only in very rare circumstances that the Registrar would consider it appropriate to grant a representation order for the proceedings before a single Judge at an oral hearing, but counsel may appear to argue the applications before the single Judge where instructed to do so, usually appearing either pro bono or privately funded. Oral applications for leave and bail are usually heard at 9.30a.m. before the normal court sittings. Counsel appears unrobed. If counsel considers that an application may take longer than 20 minutes, the Registrar must be informed.

A10   Powers of the single Judge

A10-1   The single Judge may grant the application for leave, refuse it or refer it to the full Court. In conviction cases and in sentence cases where appropriate, the single Judge may grant limited leave i.e. leave to argue some grounds but not others. If the grounds upon which leave has been refused are to be renewed before the full Court, Counsel must notify the Registrar within 14 days. In the absence of any notification of renewal, it will be assumed that the grounds upon which leave was refused will not be pursued.

The single Judge may also grant, refuse or refer any ancillary application.

A11   Grant of leave or reference to full Court

A11-1   Where the single Judge grants leave or refers an application to the Court, it is usual to grant a representation order for the preparation and presentation of the appeal. This is usually limited to the services of counsel only, in which event counsel will be assigned by the Registrar. In such a case the Registrar will provide a brief but does not act as an appellant's solicitor. Counsel who settled grounds of appeal will usually be assigned. However, the Registrar may assign one counsel to represent more than one appellant if appropriate. If it is considered that a representation order for two counsel and/ or solicitors is required, counsel should notify the Registrar and provide written justification in accordance with the Criminal Defence Service (General) (No.2) Regulations 2001.

A11-2   If solicitors are assigned, it should be noted that by virtue of General Regulation 13 Criminal Defence Service (General) (No 2) Regulations 2001, a representation order can only be issued to a solicitor if he holds a General Criminal Contract (Crime Franchise) with the LSC. A solicitor not holding such a franchise may apply to the LSC for an individual case contract (by virtue of which the solicitor is employed on behalf of the LSC to represent an appellant in a given case). Such a contract is sufficient for the purposes of General Regulation 13.

A11-3   In some circumstances, the Registrar may refer an application to the full Court. This may be because there is a novel point of law or because in a sentence case, the sentence passed is unlawful and regardless of the merits, the sentence should be amended. A representation order for counsel is usually granted. Counsel for the prosecution usually attends a Registrar's referral.

A12   Refusal by the single Judge

A12-1   Where the single Judge refuses leave to appeal, the Registrar sends a notification of the refusal, including any observations which the Judge may have made, to the appellant, who is informed that he may require the application to be considered by the Court by serving a renewal notice [Form SJ-Renewal] upon the Registrar within 14 days from the date on which the notice of refusal was served on him.

A12-2   A refused application which is not renewed within 14 days lapses. An appellant may apply for an extension of time in which to renew his application for leave: Rule 65.5(2) and s.31 Criminal Appeal Act 1968. The Registrar will normally refer such an application to the Court to be considered at the same time as the renewed application for leave to appeal. An application for extension for time in which to renew must be supported by cogent reasons.

A12-3   If it is intended that counsel should represent the appellant at the hearing of the renewed application for leave to appeal, whether privately instructed or on a pro bono basis, such intention must be communicated to the CAO in writing as soon as that decision has been made. Whilst a representation order is not granted by the Registrar in respect of a renewed application for leave, counsel may apply at the hearing to the Court for a representation order to cover that appearance. In practice, this is only granted where the application for leave is successful.

A13   Directions for loss of time

A13-1   S.29 Criminal Appeal Act 1968 empowers the Court to direct that time spent in custody as an appellant shall not count as part of the term of any sentence to which the appellant is for the time being subject. The Court will do so where it considers that an application is wholly without merit. Such an order may not be made where leave to appeal or a trial judge's certificate has been granted, on a reference by the C.C.R.C or where an appeal has been abandoned.

A13-2   The mere fact that counsel has advised that there are grounds of appeal will not be a sufficient answer to the question as to whether or not an application has indeed been brought which was wholly without merit. Hart & others [2006] EWCA Crim 3239.

A13-3   The Form SJ, on which the single Judge records his decisions, and the reverse of which is used by appellants to indicate their wish to renew, includes:

- a box for the single Judge to initial to indicate that that the full Court should consider loss of time if the application is renewed and

- a box for the applicant to give reasons why such an order should not be made, whether or not an indication has been given by a single Judge.

A14   Abandonment

A14-1   An appeal or application may be abandoned at any time before the hearing without leave by completing and lodging Form A. An oral instruction or letter indicating a wish to abandon is insufficient.

A14-2   At the hearing, an application or appeal can only be abandoned with the permission of the Court: Rule 65.13(2). An appeal or application which is abandoned is treated as having been dismissed or refused by the full Court, as the case may be: Criminal Procedure Rule 65.13(4)(c).

A14-3   A notice of abandonment cannot be withdrawn nor can it be conditional. A person who wants to reinstate an application or appeal after abandonment must apply in writing with reasons: Criminal Procedure Rule 65.13(5). The Court has power to allow reinstatement only where the purported abandonment can be treated as a nullity (*see Medway* (1976) 62 Cr.App.R.85; *Burt*, The Independent, December 3, 2004; *Grant* (2005) 149 S.J.1186)

A15   Case Management Duties

A15-1   Criminal Procedure Rule 65.2 gives the Court and parties the same powers and duties of case management as in Part 3 of the Rules. In accordance with those duties, for each application received, the Registrar nominates a case progression officer, (the 'responsible officer'). There is also a duty on the parties actively to assist the court to progress cases. Close contact between counsel and solicitors and the responsible officer is encouraged in order to facilitate the efficient preparation and listing of appeals, especially in complex cases and those involving witnesses.

A15-2   Powers exercisable by the single Judge and the Registrar are contained in s.31 Criminal Appeal Act 1968 (*as amended by s.87 Courts Act 2003, s.331 & Sched.32 Criminal Justice Act 2003 and Sched.8 Criminal Justice and Immigration Act 2008*). These powers include the power to make procedural directions for the efficient and effective preparation of an application or appeal and the power to make an order under s.23(1)(a) CAA 1968 for the production of evidence etc. necessary for the determination of the case.

A15-3   Procedural directions given by the Registrar may be appealed to a single Judge. Those given by a single Judge, including a single Lord Justice, are final.

B   INTERLOCUTORY APPEALS AGAINST RULINGS IN PREPARATORY HEARINGS

Appeal against a ruling under s.9 of the Criminal Justice Act 1987 or a decision under s.35 of the Criminal Procedure and Investigations Act 1996 [Part 66 Criminal Procedure Rules 2007]

B1   Where a judge has ordered a preparatory hearing, he may make a ruling as to the admissibility of evidence; any other question of law relating to the case or any question as to the severance or joinder of charges. (s.9(3)(b) (c) & (d) CJA 1987/s.31(3)(a) (b) & (c) CPIA 1996)

B2   Under s.9(11) CJA 1987/s. 35(1) CPIA 1996 the defence or the prosecution may appeal to the CACD (and ultimately to the House of Lords) against such a ruling, but only with the leave of the trial Judge, single Judge or the full Court. As to the scope of a judge's powers in relation to a preparatory hearing and thus the extent of appeal rights: see the decision of the House of Lords in *H* [2007] UKHL 7 on appeal from [2006] EWCA Crim 1975.

B3   If the trial date is imminent and the application is urgent, the Registrar should be notified so that he may consider referring the application directly to the full Court and make arrangements for listing.

B4   If an application for leave to appeal is made to the trial Judge, it should be made orally immediately after the ruling, or within two business days by serving a notice of an application on the appropriate officer of the Crown Court and all parties directly affected: Rule 66.4. Notice of appeal or application for leave to appeal [Form NG (Prep)] is to be served on the Registrar, the Crown Court and the parties within five business days of the ruling or the trial Judge's decision whether to grant leave: Rule 66.2.

B5   The notice and grounds of appeal having been served on the other parties, grounds of opposition should be served in a respondent's notice [Form RN (Prep)] within five business days of service of the appeal notice: Rule 66.5.

B6   Defence representatives are usually covered by the Crown Court representation order if one is in force. (Paragraph 2(2), Schedule 3, Access to Justice Act 1999)

B7   If the relevant time limits are not complied with, the court has power to grant an extension of time, but cogent grounds in support of the application will be required. Where a single Judge refuses leave to appeal or an extension of time within which to serve a notice, the application may be renewed for determination by the full Court by serving the notice of refusal, appropriately completed, upon the Registrar within five business days of the refusal being served (Rule 66.7).

C   APPEALS BY A PROSECUTOR AGAINST A 'TERMINATING' RULING

S.58 Criminal Justice Act 2003 [Part 67 Criminal Procedure Rules 2007]

C1   S.58 Criminal Justice Act 2003 gives the prosecution a right of appeal in relation to a 'terminating' ruling: in effect where the prosecution agrees to the defendant's acquittal if the appeal against the ruling is not successful. (*Y* [2008] EWCA Crim 10) This is wide enough to encompass a case-management decision (*C* [2007] EWCA Crim 2532).

C2   There is no right of appeal in respect of a ruling that the jury be discharged or a ruling in respect of which there is a right of appeal to the Court of Appeal by virtue of another enactment (s.57(2)). The prosecution should therefore consider whether there is a right of appeal under s.9 CJA 1987 or s.35 CPIA 1996.

C3   The prosecution must inform the Court that it intends to appeal or request an adjournment to consider whether to appeal (s.58(4)), which will be until the next business day (Rule 67.2(2)). The judge has a discretion to adjourn for longer if there is a real reason for doing so. (*H* [2008] EWCA Crim 483) The prosecution can then ask the trial Judge to grant leave to appeal (Rule 67.5), although leave to appeal can be granted by the trial Judge, the single Judge or the full Court. The Crown must give the undertaking (as to the defendant's acquittal if the appeal is abandoned or leave to appeal is not obtained) at the time when it informs the Court of its intention to appeal. The failure to give it then is fatal to an application to the Court of Appeal for leave:

s.58(8); *LSA* [2008] EWCA Crim 1034.

C4   Whether or not leave is granted, the trial Judge must then decide if the appeal is to be expedited and if so, adjourn the case. If he decides that the appeal should not be expedited, then he can adjourn the case or discharge the jury (s.59). Leave should be granted only where the trial Judge considers there is a real prospect of success and not in an attept to speed up the hearing of the appeal. (*JG* [2006] EWCA Crim 3276)

C5   Whether the appeal is expedited or not affects the time limits for service of the notice of appeal [Form NG (Pros)] and respondent's notice [Form RN(Pros)]. If expedited, the appeal notice must be served the next business day after the decision, if not expedited, it must be served within five business days. Similar time limits apply to the service of the respondent's notice. Defence representatives are usually covered by the Crown Court representation order if one is in force (such proceedings being considered incidental within Paragraph 2(2), Schedule 3, Access to Justice Act 1999). If the relevant time limits are not complied with, the court has power to grant an extension of time.

C6   Expedition does not impose time limits on the Registrar or Court of Appeal. However, if leave has not been granted by the trial Judge, the application may be referred to the full Court by the Registrar to enable the application and appeal to be heard together to ensure that the matter is dealt with quickly.

C7   The Registrar endeavours to list prosecution appeals where a jury has not been discharged as quickly as possible. He is unlikely to be able to list an appeal in less than a week from the ruling because it is necessary for the prosecution to obtain transcripts, papers to be copied and the judges to read their papers. It is of great assistance if it is anticipated that there is to be an appeal against a ruling where the jury has not been discharged, that a telephone call is made to the Registrar or CAO General Office (020 7947 6011) notifying the office even before the appeal notice is sent, so that the List Office may be put on notice. The listing of an urgent appeal invariably means that other cases have to be removed from the list.

D OTHER APPEALS

D1 *Prosecution appeal against the making of a confiscation order or where the court declines to make one (save on reconsideration of benefit)*

- S.31 Proceeds of Crime Act 2002.

- Parts 71 and 72 Criminal Procedure Rules.

- From 1st April 2008 only the prosecution can appeal.

- Proceedings are commenced by serving a Form PoCA 1 on the defendant and the Crown Court within 28 days of the decision appealed against. [Article 3(2)(a) Proceeds of Crime Act (Appeals under Part 2) Order 2003]

- A respondent's notice PoCA 2 is to be served on the Registrar of Criminal Appeals and the appellant not later than 14 days after receiving PoCA 1.

- An undischarged Crown Court representation order will cover advice and assistance on the merits of opposing the appeal and drafting the respondent's notice, otherwise an application for a representation order can be made to the Registrar [s.12(2)b and s.26 Access to Justice Act 1999]. In any event, where an application for a representation order is made on PoCA 2, the Registrar will consider a representation order for the hearing.

- Leave to appeal can be granted by a single Judge or the full Court.

D2   *Appeal in relation to a restraint order*

- S.43 Proceeds of Crime Act 2002.

- Parts 71 and 73 Criminal Procedure Rules.

- The prosecution or an accredited financial investigator can appeal a refusal to make a restraint order. A person who applied for an order or who is affected by the order can apply to the Crown Court to vary or discharge the order and then appeal that decision to the Court of Appeal.

- Proceedings are commenced by serving a form PoCA 3 on the Crown Court within 14 days of the decision being appealed. PoCA 3 must then be served on any respondent, and on any person who holds realisable property to which the appeal relates, or is affected by the appeal, not later than seven days after the form is lodged at the Crown Court. The documents which are to be served with PoCA 3 are set out in Rule 73.2(3).

- A respondent's notice PoCA 4 is to be served on the Registrar of Criminal Appeals not later than 14 days after the respondent is notified that the appellant has leave to appeal or notified that the application for leave and any appeal are to be heard together. PoCA 4 is then to be served on the appellant and any other respondent as soon as is practicable and not later than seven days after it was served on the Registrar.

- An application for a restraint order can be made as soon as a criminal investigation has begun. The proposed defendant may not have been charged: s.40 Proceeds of Crime Act 2002. This affects the type of public funding.

  If a defendant has been charged with a criminal offence connected to the restraint order then the restraint proceedings are regarded as incidental to the criminal proceedings and are treated as criminal proceedings for funding purposes [Reg.3(3)(c) Criminal Defence Service (General)(No2) Regulations 2001] and the Registrar can grant a representation order if a defendant appeals a decision on an application to vary or discharge the restraint order.

If the prosecution apply for a restraint order in the Crown Court before the subject of the restraint order has been charged with a criminal offence and the subject of that order wishes to appeal a decision on an application to vary or discharge the restraint order then civil legal aid may be available as these proceedings fall within para.3 Schedule 2 Access to Justice Act 1999. The Legal Services Commission should be contacted for funding within the Community Legal Service scheme.

Similarly, a person affected by the order who wishes to appeal a decision on an application to vary or discharge the restraint order should apply to the Legal Services Commission for funding within the Community Legal Service scheme.

- Leave to appeal can be granted by a single Judge or full Court.

D3   *Appeal in relation to a receivership order*

- S.65 Proceeds of Crime Act 2002.

- Parts 71 and 73 Criminal Procedure Rules.

- An appeal can be brought by

    a)   The person who applied for the order

    b)   A person who is affected by the order or c) The receiver.

    The orders against which an appeal will lie are

    1)   The appointment or non-appointment of a receiver

    2)   The powers of a receiver

    3)   An order giving a direction to a receiver and

    4)   The variation or discharge of a receivership order

- Proceedings are commenced by serving a Form PoCA 3 on the Crown Court within 14 days of the decision being appealed. PoCA 3 must then be served on any respondent and on any person who holds realisable property to which the appeal relates, or is affected by the appeal, not later than seven days after the form is lodged at the Crown Court. The documents which are to be served with PoCA 3 are set out in Rule 73.2(3).

- A respondent's notice PoCA 4 is to be served on the Registrar of Criminal Appeals not later than 14 days after the respondent is notified that the appellant has leave to appeal or is notified that the application for leave and any appeal are to be heard together. PoCA 4 is then to be served on the appellant and any other respondent as soon as is practicable and not later than seven days after it was served on the Registrar.

- If a defendant has been charged with a criminal offence connected to a receivership order then the receivership proceedings are regarded as incidental to the criminal proceedings and are treated as criminal proceedings for funding purposes [Reg.3(3)(c) Criminal Defence Service (General)(No2) Regulations 2001] and the Registrar can grant a representation order if a defendant appeals a decision relating to a receivership order.

  If a management receivership order or an application for such an order is made in the Crown Court before the a criminal offence has been charged and a person affected by the order (including the proposed defendant) wishes to appeal a decision then civil legal aid may be available as these proceedings fall within para.3 Schedule 2 Access to Justice Act 1999. The Legal Services Commission should be contacted for funding within the Community Legal Service scheme.

- Leave to appeal can be granted by a single Judge or the full Court.

D4   Appeal against an order of the Crown Court in the exercise of its jurisdiction to punish for contempt – usually a finding of contempt or sentence for contempt

- S.13 Administration of Justice Act 1960.

- Part 68 Criminal Procedure Rules.

- Anyone dealt with by the Crown Court for contempt may appeal.

- Proceedings are commenced by lodging a Form NG at the Crown Court not more than 28 days after the order to be appealed.

- The Registrar may direct a respondent's notice Form RN or the Crown may serve one if they wish to make representations to the Court.

- An undischarged Crown Court representation order will cover advice and assistance on appeal. The Registrar will usually grant a representation order for the hearing: s.12(2)(b) Access to Justice Act 1999.

- No leave to appeal is required. The appeal is as of right.

- Appeals occur most frequently when an appellant wishes to appeal a sentence for failing to appear at the Crown Court as the failing to appear is dealt with as if it were contempt.

D5 *Appeal against a minimum term set or reviewed by a High Court judge*

- Para. 14 of Schedule 22 Criminal Justice Act 2003.

- Part 68 Criminal Procedure Rules.

- A defendant with a mandatory life sentence imposed before 18th December 2003 who has had his minimum term set or reviewed by a High Court judge can appeal.

- Proceedings are commenced by service of Form NG (MT) on the Registrar not more than 28 days after the decision.

- The Registrar may direct a respondent's notice Form RN or the Crown may serve one if they wish to make representations to the Court.

- An application for a representation order can be made to the Registrar [s.12(2)(b) Access to Justice Act 1999].

- Leave to appeal is required and can be granted by the full Court or a single Judge: Part 2 Para.8 Criminal Justice Act 2003 (Mandatory Life Sentences: Appeals in Transitional Cases) Order 2005 (S.I. 2005/2798).

D6 *Attorney General's reference of an unduly lenient sentence*

- S.36 Criminal Justice Act 1988.

- Part 70 Criminal Procedure Rules.

- The Attorney General can refer sentences only in relation to specific offences or sentences [ss.35 & 36 Criminal Justice Act 1988 and Criminal Justice Act 1988 (Reviews of Sentencing) Order 2006] including a minimum term, set or reviewed by a High Court Judge [Para 15. Schedule 22 Criminal Justice Act 2003]

- Although Rule 70.3(1) implies there is a specific form to commence proceedings, in practice a standard letter with supporting documents is sent by the Attorney General's Office no more than 28 days after sentence.

- If the defendant wishes to make representations to the court he must serve a respondent's notice within 14 days of the Registrar serving the application upon him. Again, there is no specific form designated.

- Representation orders are not issued to respond to an Attorney General's reference but a defendant who appears by counsel is entitled to his reasonable costs from central funds. The cost of instructing leading counsel in addition to or instead of junior counsel is generally not considered reasonable unless there is a compelling reason. It is advisable to consult with the Registrar before leading counsel is instructed.

- The leave of the Court of Appeal is required.

D7   Attorney General's reference of a point of law on an acquittal

- S.36 Criminal Justice Act 1972.

- Part 70 Criminal Procedure Rules.

- The Attorney General can refer a point of law to the Court of Appeal for an opinion on the acquittal on indictment of the defendant.

- Although Rule 70.3(1) implies there is a specific form to commence proceedings, there is no such form and Rule 70.3 sets out what should be included in the reference. The defendant should not be identified.

- There is no time limit.

- If the defendant wishes to make representations to the court he must serve a respondent's notice within 28 days of the Registrar serving the application upon him. Again there is no specific form.

- Representation orders are not issued to respond to an Attorney General's reference but a defendant who appears by counsel is entitled to his reasonable costs from central funds.

- Leave is not required.

D8   Appeal against a finding of unfitness to plead or a finding that the accused did the act or made the omission charged

- S.15 Criminal Appeal Act 1968.

- Part 68 Criminal Procedure Rules.

- The accused can appeal (by the person appointed to represent the accused) against

  -   a finding of unfitness to plead (but not fitness to plead as the defendant can appeal any subsequent conviction in the usual way on the basis he was not fit to plead) or

  -   that he did the act or made the omission charged or

  -   both findings.

  The appeal does not lie until both findings have been made.

- Proceedings are commenced by the service of Form NG on the Crown Court not more than 28 days after the finding made which the accused wishes to appeal.

- The Crown should serve a respondent's notice Form RN if directed by the Registrar or if they wish to make representations to the Court.

- There does not appear to be any statutory provision empowering the grant of a representation order. S.19 Prosecution of Offences Act 1985 refers to costs from central funds being available to cover the fees of a person appointed by the Crown Court under s.4A of the Criminal Procedure (Insanity) Act 1964. In *Antoine* ([1999] 2 Cr.App.R 225 Court of Appeal) this was interpreted to include the costs of an appeal. S.16(4) Prosecution of Offences Act 1985 provides that where the Court of Appeal allows an appeal under Part 1 of the Criminal Appeal Act 1968 against… a finding under the Criminal Procedure (Insanity) Act 1964 that the appellant is under a disability, or that he did the act or made the omission charged against him… the court may make a defendant's costs order in favour of the accused.

- Leave to appeal may be granted by the Crown Court Judge, a single Judge or the full Court.

D9   Appeal against a verdict of not guilty by reason of insanity

- S.12 Criminal Appeal Act 1968.

- Part 68 Criminal Procedure Rules.

- The defendant can appeal a verdict of not guilty by reason of insanity.

- Proceedings are commenced by the service of Form NG on the Crown Court not more than 28 days after the verdict.

- The Crown should serve a respondent's notice Form RN if directed by the Registrar or if they wish to make representations to the Court.

- There does not appear to be any statutory provision empowering the grant of a representation order. S.16(4) Prosecution of Offences Act 1985 provides that where the Court of Appeal allows an appeal then the court may make a defendant's costs order. If the appeal is not allowed costs from central funds should be available on the same basis as was allowed in *Antoine* (above) in the absence of any statutory provision.

- Leave to appeal may be granted by the Crown Court Judge, a single Judge or the full Court.

D10   Appeal against the order following a verdict of not guilty by reason of insanity or a finding of unfitness to plead

- S.16A Criminal Appeal Act 1968.

- Part 68 Criminal Procedure Rules.

- An accused who, as a result of a verdict of not guilty by reason of insanity or a finding of fitness to plead has a hospital order, interim hospital order or supervision order made against him may appeal against the order.

- Proceedings are commenced by the service of Form NG on the Crown Court not more than 28 days after the order.

- The Crown should serve a respondent's notice Form RN if directed by the Registrar or if they wish to make representations to the Court.

- There does not appear to be any statutory provision empowering the grant of a representation order. S.16(4) Prosecution of Offences Act 1985 provides that where the Court of Appeal <u>allows an appeal</u> then the court may make a defendant's costs order. If the appeal is not allowed costs from central funds should be available on the same basis as was allowed in *Antoine* (above) in the absence of any statutory provision.

- Leave to appeal may be granted by the Crown Court Judge, a single Judge or the full Court.

D11   *Appeal against review of sentence*

- S.74(8) Serious Organised Crime and Police Act 2005.

- Part 68 Criminal Procedure Rules.

- A defendant or specified prosecutor may appeal.

- Proceedings are commenced by serving a Form NG (RD) on the Crown Court not more than 28 days after the review.

- A respondent's notice Form RN should be served if directed by the Registrar or if the respondent wishes to make representations to the Court.

- An application for a representation order can be made to the Registrar: s.12(2)(b) Access to Justice Act 1999.

- Leave to appeal can be granted by the single Judge or full Court [Serious Organised Crime and Police Act 2005 (Appeals under s.74) Order 2006/21]

D12   *Appeal against an order for trial by jury of sample counts*

- S.18 Domestic Violence, Crime and Victims Act 2004.

- Part 66 Criminal Procedure Rules.

- The defendant can appeal.

- An application for the jury to try some counts as sample counts and the judge to try the remainder if the jury convict, must be determined at a preparatory hearing and s.18 confers rights of interlocutory appeal. A Form NG (Prep) must be served on the Crown Court, the Registrar and any party directly affected not more than five business days after the order or the Crown Court Judge granting or refusing leave. *(For applications to the Crown Court Judge see Part B above)*

- A respondent's notice Form RN (Prep) should be served if the Court directs or the Crown (or any party affected) wants to make representations to the court.

- Defence representatives are usually covered by the Crown Court representation order if one is in force. [Paragraph 2(2), Schedule 3, Access to Justice Act 1999]

- The Crown Court Judge, single Judge or full Court can grant leave to appeal.

D13 Appeal against an order relating to a trial to be conducted without a jury where there is a *danger* of jury tampering

- S.45(5) and (9) Criminal Justice Act 2003 amending s.9(11) Criminal Justice Act 1987 and s.35(1) Criminal Procedure and Investigations Act 1994.

- Part 66 Criminal Procedure Rules.

- The prosecution can appeal the refusal to make an order; the defence can appeal the making of an order.

- A Form NG (Prep) must be served on the Crown Court, the Registrar and any party directly affected not more than five business days after the order or the Crown Court Judge granting or refusing leave. *(For applications to the Crown Court Judge see Part B above)*

- A respondent's notice Form RN (Prep) should be served if the Court directs or the Crown (or any party affected) wants to make representations to the Court.

- Defence representatives are usually covered by the Crown Court representation order if one is in force. [Paragraph 2 (2), Schedule 3, Access to Justice Act 1999]

- Leave is required. The Crown Court Judge, single Judge or full Court can grant leave to appeal.

D14 Appeal against an order that a trial should continue without a jury or a new trial take place without a jury *after* jury tampering

- S.47 Criminal Justice Act 2003.

- Part 66 Criminal Procedure Rules (relating to appeals against an order made in a preparatory hearing notwithstanding the ruling will not have been in the context of a preparatory hearing).

- The defendant can appeal.

- A Form NG (Prep) must be served on the Crown Court, the Registrar and any party directly affected not more than five business days after the order or the Crown Court Judge granting or refusing leave. *(For applications to the Crown Court Judge see Part B above)*

- A respondent's notice Form RN (Prep) should be served if the Court directs or the Crown (or any party affected) wants to make representations to the court.

- Defence representatives are usually covered by the Crown Court representation order is one is in force. [Paragraph 2 (2), Schedule 3, Access to Justice Act 1999]

- The Crown Court Judge, single Judge or full Court can grant leave to appeal.

D15 *Appeal against orders restricting or preventing reports or restricting public access*

- S.159 Criminal Justice Act 1988

- Part 69 Criminal Procedure Rules

- A person aggrieved may appeal.

- Applications against orders <u>restricting reporting</u> shall be made within 10 business days after the date on which the order was made by Form NG (159) on the Registrar, the Crown Court, the prosecutor and defendant and any other affected person. Applications against orders to <u>restrict public access</u> must be made the next business day after the order was made. If advance notice of an order restricting public access is given, then advance notice of an intention to appeal may be made not more than five business days after the advance notice is displayed.

- A person on whom an appeal notice is served should serve a respondent's notice Form RN (159) within three business days if he wishes to make representations to the Court or the Court so directs.

- The Court may make such order as to costs as it thinks fit (s.159(5)(c) Criminal Justice Act 1988), but not out of central funds – *Holden and others v. CPS No.2* [1994] 1 AC 22.

- A single Judge or the full Court can grant leave to appeal: s.31(2B) Criminal Appeal Act 1968.

- Applications for leave to appeal and appeals in relation to reporting restrictions <u>may</u> be heard in private (Rule 65.6 (1)). Applications for leave to appeal and appeals relating to restricting public access must be determined <u>without</u> a hearing (Rule 65.6(3)).

D16 Appeal against a wasted costs order and appeal against a third party costs order

- Regulation 3C (costs wasted) and 3E (third party costs) Costs in Criminal Cases (General) Regulations 1986.

- A legal or other representative against whom a wasted costs order has been made in the Crown Court or a third party against whom a third party costs order has been made may appeal.

- Notice of appeal should be served on the Crown Court within 21 days of the order being made. There is no specific form. The notice should be served on any interested party (including, if appropriate, the Ministry of Justice).

- Any interested party can make representations orally or in writing.

- There is no power to grant a representation order or to order costs out of central funds as these proceedings are civil in nature.

- Leave to appeal is not required.

D17 Appeal relating to Serious Crime Prevention Orders

- S.24 Serious Crime Act 2007.

- Part 68 Criminal Procedure Rules.

- A person subject to the order, an applicant authority or anyone given the opportunity to make representations at the Crown Court about the making, refusal to make, variation or non-variation of an order may appeal.

- Proceedings are commenced by the service of Form NG (SCPO) on the Crown Court not more than 28 days after the order.

- A respondent's notice Form RN (SCPO) should be served if directed by the Registrar or if the respondent wishes to make representations to the Court.

- Proceedings before the Crown Court or the Court of Appeal relating to serious crime prevention orders and arising by virtue of ss.19, 20, 21 or 24 of the Serious Crime Act 2007 are criminal proceedings for the purposes of s.12(2)(g) of the Access to Justice Act 1999 [see Criminal Defence Service (General) (No.2) (Amendment) Regulations (SI 2008/725)]. Accordingly, the Registrar may grant a representation order to a person subject to the order. A person who made representations at the Crown Court can apply to the LSC for funding. The Court has discretion to order costs as it thinks fit. [Part 3 Orders as to Costs Serious Crime Act 2007 (Appeals under s.24) Order 2008/1863]

- Leave to appeal can be granted by the Crown Court Judge, full Court or single Judge [Art.9 Serious Crime Act 2007 (Appeals under s.24) Order 2008/1863]

D18   *Appeal against the non-making of a football banning order*

- S.14A(5A) Football Spectators Act 1989.

- Part 68 Criminal Procedure Rules.

- The prosecution can appeal.

- The appeal notice should be served on the Crown Court within 28 days of the decision not to make an order. However, there is no designated form.

- A respondent's notice should be served if directed by the Registrar or if the respondent wishes to make representations to the Court. However, again there is no designated form.

- An application for a representation order may be made to the Registrar – s.12(2)(b) Access to Justice Act 1999.

- Currently, the Court of Appeal has been given no powers to deal with these appeals.

E   APPLICATION FOR A RETRIAL FOR A SERIOUS OFFENCE

E1   *Application by a prosecutor to quash an acquittal and seek a retrial for a qualifying offence*

S.76(1) Criminal Justice Act 2003 [Part 41 Criminal Procedure Rules]

E1-1   There must be new and compelling evidence and it must be in the interests of justice for the acquitted person to be re-tried for a qualifying offence as listed in Part 1 Sch. 5 Criminal Justice Act 2003. (Ss.78 and 79 Criminal Justice Act 2003 see *Dunlop* [2006] EWCA Crim 1354 and *Sanjuliano* [2007] EWCA Crim 3130)

E1-2   Proceedings can begin in one of two ways:

(1)   By serving notice of the application under s.76 on the Court of Appeal and within two days serving the notice on the acquitted person (s.80). This notice charges him with the offence. It requires the personal written consent of the Director of Public Prosecutions (DPP) (s.76(3)).

If the acquitted person is not in custody the prosecution can ask the Crown Court to issue:

    i)   A summons for the acquitted person to appear before the Court of Appeal for the hearing of the application or

    ii)   A warrant for his arrest (s.89(3)).

Once arrested on the warrant the acquitted person must be brought before the Crown Court within 48 hours (s.89(6)).

(2)   An acquitted person may be charged with the offence before an application under s76 has been made. This may be after an arrest in an investigation authorised by the DPP (s.85(2)) or where no authorisation has been given, after arrest under a warrant issued by a justice of the peace. (s.87(1)). Having been charged, the acquitted person must be brought before the Crown Court to consider bail within 24 hours (s.88(2)). He can then be remanded in custody or on bail for 42 days whilst an application under s.76 is prepared: s.88(6) unless an extension is granted under s.88(8). Once a notice of application under s.76 has been served, stating that the acquitted person has previously been charged with the offence, the acquitted person must be brought before the Crown Court to consider bail within 48 hours of the notice being given to the Registrar, if the acquitted person is already in custody under s.88 (above) (s.89(2)).

E1-3   Thus in either case, bail is dealt with largely by the Crown Court. The Court of Appeal only considers bail on the adjournment of the hearing of the application under s.76 (s.90 (1)).

E1-4   The notice [Form Notice of a s.76 application required by s.80(1) CJA 2003] should where practicable be accompanied by the witness statements which are relied on as the new and compelling evidence, the original witness statements, unused statements, indictment, paper exhibits from the original trial, any relevant transcripts from the original trial and any other documents relied on: Rule 41.2(2).

E1-5   An acquitted person who wants to oppose a s.76 application must serve a response [Form Response of the acquitted person under s.80 CJA 2003] not more than 28 days after receiving the notice: Rule 41.3(2).

E2   *Application by a prosecutor for a determination whether a foreign acquittal is a bar to a trial and if so, an order that it not be a bar*

S.76(2) Criminal Justice Act 2003 [Part 41 Criminal Procedure Rules]

E2-1   The prosecution can apply, with the personal written consent of the DPP (s.76(3)) for a determination whether an acquittal outside the UK is a bar to the acquitted person being tried in England and Wales and if it found to be so, an order that the acquittal not be a bar. Proceedings can begin in the same way as for an application under s.76(1).

E3   Application for restrictions on publication relating to an application under s.76

S.82 Criminal Justice Act 2003 [Part 41 Criminal Procedure Rules]

E3-1   An application can be made by the DPP for reporting restrictions. This can be made after a notice of an application for a re-trial has been made and may also be made by the court of its own motion (s.82(5)). An application can also be made by the DPP for reporting restrictions before a notice of an application for a retrial if an investigation has been commenced: s.82(6). The application for reporting restrictions must be served on the Registrar [Form Application for restrictions on publication under s.82 CJA 2003] and (usually) the acquitted person (Rule 41.8(1)).

E3-2   A party who wants to vary or revoke an order for restrictions on publication under s.82(7) may apply to the Court of Appeal in writing at any time after the order was made. (Rule 41.9(1))

E4   Representation orders

E4-1   The Registrar will usually grant a representation order to the acquitted person for solicitors and counsel to respond to any of the above applications.

A Guide to Commencing Proceedings in the Court of Appeal Criminal Division

Her Majesty's Courts Service – October 2008

Vk RCJ100 © Crown copyright

Sample pleadings

1 SAMPLE GROUNDS OF APPEAL AGAINST CONVICTION AND APPLICATION TO EXTEND THE TIME LIMITS

The following is a sample that has been drafted in order to indicate a possible approach to a straightforward application for leave to appeal against conviction and an application for extension of the time limit within which to give notice of application for leave to appeal. It is not intended as a rigid blueprint.

IN THE COURT OF APPEAL

CRIMINAL DIVISION

REGINA

-v-

NED KELLY

GROUNDS OF APPEAL AGAINST CONVICTION AND APPLICATION FOR EXTENSION OF TIME WITHIN WHICH TO APPLY LEAVE TO APPEAL

Introduction

1. The Applicant appeals against his conviction for possessing an offensive weapon. He does so on the grounds of a material misdirection at his trial, whereby the Judge failed to tell the jury what, in law, they would have to find proved to be sure the petrol bomb was an 'offensive weapon'. Had the jury been directed that it was for the prosecution to make them sure that the bomb was made to injure a person, they may well have doubted whether the prosecution had proved its case.

2. The Applicant also apples for an extension of time within which to apply for leave, given these *Grounds* are submitted approximately 18 months after conviction. That application is dealt with as a discrete topic at the end of these *Grounds*.

Facts

1. The allegations concerned an incident that took place on 11 August 2011. Police in the London Borough of Tower Hamlets were patrolling the local area in a police carrier as violent disturbances took place across London. At around 1:20 am, the carrier was travelling along Mile End Road, E1 the location of the rear entrance to Stepney Police Station. Officers saw four to six males standing near to the rear gates of the police station. On seeing the carrier, the males ran and entered a parked Ford Escort car. The Applicant, who had been part of that group, did not enter the car but ran off. It later transpired that the car belonged to him.

2. The carrier attempted to stop the car but was unable to do so. One of the officers chased and caught up with the Applicant. He stopped, turned towards the officer and raised his hands above his head. He was detained. An officer found a pair of gloves on the route that the Applicant had run. While speaking to the Applicant it was noted that he smelt of petrol.

3. A search of the area around the rear of the police station revealed four petrol bombs. The Applicant was arrested for possession of an offensive weapon. He was taken back to the police stationed and interviewed. In interview, the Applicant denied the offence saying that he had been walking towards his girlfriend's house when he had been confronted by a group of young men wearing gloves and masks. He denied that it was his vehicle that the men had fled into and that he had ever seen the petrol bombs before.

4. Further enquiries by the police demonstrated that much of what the Applicant had said in interview was untrue. At trial, he accepted that he had travelled to the police station in his car. He claimed that he had been kidnapped and taken there by drug dealers to whom he owed money. Once at the scene he had been forced to assist in making petrol bombs by pouring petrol into beer bottles. He had no involvement with the bombs thereafter and had just been standing alongside the group when the police carrier had turned the corner.

The trial

1. The Applicant stood trial before His Honour Judge Jones at Inner London Crown Court in February 2012 charged with the following two counts:

    (1) Count 1. Possessing petrol bombs with intent to destroy or damage property, contrary to section 3(a) of the Criminal Damage Act 1971.

    (2) Count 2. Possessing an offensive weapon, the petrol bombs, contrary to section 1 of the Prevention of Crime Act 1953.

2.   The two counts were in the alternative. In opening the case Prosecution Counsel said in terms:[1]

'You will see there are two counts on the indictment and these counts are in the alternative … If [count 1] is proved ... then you don't need to consider count 2.'

3.   In summing up the Judge:

    (1)   Made clear the two counts were in the alternative.[2]

    (2)   Directed the jury that petrol bombs were offensive weapons and 'no-one has suggested" otherwise, given "there is no lawful or peaceful reason to put petrol in a bottle with a paper wick that anyone can think of. It is designed specifically for use as a weapon, as a missile, to cause fire and damage'.[3]

    (3)   Explored the issues the jury would need to consider on count 1, including 'did he share the intention in count 1 to destroy or damage property, whether the police station or some other building or a car or whatever, by the use of those items?'[4]

4.   After lengthy deliberations and following a majority direction, the jury acquitted the Applicant of count 1, but convicted him of count 2 by a majority of 10 to 2 on 20 February 2012.

Events after trial

1.   After the Applicant was convicted and imprisoned he and his family sought fresh advice. After some delay those now acting for the Applicant were supplied with the papers in the case and have settled these *Grounds*. The history of the new representation is dealt with in more detail in the final section below, seeking an extension of the normal leave period.

2.   Pursuant to the Court's guidance in *R v McCook* [2014] EWCA Crim 734, those now representing the Applicant, who did not act at trial, have sent these *Grounds* in draft form to the trial advocate; his reply is attached to this document. In essence he accepts that it would have been preferable had he raised the point taken in these *Grounds* with the trial judge before the summing up. The Applicant is grateful for that concession and would note that the judge and prosecuting advocate fell into what is submitted to be the same error.

---

1   Transcript 1, 5B then 6B.
2   Transcript 2, 6B and 27D
3   Transcript 2, 6E to H
4   Transcript 2, 9A

Appendix D   *Sample pleadings*

Submissions

1. Section 1 of the Prevention of Crime Act 1953 [as amended], insofar as relevant to this appeal, states:

   '(1) Any person who without lawful authority or reasonable excuse, the proof whereof shall lie on him, has with him in any public place any offensive weapon shall be guilty of an offence …

   …

   (4) In this section … "offensive weapon" means any article made or adapted for use for causing injury to the person, or intended by the person having it with him for such use by him or by some other person.'

2. In *R v Simpson* (1984) 78 Cr App R 115, Lord Lane CJ identified three categories of offensive weapon: those made for use for causing injury to the person (offensive per se), those adapted for such a purpose, and those not so made or adapted, but carried with the intention of causing injury to the person. In the first two categories, the prosecution do not have to prove that the defendant had the weapon with him for the purpose of inflicting injury. Once a jury are sure that the weapon is offensive per se, the defendant will only be acquitted if he establishes lawful authority or reasonable excuse.

3. The jury at the Applicant's trial were told that petrol bombs were offensive weapons and 'no-one has suggested' otherwise, given 'there is no lawful or peaceful reason to put petrol in a bottle with a paper wick that anyone can think of. It is designed specifically for use as a weapon, as a missile, to cause fire and damage'.[5]

4. It is submitted this is wrong. An incendiary device can be made either to injure people or damage property. Indeed, it was the prosecution case that the latter was probably what was intended here; see the nature of count 1 and the summing up in respect of that count:

   'did he share the intention in count 1 to destroy or damage property, whether the police station or some other building or a car or whatever, by the use of those items?'[6]

5. There may be many cases in which the circumstances of the possession of a petrol bomb may provide an irresistible basis for an inference that it was made with the intent of injuring a person or persons. However, on the facts of this case there was an alternative possibility, that the Applicant was in possession of the bomb with the intention of causing damage to

---

5   Transcript 2, 6E to H
6   Transcript 2, 9A

276

property; indeed that alternative was the main thrust of the prosecution case.

6.   It follows that had the issue been left to the jury they may have entertained at the very least a doubt, and consequently the conviction for count 2 is unsafe and this appeal should be allowed.

Application for an extension of leave period

1.   The Solicitor who now acts for the Applicant has made a witness statement, attached to these *Grounds*, setting out the history of the passage of time between the Applicant's conviction and these *Grounds* being lodged. In essence the time was taken up as follows:

   (1)   Trial Counsel advised that there were no grounds of appeal; given the concession now made by Counsel, it is submitted that that advise may not have been correct.

   (2)   Thereafter the Applicant and his family made numerous efforts to seek fresh advice. Those efforts were handicapped both by their lack of wealth and the fact that, perhaps unsurprisingly, they did not spot the technical legal point now pursued.

   (3)   Some months later they made contact with the Solicitor now acting who agreed to consider whether there were grounds for an appeal. There was then a very considerable delay while the trial papers were obtained from the previous solicitors. Those papers were 'chased' on numerous and regular occasions.

   (4)   Once the papers were located and passed on, Counsel was instructed and she advised that a transcript of the summing up was required. The Legal Aid Authority then refused the application for funding and that refusal had to be appealed to the area Committee.

   (5)   Once the transcript was finally obtained and supplied to Counsel along with all the trial papers, these *Grounds* were drafted and lodged within three weeks.

Conclusion

1.   In conclusion, it is submitted that this Applicant has always protested his innocence and he and his family have done all that was practically possible to get fresh advice. Once new lawyers were in place it is submitted that they acted properly and efficiently in getting these *Grounds* in a fit state to be lodged. For all these reasons it is submitted that the Court should allow the extension now sought.

[Signed by the advocate drafting]
Quality Street Chambers
25 September 2014

2   SAMPLE GROUNDS OF APPEAL AGAINST SENTENCE

This is a sample that has been drafted in order to indicate a possible approach to a straightforward application for leave to appeal against sentence. It is not intended as a rigid blueprint.

IN THE COURT OF APPEAL

CRIMINAL DIVISION

REGINA

-V-

KARON JOSEPH

GROUNDS OF APPEAL AGAINST SENTENCE

Introduction

1. The Applicant applies for leave to appeal against her sentence of seven years' imprisonment, passed by HHJ Jolly at Acton Crown Court on 13 February 2014. In summary the grounds advanced are:

    (1) The Judge was wrong to reject the basis of plea without at least warning that he was minded to do so. Such a warning would have allowed the Applicant's advocate to make submissions and inform the Judge of unused material of which he was unaware.

    (2) The Judge was wrong to only allow a reduction of 12.5 per cent for the Applicant's guilty plea at the pleas and case management hearing.

Facts

1. The Applicant was arrested on 23 September 2013 after police officers entered and searched the address where she lived. They found a knotted carrier bag under the Applicant's bed that contained some 25 wraps of crack cocaine. Each wrap was made from cling film, with a total weight of 120 grams. They also found electronic scales with two pans that a scientist was later to say had 'very probably' been used to make crack cocaine from the powered form of the drug, 14 rolls of cling film [all in the kitchen] and three mobile phones in the sitting room that rang on numerous occasions during the search. A police officer attempted to answer these calls but when he did so the calls were immediately terminated. These facts were all evident from the prosecution papers that were supplied to the Judge.

2.   The unused material contained the following material [as attached to these *Grounds*] that was not served on the Court and consequently was not known to the Judge:

   (1)   Various documents that suggested at least three other people lived in the same house, including Martin Jones and Ken Owen.

   (2)   Jones had a number of previous convictions for supplying cannabis and heroin, and a recent conviction for possession of a small amount of cocaine.

   (3)   Owen had two previous convictions for possessing cocaine and cannabis and seven for offences of violence, mainly of a low level but he had served a six-year sentence for wounding with intent some eight years before the time of the search.

3.   The Applicant did not speak at all when the house was being searched or when she was arrested on suspicion of possession with intent to supply the crack cocaine. She was later interviewed under caution and answered 'no comment' to all the questions asked of her. She had one previous conviction for assault police some five years previously for which she had received a community order. She was aged 27 at the time of sentence and worked part time as a carer.

4.   In preparing the case her solicitor had taken a number of statements from her mother, father and elder sister who between them suggested that she had little money and would often borrow small sums of money from them or allow them to buy her drinks on social occasions.

5.   The Applicant was committed to the Crown Court. At a preliminary hearing no plea was entered despite HHJ Dour QC reminding her and her advocate that under the authority of *Caley*, maximum credit for any guilty plea could only be guaranteed by a plea indicated or entered at that hearing.

6.   At the PCMH the Applicant pleaded guilty to the single count she faced, that of possessing cocaine with intent to supply. She did so on the basis of a written basis of plea [copy attached] that included the passage:

   'The defendant was not a drug dealer in the sense that she did not sell to drug users or anybody else, but she admits by her plea that she possessed the drugs intending to supply them; another person had given her the drugs to look after. While she does not claim to have been acting under duress, she did feel obliged to help out another who lived in the same house from time to time, so she put the drugs under her bed until that other person would ask for them back.'

7.   The Prosecution opened the facts of the case to HHJ Jolly, but made clear they 'could not gainsay' the basis of plea and did not seek a *Newton* hearing. The mitigation advanced on behalf of the Applicant included:

(1)   Reliance on the basis of plea and the submission that this placed the Applicant in the category of 'lesser role' in the sentencing guidelines. Given the Prosecution's stance and the very heavy list that HHJ Jolly was dealing with, no further time was taken up rehearsing the items of unused material or familial evidence, as set out above, such as supported the basis.

(2)   A submission that the Applicant, as a woman of almost good character, could be forgiven for being too scared of the inevitable custodial sentence that would follow to plead at the preliminary hearing, and that therefore the Court should grant her maximum, or close to maximum, credit for her timely plea at the PCMH.

8.   In passing sentence HHJ Jolly said:

(1)   He did not believe a word of the basis of plea. The Defendant was a grown woman. It was all too easy for any major drug dealer to claim, when caught red handed, that they were only minding the drugs for no profit. Yet here was a defendant arrested in her own house, surrounded by all the accoutrements of a busy commercial drug dealer. She had not said a word about any lesser role either upon arrest or in her interviews under caution. Therefore he would take her role to be a 'leading role' under the sentencing guidelines. Given that the drugs were clearly being packaged and prepared for sale to street level users [which was not in dispute] this was a category 3 case. He therefore adopted a starting point of eight years six months.

(2)   *Caley* makes clear the sentencing judge is not deprived of all flexibility; this was a defendant who had chosen to stay silent at interview, had not indicated a plea at the preliminary hearing despite being specifically warned, and now entered a guilty plea when confronted with overwhelming evidence of guilt; the drugs, the wrappings, the scales, the pans and the 'dealer phones'. As such while he would of course make a reduction for the guilty plea, it would be a moderate one.

9.   The judge then took the above starting point, eight years six months, deducted six months for the defendant's lack of relevant previous convictions and deducted one year (thus an eighth or 12.5 per cent) for the guilty plea. The Judge consequently passed a sentence of seven years imprisonment.

Submissions

1.   It is submitted the Judge was wrong to disregard the basis of plea without at least warning the Applicant that he was minded to do so, see *R v Smith (Patrick)* (1988) 87 Cr App R 393 and *R v Dudley* [2012] 2 Cr App R (S) 15. Similarly, paragraph B10, *Criminal Practice Directions (Sentencing)*

[2013] 1 WLR 3164 states in terms that, 'A Judge is not entitled to reject a defendant's basis of plea absent a Newton hearing unless it is determined by the court that it is manifestly false'. It is submitted that the basis advanced was not manifestly false and, in any event, if the Judge were of that belief he was still obliged to warn the Applicant of that view.

2. This was not merely a technical failing. The unused and defence material, as set out above, would have allowed submissions to be made that:

   (1) There was an obvious better candidate for the person with the senior position in the drugs supply from that house, Martin Jones.

   (2) Another person who was a perfectly sensible candidate for playing a role in the supply of drugs, also linked to the house was Ken Owen. His history of violence provided a perfectly credible explanation for why the Applicant might not have been keen to set out the history of her limited involvement with the drugs either on arrest or in interview.

   (3) The evidence from the Applicant's family would have gone beyond merely providing other possible candidates for the main drug dealing, and would have been positive evidence that she was not engaged in what is obviously a highly lucrative trade.

3. It is therefore submitted that the Judge was wrong not to warn of his view of the facts. Had he done he may well have been persuaded that he should accept the Applicant's basis of plea was the proper basis for sentence.

4. As such, it is submitted, the proper starting point in the Applicant's case, from the sentencing guidelines, for a defendant with a lesser role in category 3, one of three years' custody.

5. This Court will be very familiar with the case of *Caley* [2013] Cr App R (S) 47 and the Sentencing Guidelines Council guidelines on credit for guilty pleas. To summarise the relevant parts for the purposes of this appeal [with paragraph numbers from *Caley*]:

   (1) Whilst the sentencing judge does have flexibility as to the first reasonable time for a guilty plea to be indicated or entered, the criminal justice system should aim to be consistent between defendants, thus allowing those who act for them to advise properly [9].

   (2) The Court specifically rejected using the police interview as the first opportunity [12]

   (3) The reduction for a plea at the PCMH will be about a quarter [19]

   (4) The Courts need to be very slow and cautious before concluding a case is overwhelming and withholding the normal reduction. Even in a truly overwhelming case where the sentencing court was

entitled to reduce the credit, it would still not go below 20 per cent for a plea at the first opportunity [23 and 24].

6.   Applying the above to the facts of the instant application, it is submitted:

(1)   The Judge was quite entitled to reject the defence application for full, 33 per cent, credit as there had been no plea at the preliminary hearing.

(2)   The Judge was wrong to attach significance to the Applicant remaining silent in interview and at the scene, given the views of this Court in *Caley*.

(3)   This was not an overwhelming case. Although it was obvious that the house was being used as a centre for drug dealing, the existence of other candidates who were identified as users of the house, including a man who had been convicted of serious offences of violence and the Applicant's very limited criminal history may have lead some defendants in her position to seek to advance the defence of duress. As such the Applicant should have received the usual 25 per cent reduction. If this Court accepts that argument, the final sentence should have been in the region of 23 months [in other words three years as above, reduced by 25 per cent] plus any allowance such as the Judge made for the lack of any relevant convictions.

(4)   Even if the case were overwhelming, it is submitted the reduction the Judge allowed, of 12.5 per cent, was simply insufficient for a plea at the PCMH.

7.   For all these reason it is submitted this Applicant should be granted leave and her sentence should be very significantly reduced.

Anthony Advocate
Criminal Solicitors
Date

3   DRAFT STATEMENT OF FACTS AND STATEMENT OF ALLEGED VIOLATION AND LEGAL ARGUMENTS FOR AN APPLICATION TO THE EUROPEAN COURT OF HUMAN RIGHTS

An application to the European Court of Human Rights must be made using the Court's own application form. However, the substance of the application will be contained in the statement of facts and the statement of alleged violation(s) and relevant legal arguments that will accompany the form itself. This is a sample that is intended to indicate a possible approach to both drafting exercises. It is not intended to be a blueprint.

Statement of the facts

1. On 10 September 2010, Alfred Jones was the victim of various offences. He gave police an account of being parked outside his home waiting for his friend Ralph to join him when he was kidnapped and placed into a van. Thereafter he was driven around, assaulted, robbed and demands were made to his friends via his own mobile phone to bring large amounts of cash to a meeting place. His car was also stolen. He was able to escape some hours later. He supposedly identified the Applicant Davies as the man who first approached him as part of the kidnap and identified a blue Suzuki van as the vehicle used in the kidnap, false imprisonment and blackmail. There were a series of links between the Applicant Dawes and that van.

2. The purported identification of Davies was, at its highest, qualified. In essence, Mr Jones stated at the identification procedure that he could not be sure ['Out of all of them number 3 gave me an inkling ... Can't be 100 per cent sure but I'd say number 3', number 3 being the position in the video line up at which the Applicant Davies was shown] but by stages ended up claiming in a later witness statement that he was sure of his identification of Davies as the man who had first approached him.

3. There were various alleged links between the Applicant Dawes and a blue Suzuki van. After describing the van used by his abductors in terms no more than, at best, consistent with the blue Suzuki van ['a Rascal ... a little Nissan van ... a little blue thing ... that royal kind of blue ... a transit'], six months later he was shown photographs of that van and said, 'This is the type of van I was kidnapped in ... I can say that this is exactly the van that it was'.

4. In the course of the kidnap Mr Jones was asked to tell the kidnappers where his cocaine was to be found and the abductors clearly assumed that his friends would have ready access to large amounts of cash. Peter Huseyin, a friend of Jones who became a prosecution witness, first became aware of these events when the friend Ralph drove up and said that 'someone's tried to rob me and Alf outside his flat. I saw some guys near Alf's car but I don't know where he is'. Huseyin then drove for a few minutes to the area of Jones' flat. Ralph did not assist the police and was not a witness. Neither Ralph nor Huseyin called the police. Jones' girlfriend eventually called the police and the call was logged as being received at 00:20.

5. In addition to the identifying evidence from Jones, the prosecution relied on phone calls between the three defendants' mobile phones, and all three phones being cell sited in the same general area where the offences were taking place. It is noted in passing that the Applicant Davies was acquitted of counts 2 and 3 [false imprisonment and blackmail] and the co-defendant Phipps acquitted of all counts. Thus the jury did not regard the cell site alone evidence as sufficient proof of guilt on any count.

6.   Counts 4 and 5 on the trial indictment alleged that the Applicant Dawes and the co-defendant Phipps had committed an aggravated burglary on 24 September. That allegation was based on phone evidence, the use of the car stolen from Jones in the course of counts 1 to 3, and the possession of a blackberry mobile phone, stolen in the aggravated burglary, by Phipps shortly afterwards. Both men were acquitted.

7.   Count 6 alleged a robbery of a lorry delivering cigarettes on 24 November 2010. A camera in that lorry showed that the Suzuki van to which Dawes had the links was used by the robbers and a photograph from the same source was said to be him; he was found guilty of that count.

8.   The trial was fixed for 7 June 2012. In the days before trial Mr Jones notified the police that he would not attend Court to give evidence. He alleged that on Monday 30 May his mother received a call on her landline number asking to speak to him. He then received a phone call on his mobile phone. According to Mr. Jones' statement 'It was from a private number on my mobile phone number ending 138. A male voice said, "I would advise you not to go to trial. There are a lot of people upset, they are on standby waiting for the word". I did not recognise this voice. It sounded black. I hung up the phone. Straightaway the phone rang back with private number. I answered the call but did not say anything. I did not listen to the phone and hung up. The phone rang again and my girlfriend Simone answered the call. They told her the same things and said they were in ********. She told them not to ring again and hung up the phone. During the first phone call the person told me details about the case such as what I said in my statement and details about the identity parade. I do not know if I want to go to court now. I am scared for my family. I am worried that they know details about the case.'

9.   Mr Jones was visited by Detective Constable Stewart who offered him various forms of witness protection and told him he might be witness summonsed; he replied that in that case he would not say anything in Court and would not give his evidence.

10.   The prosecution did not seek a summons or warrant but applied to read Mr Jones' evidence under section 116 of the Criminal Justice Act 2003.

11.   The application was opposed and the arguments advanced encompassed the conditional or mixed nature of the identifying claims made by the witness. Further, as regards the potential for the defendants to have been responsible for the threats, it was known that at the time that the Appellant Davies was in custody and in solitary confinement and the Appellant Dawes, being under 21, was in a Young Offenders Institution, separate from both his co-defendants.

12.   In addition, there was submitted to be another candidate for having made the threats; Darren Davies was a cousin of both Applicants. He was, at the time leading up to the trial, wanted as a suspect with regard to all the

counts on the indictment and was indeed named as another offender on count 6 of the trial indictment. He was arrested a few days prior to trial and found to have the trial committal bundle stored on his laptop, with the statements by Alfred Jones highlighted. He was charged, but at a later stage the Prosecution dropped all charges against him.

13. The trial Judge ruled that the evidence could be adduced. His decision was based on his finding that the Appellants had played some part in the threats being made. The terms of that finding were:

> '(1) On basis of material available to me at the moment, I conclude as a matter of fact, so that I am sure about it, that Mr. Jones was put in a state of extreme fear by these defendants or by somebody associated with them and with their knowledge and/ or approval. In other words, these defendants are associated with those threats. I find that as a fact to the criminal standard.
>
> (2) I have found as a fact it is through deliberate actions attributable to these defendants or with their approval that Mr. Jones is absent.'

14. The Judge also accepted that Mr Jones' evidence was 'sole or decisive' in one sense, though there was supporting evidence in the phone evidence. This ruling also, in effect, admitted the partial identifications, as it considered that aspect and made reference to section 78 of the Police and Criminal Evidence Act 1984. The Judge also referred to both *Horncastle* and *Al-Khawaja*.

15. In terms of whether the evidence was reliable, the Judge did not deal with the later recognition of the van, but dealt with the identification of the Appellant Davies; he held that the stages of the move from the uncertain terms of the identification procedure to the later witness statements were all documented and provided a 'clear line of reasoning' for his doing so, concluding that in his judgment, 'the evidence of Mr Jones is reliable in the senses that I have described. It is documented, it is reasoned, it can be tested and it can be fully commented upon'.

16. The trial proceeded. The defendants all gave evidence and proffered various reasons for their phone contact and the presence of their phones in or around the general area of the kidnap. In summary, Dawes spoke of being in the area driving around selling cannabis. Davies testified that he had left his phone at the home of his cousin Darren Davies and it was being returned to him. The co-defendant Phipps spoke of being in the area and calling Dawes to try to buy some cannabis from him.

17. The Judge summed up and gave warnings as to the difficulties faced by the defence through the absence of the witness. He also gave a traditional Turnbull direction, to warn the jury of the dangers of identification evidence, namely that an honest witness can nonetheless be mistaken. In

dealing with Mr Jones' 'identification' of the blue Suzuki van, the Judge again warned the jury of the disadvantage the defence said they faced, but went on to suggest that the other links between the Appellant Dawes and the van could support the identification [whereas, it is submitted they were the distinct next link in the evidential chain, which only became relevant once the jury accepted that first identification]:

'The question for you, I would suggest, is that the van, that particular blue van, linked to the crimes? I have reminded you, I think though, on Mr Jones' evidence he gives a general description of the van for you to consider. He is then shown photographs and I have reminded you about those and what he has said about it, and how the defence say they have been disadvantaged by him not having him here to question him. But you also have, have you not, other evidence, if you accept it, which links Mr. Dawes to that particular van, where police observations of him in the street going to it are on two occasions at least.'

18.   After their retirement the jury posed a question about the identification of the van by Alfred Jones, namely:

'In reference to admission 5, do the defence say that Alfred Stevens positively identified the Suzuki van with the registration X493LBJ? We feel there is a contradiction between paragraph 5 of the admissions and Mr Dunn's [defence Counsel at trial for Dawes] closing statement regarding the positive identification of the particular van.'

19.   The Judge answered the question, pointing out that the admissions merely gave the date, 18 March 2011, when Alfred Jones 'wrote a statement concerning the Suzuki Supercarry panel van X493LBJ'. He added a reminder of the disadvantage that the defendant faced given the inability to question Mr Jones about that identification.

20.   Amongst the varied verdicts, the jury acquitted of a number of counts that were founded on phone use and cell site evidence placing phones connected to the three defendants in the area of the false imprisonment, namely counts 2 and 3 against the Appellant Davies, and counts 1 to 3 against the defendant Phipps.

21.   All the convictions that are the subject of these appeals were by way of majority verdicts.

22.   The Applicant's appealed against their convictions. Both were given leave to appeal against their convictions on the basis of the trial Judge's admission of Alfred Stephen's evidence. In summary, their grounds of appeal submitted:

(1)   There was no evidential basis such as allowed for the conclusion reached by the trial Judge that the Defendants were behind threats made to the complainant Alfred Jones such as prevented him from attending to give evidence at trial.

(2)   Further, it is submitted that the combined effect of *Horncastle* in the Supreme Court and *Al-Khawaja and Tahery* in the Grand Chamber of the European Court of Human Rights was such that in the absence of an individual defendant threatening a witness away from trial, 'sole or decisive' evidence should not be admitted as hearsay unless there is exceptional and compelling support such as to suggest it is truthful and accurate.

23.   The Applicants were granted leave to appeal. The Court of Appeal heard their case on 7 September 2012. The Court dismissed their appeal, finding:

(1)   The trial Judge should have required the prosecution to make attempts to get Mr Jones to come to court, but that failing was not fatal to the conviction.

(2)   The trial Judge's finding that the Applicants could be blamed for the fear of Mr Jones was impeccable. The Court did not identify what, if any, evidence could possibly be the basis for such a finding.

(3)   The Court held that the evidence was admissible under the test expounded in *R v Riat* [see below].

24.   On the same day, the Applicants applied to the Court of Appeal for the following question to be certified as a point of law of general public importance [thus allowing the Applicants to apply for permission to appeal to the UK Supreme Court]:

'Should the sole or decisive evidence of an absent witness be admitted as hearsay if it is not demonstrably reliable?'

25.   Later that day the Court of Appeal indicated, by way of phone calls between Lady Justice Thorne's clerk and defence Counsel's clerks that the Court would not certify the question.

26.   In the light of the refusal to certify, there was no further avenue of appeal open to the Applicant's in the domestic Courts.

Statement of alleged violation(s) of the convention and relevant arguments

The law

RELEVANT STATUTORY PROVISIONS

1.   Section 116 of the *Criminal Justice Act* 2003 states as follows:

'116.   Cases where a witness is unavailable

(1)   In criminal proceedings a statement not made in oral evidence in the proceedings is admissible as evidence of any matter stated if—

(a) oral evidence given in the proceedings by the person who made the statement would be admissible as evidence of that matter,

(b) the person who made the statement (the relevant person) is identified to the court's satisfaction, and

(c) any of the five conditions mentioned in subsection (2) is satisfied.

(2) The conditions are–

(a) that the relevant person is dead;

(b) that the relevant person is unfit to be a witness because of his bodily or mental condition;

(c) that the relevant person is outside the United Kingdom and it is not reasonably practicable to secure his attendance;

(d) that the relevant person cannot be found although such steps as it is reasonably practicable to take to find him have been taken;

(e) that through fear the relevant person does not give (or does not continue to give) oral evidence in the proceedings, either at all or in connection with the subject matter of the statement, and the court gives leave for the statement to be given in evidence.

(3) For the purposes of subsection (2)(e) "fear" is to be widely construed and (for example) includes fear of the death or injury of another person or of financial loss.

(4) Leave may be given under subsection (2)(e) only if the court considers that the statement ought to be admitted in the interests of justice, having regard–

(a) to the statement's contents,

(b) to any risk that its admission or exclusion will result in unfairness to any party to the proceedings (and in particular to how difficult it will be to challenge the statement if the relevant person does not give oral evidence),

(c) in appropriate cases, to the fact that a direction under section 19 of the Youth Justice and Criminal Evidence Act 1999 (special measures for the giving of evidence by fearful witnesses etc) could be made in relation to the relevant person, and

(d) to any other relevant circumstances.

(5) A condition set out in any paragraph of subsection (2) which is in fact satisfied is to be treated as not satisfied if it is shown that the circumstances described in that paragraph are caused–

(a) by the person in support of whose case it is sought to give the statement in evidence, or

(b)   by a person acting on his behalf,

in order to prevent the relevant person giving oral evidence in the proceedings (whether at all or in connection with the subject matter of the statement).'

RELEVANT ARTICLE OF THE CONVENTION

1.   Article 6 states:

'(1)   In the determination of his civil rights and obligations or of any criminal charge against him, everyone is entitled to a fair and public hearing within a reasonable time by an independent and impartial tribunal established by law. Judgment shall be pronounced publicly but the press and public may be excluded from all or part of the trial in the interest of morals, public order or national security in a democratic society, where the interests of juveniles or the protection of the private lives of the parties so require, or to the extent strictly necessary in the opinion of the court in special circumstances where publicity would prejudice the interests of justice.

(2)   Everyone charged with a criminal offence shall be presumed innocent until proved guilty according to law.

(3)   Everyone charged with a criminal offence has the following minimum rights:

(a)   to be informed promptly, in a language which he understands and in detail, of the nature and cause of the accusation against him;

(b)   to have adequate time and facilities for the preparation of his defence;

(c)   to defend himself in person or through legal assistance of his own choosing or, if he has not sufficient means to pay for legal assistance, to be given it free when the interests of justice so require;

(d)   to examine or have examined witnesses against him and to obtain the attendance and examination of witnesses on his behalf under the same conditions as witnesses against him;

(e)   to have the free assistance of an interpreter if he cannot understand or speak the language used in court.'

Case law

1.   A series of cases in the European Court of Human Rights considered the meaning of the Article 6(3)(d) right to 'examine or have examined witnesses against him'. In *Luca v Italy* (2003) 36 EHRR 46 at paragraph 40, the Court stated as follows:

'If the defendant has been given an adequate and proper opportunity to challenge the depositions, either when made or at a later stage, their admission in evidence will not in itself contravene Article 6.1 and 3(d). The corollary of that, however, is that where the conviction is both solely or to a decisive degree based on depositions that had been made by a person whom the accused has had no opportunity to examine or to have examined, whether during the investigation or at the trial, the rights of the defence are restricted to an extent that is incompatible with the guarantees provided by Article 6.'

2.   This line of authority was ultimately considered by the Supreme Court in *R v Horncastle* [2010] 1 Cr App R 17. The Court rejected the 'sole or decisive' test, Lord Phillips holding at paragraph 108:

'In these circumstances I have decided that it would not be right for this court to hold that the sole or decisive test should have been applied rather than the provisions of the 2003 Act, interpreted in accordance with their natural meaning.'

3.   The Court declined to follow the earlier ECHR section judgment in *Al-Khawaja and Tahery*, in the following terms [paragraph 11]:

'There will, however, be rare occasions where this court has concerns as to whether a decision of the Strasbourg Court sufficiently appreciates or accommodates particular aspects of our domestic process. In such circumstances it is open to this court to decline to follow the Strasbourg decision, giving reasons for adopting this course. This is likely to give the Strasbourg Court the opportunity to reconsider the particular aspect of the decision that is in issue, so that there takes place what may prove to be a valuable dialogue between this court and the Strasbourg Court. This is such a case.'

4.   That reconsideration duly occurred when the Grand Chamber gave judgment in the UK government's appeal, *Al-Khawaja and Tahery* [2012] 54 EHRR 53. In essence, the Grand Chamber reaffirmed the 'sole or decisive' rule but modified the rigidity with which it should be applied. Thus at paragraph 147:

'The Court therefore concludes that, where a hearsay statement is the sole or decisive evidence against a defendant, its admission as evidence will not automatically result in a breach of Article 6 § 1. At the same time where a conviction is based solely or decisively on the evidence of absent witnesses, the Court must subject the proceedings to the most searching scrutiny'

5.   Neither of the absent witnesses in *Al-Khwaja and Tahery* had been kept from court by the acts of the accused, but in discussing that situation the Grand Chamber stated [at paragraph 123]:

'When a witness's fear is attributable to the defendant or those acting on his behalf, it is appropriate to allow the evidence of that witness

290

to be introduced at trial without the need for the witness to give live evidence or be examined by the defendant or his representatives – even if such evidence was the sole or decisive evidence against the defendant. To allow the defendant to benefit from the fear he has engendered in witnesses would be incompatible with the rights of victims and witnesses. No court could be expected to allow the integrity of its proceedings to be subverted in this way. Consequently, a defendant who has acted in this manner must be taken to have waived his rights to question such witnesses under art. 6(3)(d). The same conclusion must apply when the threats or actions which lead to the witness being afraid to testify come from those who act on behalf of the defendant or with his knowledge and approval.'

6.   In applying the modified test as to when 'sole or decisive' hearsay might be admitted, the Grand Chamber discussed the facts of the two cases. In *Al-Khawaja* the Court allowed the UK's appeal, finding that it 'would be difficult to conceive of stronger corroborative evidence' [paragraph 156] for the accuracy and truthfulness of the absent witness. In contrast, in *Tahery* the finding of a violation was upheld; in that case the victim had been stabbed but was unable to say which of the various men in the vicinity had stabbed him. The only witness who claimed that Tahery was the stabber made a statement to police within two days, then refused to attend court through a fear of being seen as an informer, which fear could not be shown to be brought about by Tahery. The Grand Chamber spoke of his evidence in these terms: 'Even though the testimony may have been coherent and convincing on its face it cannot be said to belong to the category of evidence that can be described as "demonstrably reliable"' [paragraph 160].

7.   In *R v Ibrahim* [2012] EWCA Crim 837, the Court of Appeal considered the differing conclusions of *Horncastle* and the Grand Chamber judgment and suggested [at paragraph 89]:

'This difference may be more one of form than substance, however. Thus, the Court of Appeal talked of a conviction being based "solely or to a decisive degree on hearsay evidence admitted under the CJA" and the Supreme Court talked of the hearsay evidence being "critical evidence". That may not be very different from the Grand Chamber's concept of "sole or decisive". Next, the Court of Appeal and the Supreme Court both emphasise that when the untested hearsay evidence is "critical", the question of whether the trial is fair will depend on three principal factors. First, the English courts accept that there has to be good reason to admit the untested hearsay evidence. To decide this under English law there must be compliance with the statutory code. The Grand Chamber necessarily puts this requirement on a more general basis, but it emphasised the need for "justification". Secondly, and we think most importantly, all three courts stipulate that there must be an enquiry as to whether that evidence can be shown to be reliable. Thirdly, all three courts are concerned with the extent to which there are "counterbalancing measures" and if so whether they have been properly applied in deciding whether to admit the "critical" untested hearsay evidence or to allow the case to proceed. In the case of England and Wales those "counterbalancing measures" must include all the statutory safeguards in the "code", as well as a proper application of common law safeguards, such as proper directions in the summing up. The Grand Chamber emphasised the same thing at paragraph 144 and particularly in its "general conclusion on the sole or decisive rule" at paragraph 147'

8. In the subsequent case of *R v Riat* [2012] EWCA Crim 1509, the Court of Appeal considered a number of appeals in the light of the Supreme Court judgment in *Horncastle*, the Grand Chamber decision in *Al-Khawaja and Tahery*, and the Court of Appeal's judgment in *Ibrahim*. At paragraphs 4–6 and 17, the Court explained that if *Horncastle*, *Al-Khawaja* and *Ibrahim* had been understood to suggest that evidence that was central or sole and decisive should only be admitted if it was clearly or manifestly reliable, that is to say accurate, then that was a misunderstanding. In fact, the position is that evidence can be admitted either if it is manifestly reliable or if any possible unreliability is such as can be tested by the jury.

Submissions: alleged violations of Article 6 of the Convention

1. The Grand Chamber in *Al Khawaja and Tahery* constructed a delicate accommodation so as to guard the rights of those within signatory states and yet to concede a degree of sovereignty to national courts as to the manner in which such rights are protected. It is submitted, with regret, that the decision in this case show that the English Court of Appeal has disregarded that delicate balance and that the current state of law now propounded by the UK Court of Appeal permits flagrant breaches of the right to a fair trial. It is further submitted that the response of the UK perhaps, with respect, confirms the fears of honourable dissenting Judges in the Grand Chamber decision, that:

   'The sole or decisive rule that has been followed so far was intended to protect human rights against the "fruit of the poisonous tree" … The adoption of the counterbalancing approach means that a rule that was intended to safeguard human rights is replaced with the uncertainties of counterbalancing.'

2. It is submitted that the Applicants rights under Article 6(3)(d) to 'examine witnesses against him' were violated at their trial. The witness Jones was central to the cases against both men. Without his account the prosecution could not have even begun their case. The evidence adduced

was such as to identify the Applicant Davies and to identify the vehicle closely associated with the Applicant Dawes. It is submitted to be telling that the other counts that were not supported by such identifications, both against these Applicants and against their co-defendant at trial, led to acquittals.

3.   In the Grand Chamber of *Al-Khawaja and Tahery* this honourable Court adopted the modified test of not absolutely barring 'sole or decisive' hearsay evidence, but subjecting such evidence to 'the most searching scrutiny'. That level of scrutiny was illustrated in the outcome of those cases, whereby the 'demonstrably reliable' evidence against the Applicant Al-Khawaja led to the UK's appeal being allowed, whereas the lack of such evidence led to the decision in *Tahery* being unchanged. To apply a similar test, the evidence of the absent witness in the Applicants' case, his identification of the Applicant Davies was a flawed example of a form of evidence, identification evidence, that is considered dangerous even when given by a 'live' witness. In the Applicant Dawes's case, a bland statement describing a very common type of van in the most general terms was then followed much later by an assertion that the vehicle linked to the Applicant was the very same van.

4.   In addition to the obvious weaknesses and potential for error in the nature of the evidence the missing witness gave, there was what could be seen as a 'drugs' background, in that his friends declined to call the police and the demands made of Mr Jones were, according to him, for cash and cocaine. Without expecting this honourable Court to make any finding adverse to that absent witness, that background of possible criminal activity by the complainant and his associates is such as to make his account even more in need of the most careful testing under cross examination.

5.   If there were any evidential basis for the trial Judge's finding that the Applicants were both responsible for the absent witness being placed in fear, then it is accepted that this case would be outside the judgment in *Al-Kahwaja and Tahery*. It is submitted that there was simply no evidence of the Applicants being those responsible. It is submitted to be telling that neither the trial Judge nor the Court of Appeal even purported to identify any evidence such as could justify such a finding. Whilst this Court will very often defer to the facts found by the trial tribunal, if the Court is to guarantee rights that are practical and effective, it must be prepared not to allow a national court to shield its breaches of Convention rights by completely indefensible findings of fact.

6.   The decision of the Court of Appeal in *Ibrahim* had the potential to resolve the dispute between this Court and the UK domestic courts by an accommodation that seemed to allow for the use of sole or decisive hearsay only it was manifestly reliable. The later judgment in *Riat* specifically 'explained away' that approach such that no such limit is now in place in the English law.

7. This Court will notice that the 'valuable dialogue' that Lord Phillips spoke of in the Supreme Court judgment in *Horncastle* has not taken place. This is because the English Court of Appeal has refused to certify a point of law of public important, thus cutting off the possibility of a further appeal within the English system, as section 33(2) of the Criminal Appeal Act 1968 states, inter alia, that an 'appeal lies only with the leave of the Court of Appeal or the Supreme Court; and leave shall not be granted unless it is certified by the Court of Appeal that a point of law of general public importance is involved in the decision'.

8. The Applicants therefore submit that they have suffered a violation of their right to a fair trial in that the trial judge's admitted sole or decisive evidence that they had no chance to challenge.

Appendix E

Useful contact details

The Court of Appeal (Criminal Division)
Criminal Appeal Office
The Royal Courts of Justice
Strand
London
WC2A 2LL
Enquiries: 020 7947 6011
Listing: 020 7947 6632, 020 7947 6781
Email enquiries: criminalappealoffice.generaloffice@hmcts.x.gsi.gov.uk
Email listing enquiries: criminalappealoffice.listoffice@hmcts.x.gsi.gov.uk

The Supreme Court
Parliament Square
London
SW1P 3BD
Tel: 020 7960 1500 or 1900
Fax: 020 7960 1901
DX: 157230 Parliament Sq 4
Registry enquiries: 020 7960 1991 or 1992.

The European Court of Human Rights
The Registrar
European Court of Human Rights
Council of Europe
F-67075 Strasbourg cedex
www.echr.coe.int

CPS Appeals Unit
Rose Court
2 Southwark Bridge
London
SE1 9HS
Tel: 020 3357 0000

Appendix E *Useful contact details*

Criminal Cases Review Commission
5 St Philip's Place
Birmingham
B3 2PW
Tel: 0121 233 1473
Email: info@ccrc.x.gsi.gov.uk
DX: 715466 Birmingham 41

The Law Society
The Law Society's Hall
113 Chancery Lane
London
WC2A 1PL

Find a solicitor service:
Tel: 020 7320 5650
http://solicitors.lawsociety.org.uk

The Bar Pro Bono Unit
48 Chancery Lane
London
WC2A 1JF
www.barprobono.org.uk

Centre for Criminal Appeals
National Pro Bono Centre,
48 Chancery Lane,
London
WC2A 1JF
www.criminalappeals.org.uk

Index

All references are to paragraph numbers

A

Absolute discharge 14.16
Abuse of process 2.14
  may be unfair conviction 3.16
Acquittal agreement 13.5
  definition 13.7
  scope of 13.8
Acquittals
  appeals against 13.2
Acts of Parliament 2.1
Address
  for correspondence 1.26
  Court of Appeal judges 1.17
Admissibility 5.5
  applications to ECtHR 11.20
Adverse publicity
  appeals founded on 3.46
Advice and assistance 8.3
  alternative sources of 8.46–52
  application for referral to CCRC 9.18
  Bar *Pro Bono* Unit 8.53
  Centre for Criminal Appeals 8.52
  claiming for work done under scheme
    8.43–44
  funding for 8.16–45
    application for 8.29–36
    applications for extension of
      8.35–36
    availability 8.18
    change of circumstances 8.19
    completing and lodging CRM1 and
      CRM2 8.29–32
    cost of public transport to visit
      client 8.36
    eligibility 8.21–25
      children 8.26
    grants under CRM 1 and CRM2 8.35
    hopeless requests 8.35
    limitations on 8.17
    necessary further work 8.35
    period of calculation 8.23

Advice and assistance – *contd*
  funding for – *contd*
    postal applications 8.35
    previous advice 8.19–20
    qualifying benefits 8.21
    for same matter from another
      provider within past six months
      8.19
    screening 8.35
    Sufficient Benefits Test (merits)
      8.27–29
      scope 8.28
    telephone advice on 8.35
  further instructions 8.45
  innocence projects 8.48–50
  submitting claim for 8.44
  unfair convictions 3.28
Advocacy 7.1–3, 7.38–39
Advocates 8.42
  advice from 8.36
  expectations of 7.39
  fees 8.36
Aggravated trespass 10.5
Alibi evidence 3.58
'Alleged violations'
  section of form for applications to
    ECtHR 11.14
Allowing appeal 3.60
Alternative verdicts
  leaving to jury 3.35
Anti-social behaviour orders 4.10
Appeals
  against conviction 6.21
    citation of authorities 6.24
  against order made under s.5 of the
    Criminal Procedure (Insanity) Act
    1964 14.16–19
  against sentence 1.13, 1.19, 5.5,
    6.22–23
    assistance provided to police 6.23
    citation of authorities 6.26
    grounds for 6.22

297

DOUGHTY STREET CHAMBERS

Criminal Appeals

doughty street chambers

Since its foundation in 1990, Doughty Street Chambers and its barristers have taken as their guiding principle the use of the law for the advancement of the protection of human rights and civil liberties. It is now amongst the very largest and most wide-ranging civil liberties practices in the world, providing specialist advice, advocacy and training in the UK and around the world. Their practice areas include crime and criminal appeals, international crime (such as war crimes), fraud and financial services regulation, extradition, prisoners' rights, actions against the police, immigration, media law, professional regulation, social welfare and housing, clinical negligence and more.

The Criminal Team is the largest practice group at Doughty Street Chambers, comprising almost half the total number of barristers at the set. Its members have long-standing experience of defending in many of the most serious and complex criminal trials, appeals and extradition cases to come before the UK Supreme Court, Privy Council, Court of Appeal and High Court, as well as their daily work in the Crown and Magistrates' Courts. Abroad they appear in the courts of Northern Ireland, Hong Kong, Singapore, the Caribbean, South America, the International Criminal Court and the European Court of Human Rights.

The Appeals Unit at Doughty Street Chambers spans all this criminal work, and is widely regarded as home to several of the best appellate lawyers in the UK. A wrongful conviction or sentence at any level can have a devastating impact on an appellant and his family, and the appeal specialists at Doughty Street Chambers advise across the full range of cases, from the relatively minor, challenging decisions of Magistrates, right up to drafting submissions to the Criminal Cases Review Commission, appeals in cases of homicide and terrorism, and appearing at all levels up to the Supreme Court and the European Court of Justice. Their work includes appeals on sentencing (including whole life tariffs and indeterminate sentences), jury irregularities, psychiatric issues (e.g. automatism, loss of control and provocation), sexual offences prevention orders, deficient trial representation, fraud and confiscation appeals, appeals by way of Case Stated and Judicial Review.

Doughty Street Chambers also offers its solicitor clients use of a Criminal Appeals Advice Line, which provides free preliminary advice and guidance for those considering potential appeals and CCRC matters. More information on this, and the criminal appeals and other barristers at Doughty Street Chambers, can be found at www.doughtystreet.co.uk or by e-mailing crime@doughtystreet.co.uk.